"Faculty in public affairs programs are steeped in the science of administration and management, yet when the time comes to serve as organizational leaders, they are frequently unprepared. *The Public Affairs Faculty Manual* addresses this paradox with smart, practice-based advice. This is a comprehensive handbook for deans, directors, and chairs – and for the academic administrators 'in waiting' whose day will come."

Matthew Auer, *University of Georgia, USA*

"This is a long overdue compilation of what an aspiring director of an MPA program needs to know before they step into the position. In one tome, Bruce McDonald and William Hatcher have pulled together insights and perspectives that often take months to learn just by doing. Read *The Public Affairs Faculty Manual* first, then accept the offer to be MPA director!"

Michael A. Pagano, *University of Illinois, USA*

THE PUBLIC AFFAIRS FACULTY MANUAL

While public affairs faculty study administration and management techniques, few administrators of public affairs programs receive formal training in the nuts and bolts of academic administration. Even those faculty who come to academia after distinguished careers in managerial positions may not be ready for the very different (and difficult) environment of university administration. *The Public Affairs Faculty Manual* argues that public affairs as a field needs to ensure that knowledge about administration and management is applied to the running of its academic programs, and brings together major leaders in the discipline to explore key features of academic administration. Many of these leaders have served as Master of Public Administration (MPA) directors, chairs, and deans at the nation's top public affairs programs.

Crucial issues of academic administration discussed include the basics of public affairs programs, models of governance, roles of different administrative leaders, planning and budgeting for programs, navigating the accreditation process, assessing and improving student learning, ensuring social equity and cultural competency, mentoring faculty, developing curriculum, and helping provide service and applied research to community partners. Themes running throughout the book's chapters are examined, and additional resources to help manage public affairs programs are offered. This collection of essays and the strategies within it are designed to encourage faculty to assume positions of leadership in their programs and manage those programs in an effective, efficient, and fair manner. *The Public Affairs Faculty Manual* is required reading for new, seasoned, and aspiring academic administrators in public administration, public policy, and nonprofit management programs, as well as schools of government.

Bruce D. McDonald, III is Associate Professor of Public Budgeting and Finance at North Carolina State University and the Co-Editor-in-Chief of the *Journal of Public Affairs Education*. He has served as the MPA director at both North Carolina State University and Indiana University South Bend. His research focuses on public budgeting and finance in the context of the fiscal health of local governments. His research has appeared in the *Journal of Public Administration Research and Theory*, *Public Administration Review*, and the *American Review of Public Administration*.

William Hatcher is Associate Professor of Public Administration and MPA Director at Augusta University. He also serves as the Co-Editor-in-Chief of the *Journal of Public Affairs Education*. He was previously on faculty at Eastern Kentucky University. His research focuses on health policy, community development, and public budgeting. His research has appeared in journals such as the *Journal of Public Affairs Education*, the *American Journal of Public Health*, the *Journal of Mental Health*, and *Public Administration Quarterly*.

Routledge Public Affairs

Editors

Bruce D. Mcdonald, III
Associate Professor of Public Budgeting and Finance
North Carolina State University, Raleigh NC

William Hatcher
Associate Professor of Public Administration
Augusta University, Augusta GA

The Routledge Public Affairs Education series, edited by William Hatcher and Bruce D. McDonald, III, publishes books designed to assist faculty in the classroom and in the management of public administration, public affairs, and public policy programs. To accomplish this, the book series explores evidence-based practices, commentary about the state of public administration education, and pedagogical perspectives. The Routledge Public Affairs Education series examines the future of public administration education, teaching practices, international public administration education, undergraduate public administration programming, and other relevant topics to advance the fieldís knowledge. For more information about the series, or to submit a book proposal, please contact series editors William Hatcher at wihatcher@augusta.edu and Bruce D. McDonald, III at bmcdona@ncsu.edu.

Recently Published Books:

The Public Affairs Faculty Manual
Bruce D. McDonald, III and William Hatcher

THE PUBLIC AFFAIRS FACULTY MANUAL

A Guide to the Effective Management of Public Affairs Programs

Edited by
Bruce D. McDonald, III
and William Hatcher

 Routledge
Taylor & Francis Group

NEW YORK AND LONDON

First published 2020
by Routledge
52 Vanderbilt Avenue, New York, NY 10017

and by Routledge
2 Park Square, Milton Park, Abingdon, Oxon, OX14 4RN

Routledge is an imprint of the Taylor & Francis Group, an informa business

Library of Congress Cataloging-in-Publication Data
A catalog record for this title has been requested

ISBN: 978-0-367-89336-1 (hbk)
ISBN: 978-0-367-86196-4 (pbk)
ISBN: 978-1-003-01981-7 (ebk)

Typeset in Bembo
by Wearset Ltd, Boldon, Tyne and Wear

DEDICATION

1: 4643 2441 2442 8594 1 35255 21464
—BM

During my time as a student and scholar, I have had the pleasure to be guided by excellent program leaders in our field. I dedicate this book to these leaders.
—WH

CONTENTS

FIGURES

TABLES

CONTRIBUTORS

Hunter Bacot, Ph.D. is Professor of Political Science and Director of Graduate Programs at the University of North Carolina at Greensboro. Previously, he served as the director of the Institute of Government at the University of Arkansas at Little Rock and director of the Elon Poll at Elon University. He received his BA in Political Science from the University of North Carolina at Chapel Hill, an MPA from the University of North Carolina at Charlotte, and a Ph.D. in Political Science from the University of Tennessee. His research focuses on civic development in local governments, airport authorities, and state-level environmental policy. His research has been published in outlets such as the *Journal of Public and Nonprofit Affairs*, *Public Administration Review*, *Economic Development Quarterly*, and *Policy Studies Journal*.

Thomas J. Barth, Ph.D. is Professor of Public Administration and MPA Director at the University of North Carolina at Charlotte. Previously, he served as the MPA director at the University of North Carolina at Wilmington and the University of Memphis. He received his BA in Anthropology from the University of Notre Dame, an MA in Social Policy analysis from the University of Chicago, and a Ph.D. in Public Administration and Policy from Virginia Polytechnic Institute and State University. His research interests include public management, organization behavior, and ethics. His research has appeared in journals such as *Public Administration Review*, the *Journal of Public Affairs Education*, *Public Voices*, and *American Review of Public Administration*.

John R. Bartle, Ph.D. is Dean of the College of Public Affairs and Community Service and Professor of Public Administration at the University of Nebraska at Omaha. He is a fellow of the National Academy of Public

Administration. He received his BA in Economics from Swarthmore College, an MPA from the University of Texas at Austin, and his Ph.D. in Public Policy and Management from Ohio State University. He also has an honorary Doctorate of Humane Letters from the State University of New York. His research focuses on tax policy issues and he is the author or editor of three books: *Management Policies in Local Government Finance* (2012), *Sustainable Development for Public Administration* (2006), and *Evolving Theories of Public Budgeting* (2001).

Brandi Blessett, Ph.D. is Associate Professor of Political Science and MPA Director at the University of Cincinnati. She received her BS in Physical Education and Health from the University of Michigan, a MEd in Educational Leadership from Wayne State University, and a Ph.D. in Urban Policy and Public Administration from Old Dominion University. Her research focuses on administrative responsibility, disenfranchisement, and social equity. Her research has appeared in journals such as the *Journal of Public Affairs Education*, *Administrative Theory and Praxis*, and *Public Administration Quarterly*.

Jerrell D. Coggburn, Ph.D. is Professor of Public Administration at North Carolina State University. From 2007 to 2019 he served as chair of the Department of Public Administration. He received his BA in Political Science from Oklahoma State University and both his MPA and Ph.D. in Political Science from the University of South Carolina. His research focuses on public human resource management and public management. His research has been published in outlets such as *Public Administration Review*, *American Review of Public Administration*, and *Public Budgeting and Finance*.

Susan T. Gooden, Ph.D. is Interim Dean and Professor of Public Administration and Policy at the L. Douglas Wilder School of Government and Public Affairs at Virginia Commonwealth University. She is a fellow of the National Academy of Public Administration and is past president of the American Society for Public Administration. She received both her BA in English and an MA in Political Science from Virginia Polytechnic Institute and State University. She also earned an MA and a Ph.D. in Political Science from Syracuse University. Her research centers on social equity and has appeared in outlets such as the *Journal of Public Affairs Education*, *Public Administration Review*, and the *Journal of Public Administration Research and Theory*.

Doug Goodman, Ph.D. is Professor of Public and Nonprofit Management at the University of Texas at Dallas. Previously, he was on faculty at Mississippi State University, where he served as the graduate coordinator. He received a BA in Political Science from Brigham Young University and both his MS and Ph.D. in Political Science from the University of Utah. His research focuses on state and local government with an emphasis on sustainability, organization behavior, human resource management, and public budgeting. His research has been published in a number of outlets, including the *American Review of Public Administration, Public Administration, Review of Public Personnel Administration,* and *Political Research Quarterly.*

Kathleen Hale, Ph.D. is Professor of Political Science and Director of the Graduate Program in Election Administration at Auburn University. Previously, she served as the director of the university's MPA program. She received her Ph.D. in Public Policy and Administration from Kent State University. Her research focuses on election administration and voting and has appeared in journals such as *Government Information Quarterly, Policy Studies Journal, Public Administration Review,* and *Publius.*

Justin D. Hamel is a graduate student in the MPA program at the University of North Carolina at Charlotte, where he currently serves as a graduate assistant in the Office of Emergency Management. He received his BS in Community Development from Portland State University.

William Hatcher, Ph.D. is Associate Professor of Public Administration and MPA Director at Augusta University. He also serves as Co-Editor-in-Chief of the *Journal of Public Affairs Education.* Previously, he was on faculty at Eastern Kentucky University. He received both a BS in Political Science and an MPA from Georgia College and State University and a Ph.D. in Public Policy and Administration from Mississippi State University. His research focuses on health policy, community development, and public budgeting. His research has appeared in journals such as the *Journal of Public Affairs Education,* the *American Journal of Public Health,* the *Journal of Mental Health,* and *Public Administration Quarterly.*

Martha Humphries Ginn, Ph.D. is Professor of Political Science at Augusta University. She received a BA in Political Science from Western Kentucky University and a Ph.D. in Political Science from the University of South Carolina. Her research focuses on judicial decision-making, public opinion, and the effect of terrorism on political behavior. Her research has been published in the *Journal of Politics, Political Research Quarterly, Public Opinion Quarterly,* and *Justice Systems Journal.*

Maja Husar Holmes, Ph.D. is Associate Professor and Chair of the Department of Public Administration at West Virginia University. From 2016 to 2019 she served on NASPAA's Commission on Peer Review and Accreditation (COPRA). She received a BS in Business Management from Washington University and both her MPA and Ph.D. in Public Administration from Syracuse University. Her research focuses on public leadership, public participation and diversity, and inclusion and has been published in the *Journal of Public Administration Theory*, *Administration and Society*, the *Journal of Public Affairs Education*, and *Innovative Higher Education*.

Myung H. Jin, Ph.D. is Associate Professor of Public Administration and Chair of the MPA program at Virginia Commonwealth University. He also serves as Associate Editor for the *Journal of Public and Nonprofit Affairs*. He received his BA in Architectural Studies from the University of Illinois at Chicago and both his MPA and Ph.D. in Public Administration from Florida State University. His research focuses on organizational behavior and human resource development and has appeared in *International Review of Administrative Sciences*, *Review of Public Personnel Administration*, and *American Review of Public Administration*.

Jasmine McGinnis Johnson, Ph.D. is Assistant Professor in Public Policy and Public Administration at George Washington University. She received a BA in Sociology from Emory University, an MPA from the University of Georgia, and a Ph.D. in Public Policy from Georgia Institute of Technology and Georgia State University. Her research focuses on philanthropy and human resources and has been published in *Nonprofit and Voluntary Sector Quarterly*, *International Public Management Journal*, and *Public Personnel Administration*.

Jared J. Llorens, Ph.D. is Professor of Public Administration and Chair of the Department of Public Administration at Louisiana State University. He received a BA in English Literature from Loyola University of New Orleans, an MPAff from the University of Texas at Austin, and a Ph.D. in Public Administration from the University of Georgia. His research focuses primarily on public-sector human resource management, with particular interests in compensation and recruitment. His research has appeared in a variety of journals and he is the co-author of the textbook *Public Personnel Management: Context and Strategies* (2015).

Bruce D. McDonald III, Ph.D. is Associate Professor of Public Budgeting and Finance at North Carolina State University and Co-Editor-in-Chief of the *Journal of Public Affairs Education*. He has served as the MPA director at both North Carolina State University and Indiana University South Bend. He received his BA in Communications from Mercer University, his MA in International Peace and Conflict Resolution from American Military University, his MSc in Economic History from the London School of Economics, and his Ph.D. in Public Administration and Policy from Florida State University. His research focuses on public budgeting and finance in the context of the fiscal health of local governments. His research has appeared in the *Journal of Public Administration Research and Theory*, *Public Administration Review*, and the *American Review of Public Administration*.

D. Ryan Miller, Ph.D. is Assistant Professor of Public Administration at Nova Southeastern University. He received his Bachelor of Music Education from Florida Southern College and his MPA and Ph.D. in Public Administration and Policy from Florida State University. His research examines a variety of policy topics, as well as public administration education, and has appeared in the *Journal of Policy Modeling*, *Local Government Studies*, and the *Journal of Public Affairs Education*.

Kathryn Newcomer, Ph.D. is Professor of Public Policy and Administration and Director of the Trachtenberg School of Public Policy and Public Administration at the George Washington University. She is also a fellow of the National Academy of Public Administration. She received both her BS and MA at the University of Kansas and a Ph.D. in Political Science at the University of Iowa. Her research focuses on accountability in government, with a focus on the Federal Inspectors General. She has published five books, including *The Handbook of Practical Program Evaluation* (2015), and numerous articles in journals such as *Public Administration Review* and *American Journal of Evaluation*.

Robert W. Smith, Ph.D. is Dean of the College of Public Affairs and Administration and Professor of Public Administration at the University of Illinois at Springfield. Previously, he served as dean of the College of Liberal Arts and Social Sciences at Savannah State University and chair of the Department of Political Science and International Affairs at Kennesaw State University. He received his BA in History and Political Science from the College of Saint Rose and both his MPA and Ph.D. in Public Administration from the University at Albany. His research focuses on public budgeting processes and structure and has appeared in journals such as *Public Administration Review*, *Administration and Society*, and the *Journal of Public Budgeting, Accounting, and Financial Management*.

ABBREVIATIONS

AACSB	Association to Advance Collegiate Schools of Business
CHEA	Council for Higher Education Accreditation
COPRA	Commission on Peer Review and Accreditation
CUMU	Coalition of Urban and Metropolitan Universities
CUPSO	Consortium of University Public Service Organizations
JPAE	*Journal of Public Affairs Education*
MBA	Master of Business Administration
MNM	Master of Nonprofit Management
MPA	Master of Public Administration
MPAffairs	Master of Public Affairs
MPM	Master of Public Management
MPP	Master of Public Policy
MSW	Master of Social Work
NASPAA	Network of Schools of Public Policy, Affairs, and Administration
PA	public affairs and administration
SLOs	student learning outcomes
TPA	teaching public administration
UPS	university public service organization

1

MANAGING YOUR PUBLIC AFFAIRS PROGRAM

William Hatcher and Bruce D. McDonald, III

Have you recently assumed an administrative role in your public affairs program? Maybe you have been asked to serve as director of your institution's MPA program, or you are moving up the administrative ladder to serve as a chair or dean? Perhaps you are a faculty now, but have ambitions to lead public affairs programs? Maybe you are a seasoned academic administrator in public affairs, but you want to maintain your effectiveness in your current job? If you answered "yes" to any of these questions, this book is for you.

While public affairs faculty study administration and management techniques, we are rarely trained in the nuts and bolts of academic administration. Even those faculty who come to academia after distinguished careers in managerial positions may not be ready for the very different (and difficult) environment of university administration. Newly appointed administrators may be lost when assuming the job. Data support this assertion. In a recent survey of MPA directors (Hatcher, Meares, & Gordon, 2017), a lack of training and mentoring were identified as major barriers blocking success. The lack of training for those who manage public affairs programs should be of concern to a field that is dedicated to teaching efficient and effective administration. We should practice what we preach.

Accordingly, public affairs as a field needs to ensure that we are apply our knowledge about administration and management to the running of our academic programs. In this book, we seek to start a conversation in the field on managing academic programs. We have asked leaders in public affairs to write about key features of academic administration in the field. Many of these leaders have served as MPA directors, chairs, and deans at the nation's top public affairs programs. The book is intended to be a reference for academic administrators in our field, especially ones who are new in their leadership roles.

Today, public affairs programs face numerous challenges from a public that does not trust government and political elites that do not respect the crucial work of bureaucrats. In this time of crisis, public affairs programs have a responsibility to educate current and future managers to be efficient, effective, and fair. To accomplish this, public affairs programs need faculty who conduct cutting-edge and useful research, who are engaging and effective instructors, but who are also able, and willing, to apply evidenced-based management to their academic programs.

Challenges Facing Public Affairs Programs

In the United States (US), decades of anti-government rhetoric from political elites, the polarization of the political parties, and distrust of government among the general public has led to a maelstrom for government. The chaotic and at times anti-democratic administration of President Trump has placed additional stress on public administration in the US. Public affairs programs must educate and train the next generation of public servants to work in such an environment. To ensure that these academic programs are successful, the leaders of public affairs need to recognize that public administration is in a time of crisis. In other words, quoting Jeff Daniel's character in *The Newsroom*, "[t]he first step in solving any problem is recognizing there is one" (Sorkin & Mottola, 2012). We have a problem of governance in the US. In fact, we have multiple problems.

First, the public's distrust of government erodes the ability of public administrators to serve their organizations and communities. This distrust of government has increased significantly, making the trend one of the most pressing problems facing public affairs programs (Kettl, 2018). But public administration holds solutions. In his 2018 presidential address at the Network of Schools of Public Policy, Affairs, and Administration's (NASPAA) annual conference, Jack Meek stressed that programs need to answer the question of, "[g]iven the challenging of declining trust in government, how do we communicate the value of our programs?" (Meek, 2018, p. 151). According to Kettl (2018, 2019), this question can be answered and the problem of distrust can be addressed through citizens having positive interactions with public officials. Public administrators, focused on fairness, engaging citizens, and delivery of services to meet the needs of citizens, can make small but measurable steps toward repairing the public's trust in government (Kettl, 2019).

Second, political leaders, from both major parties, are often not supportive of public administration and the work being done by the nation's civil servants. Whether it is President Reagan saying "government is the program"[1] or President Clinton saying that "the era of big government is over," public affairs has been plagued for decades with anti-government rhetoric in the American political discourse. In recent years, "bureaucrat bashing" has taken a darker turn.

President Trump, his supporters, and aides, such as former strategist Steve Bannon, consistently discuss the need to "deconstruct the administrative state" (Katz, 2017). In 2017, for instance, President Trump even took the unprecedented step of engaging in bureaucrat bashing, while giving a foreign address in Poland, by discussing the bureaucracy as a "common" threat facing "Western democracies" (Katz, 2017). Being labeled a threat to democracy, clearly, adversely affects the work of public administrators. In one study, researchers (Garrett, Thurber, Fritschler, & Rosenbloom, 2006) found that bashing makes senior federal managers more likely to feel "hostile and frustrated" with politicians and the media (p. 228). Additionally, bashing harms morale, recruitment, and the development of employees (Garrett et al., 2006). Sadly, it appears that bureaucrat bashing negatively affects how public managers view themselves compared to their counterparts in the private sector. Chen and Bozeman (2014) found that state mangers in the US "perceive public sector inferiority with respect to worker creativity, talent, and autonomy" (p. 549).

In this environment of public distrust of government and bureaucrat bashing, public affairs programs face a number of specific challenges. The first challenge is that public affairs programs are pressured to increase their enrollments, but in recent years, due in part to the anti-bureaucracy environment, programs have experienced a decline in the number of students. In recent years, there have been declining enrollments in MPA programs (NASPAA, 2017). Declining enrollments place additional pressure on MPA directors. Universities are more likely to look to MPA programs and question their viability if enrollments are not consistently growing. Some universities may even seek to disband their MPA programs, as *Governing* magazine recounted in an article appropriately titled "Fighting to Save the MPA" (Kerrigan, 2011). In such an environment, directors have to make the case for the degree and the need for sustainable enrollments, not just uncontrolled growth.

The second challenge is that graduates from public affairs programs may be "sector switching" by finding employment in the private sector instead of working for public agencies and/or nonprofits. In recent years, a large percentage of graduates from NASPAA programs have found employment in the programs in the private sector (NASPAA, 2017). For instance, NASPAA's 2016–2017 report on accredited programs found that 19 percent of graduates are employed by the private sector (NASPAA, 2017). Additionally, many of the graduates of top programs, such as Harvard's Kennedy School of Government (Chetkovich, 2003), find employment in the private sector. And recent research has found that millennials with advanced education, like an MPA, may be motivated by pay to switch from public service to the private sector (Johnson & Ng, 2016). There are positive aspects of sector switching from public to private. The demand of public affairs graduates in the private sector demonstrates the power of the field's academic programs. Additionally, the problems of the public sector, such as declining budgets, makes the private sector more attractive to the graduates of public affairs programs, especially the ones from top universities. However, these graduates are not bringing their talent and skills to public organizations and/or nonprofits that desperately need that help, which should be a concern of public affairs programs.

This bring us to the third challenge. Public affairs programs are not adapting well to modern public administration. Just a few examples of this include: The curriculum of many public affairs programs does not offer adequate training in information technology to help public managers secure the vital data housed by public agencies and nonprofits. Many public affairs programs are not connecting the classroom with the community through service learning, community partnerships on applied research, and other experiential learning. Perhaps most concerning, public affairs programs are not working with key players to prepare for the upcoming wave of public-sector retirements in all levels of government (Maciag, 2013).

Public affairs programs face these challenges while experience declining resources for universities and public-sector employers. Public affairs programs have fiscal problems in recruiting faculty, funding travel for research, providing small class sizes, and adequately training their administrators (Hatcher et al., 2017). Employers, in particular governments and nonprofits, facing fiscal constraints have issues hiring graduates, providing internship experiences, and offering tuition reimbursements. These problems are not without solutions, of course. Over the last few years, the leaders of the nation's top policy schools (Evans, Morrison, & Auer, 2019) have been working on what public affairs education should do during the current "turbulent" times. According to these leaders, public affairs programs can address the challenges through holding to the following principles: "(1) build sustained partnerships between public and educational sectors, (2) focus on competency-based learning, (3) instill a lifelong learning mind-set in students, and (4) integrate new modalities for learning" (p. 285).

Again, the first step to solving a problem is recognizing you have one, and public affairs programs are facing many challenges. So, our programs need stellar administrators to steer through the problems and achieve success.

Roles of the Public Affairs Program Director

In an environment of crisis, we need excellent faculty to serve as administrators of public affairs programs. Let us stress, assuming a leadership role in your program is service. The directors of public affairs programs are often servant leaders in that they are doing the job not because of personal gain, monetary or prestige, but because they believe in their academic programs and strive to impact the next generation of practitioners in the field.

If you are interested in an administrative job within the academia that has multiple challenges and where you will be taking on multiple roles, then the job for you is as the director of a public affairs program. The directors of public affairs programs wear multiple hats. They are recruiters, marketers, academic advisors, career advisors, assessment officers, planners, diversity advocates, supervisors, budget directors, fundraisers, and, of course, instructors (Brainard & Infeld, 2017; Vicino, 2017). Additionally, directors need to go beyond advocating diversity and help promote inclusive learning environments for faculty and staff (Edwards, Holmes, & Sowa, 2019).

With universities pressing academic programs to increase enrollments, directors of public affairs programs often find themselves spending hours marketing their programs and recruiting students. MPA directors label the pressure to recruit new students as the most pressing concern from their home institutions (Hatcher et al., 2017). To ensure that academic programs are diverse and reflect the communities that they serve, leaders also need to be advocates of diversity in their planning and recruitment efforts (Breihan, 2007).

Public affairs directors help students plan their academic programs of study, and leaders also provide career advice to students. Programs need to show that their graduates are able to secure employment, and their directors are held accountable. Some programs even combine the career and academic advising tasks into assessments, such as portfolios, to help students advance their careers (Williams, Plein, & Lilly, 1998).

Program directors are also supervisors of administrative staffs and graduate assistants, and in this managerial role some are responsible for programmatic budgets. Through managing budgets for their programs, directors find themselves being pressured to raise funds for scholarships, student and faculty travel, or even annual expenditures.

Often public affairs must perform these roles without much formal authority over other faculty, staff, and administrators at their universities. For instance, MPA directors normally do not have the authority of evaluating the performance of faculty, over the actors that they must convince to follow assessment plans, help with recruitment, and provide quality instruction that fits within the overall vision of a program. Leaders in such a situation need to rely on their ability to make the case for their desired actions.

In such demanding roles, public affairs directors need to be concerned with professional burnout. Such a feeling of exhaustion (World Health Organization, 2019) causes employees to disengage at work, and if the burnout becomes too intense employees will leave their positions, leading to costs for organizations (Kim, 2015). When it comes to MPA directors, many serve in the role in addition to their tenured faculty position. In such an employment situation, often directors can be the ones who decide to return to being primarily faculty. Accordingly, universities and public affairs units need to help ensure that MPA directors are supported and able to balance the competing demands in their professional and personal lives.

How Do We Find These Directors?

We do not want to completely scare you away from serving your programs in a leadership role and/or being interested in the nuts and bolts of program administration. Given the demands of program leadership and the roles that directors must perform, one can see the importance of the material covered in this book. In particular, one pressing concern is finding faculty who are willing to serve as program leaders and excel in the leadership positions.

Finding academic leaders, like finding a leader for any position, is difficult. For one, it is hard to convince faculty members to give up the freedom of being able to dedicate more time to their research and classes to work in a position that may not come with much more compensation, if any, and that is often a thankless post. However, public affairs directors tend to be satisfied with their jobs. In their survey of MPA and MPP directors, Killian and Wenning (2017) found that most respondents are satisfied in their positions of academic leadership. Still, it should be noted that most surveyed directors were tenured (86 percent), and a majority were at the rank of full professor (55 percent). Such faculty may be motivated to serve as academic leaders because of intrinsic factors, such as caring about their program's mission and its students. Such intrinsic factors may not be as rewarded as peer-reviewed publications, external grants, and other accomplishments that are needed for faculty members to be tenured and advance to full professor. Thus, finding junior faculty to serve in leadership positions can be a difficult task for public affairs programs.

Our Experiences

Our experiences directing MPA programs led us to edit this book. Both of us have worked in different academic institutions. We both worked in MPA programs housed in regional teaching universities, and now we both work for research-orientated institutions. Both of us worked as MPA directors before we were tenured, which as noted by Killian and Wenning (2017) is atypical. Both of us have been pressured to achieve results without needed resources. While facing these pressures, we constantly looked for information to help us manage our programs. But beside some help from articles in the *Journal of Public Affairs Education* and from NASPAA, we were surprised by the lack of resources in our field for directors, especially new ones. This is very concerning because, as mentioned, directors note that they are not trained or mentored at their home universities when they assume their leadership roles (Hatcher et al., 2017). So, we decided to put this book together in the hopes of helping program directors and in doing so improve the quality of program administration in our field.

A Roadmap for the Book

As public administration teachers and scholars, we care about the management of public agencies and nonprofits, but we often do not apply our field's scientific findings to the administration of our academic programs. This book argues for us to apply these tools, and we do so by asking our fields top academic leaders to discuss key aspects of their jobs. These aspects include the basics of public affairs programs, models of governance, roles of different administrative leaders, planning and budgeting for programs, navigating the accreditation process, assessing and improving student learning, ensuring social equity and cultural competency, mentoring faculty, developing curriculum, and helping provide service and applied research to community partners. These topics are examined in the following chapters.

In Chapter 2, Thomas J. Barth and Justin D. Hamel of the University of North Carolina at Charlotte discuss the differences in the various approaches to studying public organizations. The authors focus primarily on Master of Public Administration, Public Affairs, Public Policy, and Nonprofit Management degrees. They include discussions of what the different programs mean for a department with regards to student recruitment and placement, as well as program and faculty needs. The chapter presents some valuable data on the number of public affairs degrees, their focus (public policy, public administration, public affairs, etc.), and their concentrations. This information lays a useful foundation for the rest of the book.

In Chapter 3, Myung H. Jin of Virginia Commonwealth University surveys models of academic governance for public affairs programs. NASPAA accreditation standards require that a program be administered by the shared governance of its faculty. The chapter discusses the fully collaborative, consultative, and distributed decision-making models of shared governance that public affairs programs may take. The discussion on academic governances helps frame the rest of the book's focus on the work of public affairs directors and leaders.

In Chapter 4, Robert W. Smith of the University of Illinois at Springfield discusses the roles and responsibilities of key administrative officers that are responsibility for public affairs programs. He focuses on the university and NASPAA's perspective on the roles involved in the daily management of public affairs programs. Dr. Smith does an excellent job of discussing not just these roles but also some of the thinking and motivation pushing faculty to advance careers in academic administration.

In Chapter 5, Jerrell D. Coggburn of North Carolina State University and Jared J. Llorens of Louisiana State University examine the strategic planning process as it applies to managing a public affairs program. The authors include an overview of the strategic planning process, how to align a program within the mission of a department, the establishment of goals for a program, and the devising of strategies to pursue those goals. The tools discussed in this chapter can be used by program leadership in their efforts to develop missions and implement initiatives in a strategic manner, including securing and maintain accreditation.

In Chapter 6, Maja Husar Holmes of West Virginia University discusses the nuts and bolts of NASPAA accreditation. Being accredited by NASPAA is an important validation of excellence for MPA programs. However, many programs are not accredited, including some of the nation's best MPA programs. This chapter describes the accreditation process for MPA programs and discusses the importance of achieving this recognition. Special attention is paid toward how programs obtain accreditation, how they can use accreditation as a tool of constant improvement, and how programs are reaccredited.

In Chapter 7, John R. Bartle of the University of Nebraska at Omaha covers the principles of budgeting as it pertains to an academic department. He includes an introduction to university budgeting and a discussion of how many MPA programs make financial decisions. Additionally, the chapter addresses the limitations of MPA directors when preparing budgets for their programs. The importance of this chapter cannot be stressed enough. Even if MPA directors do not have budgetary authority, it is important to understand academic budgeting to be able to achieve objectives for their programs.

In Chapter 8, Kathryn Newcomer and Jasmine McGinnis Johnson of George Washington University present methods of faculty development, including the establishment of research and teaching mentorships, teaching training programs, and approaches to supporting faculty accomplishments. The authors include a model of how departments can work with and support their faculty to ensure that faculty meet tenure and promotion expectations.

In Chapter 9, Doug Goodman of the University of Texas at Dallas presents ideas on how to develop a curriculum for public affairs programs, including how to match the desired outcome of a program to the selection of courses that it offers. Also, the author discusses the design of concentrations within a program and choices of program modality and linking NASPAA competences to the curriculum of programs. Developing a curriculum is an important component of being an MPA director, and it is an area where many directors have a great deal of influence in their home institutions. It is imperative that directors keep up with the latest trends in curriculum development, poll stakeholders, and build curricula that work for their faculty, students, and program supporters.

In Chapter 10, Kathleen Hale of Auburn University discusses how programs assess their performance. To be successful, MPA programs need to craft measures of success and processes to determine whether or not goals are being met. The chapter focuses on how programs prepare evaluation and assessment plans. The author discusses how programs satisfy the requirements of NASPAA and provides examples of program assessment.

In Chapter 11, D. Ryan Miller of Nova Southeastern University examines how programs ensure that their graduates are achieving desired outcomes, such as "academic achievement, degree completion, employment, and enhanced salary." The chapter details how programs can achieve desired student outcomes through the design of their admissions process, curriculum, course scheduling, and assignments.

In Chapter 12, William Hatcher and Martha Humphries Ginn of Augusta University discuss issues of recruitment and retention for public affairs programs in order to provide advice for the directors of MPA degrees and similar programs in public affairs. The authors argue that recruiting and retaining diverse student bodies contributes to the goals of fairness and effectiveness in public administration. Their chapter also provides strategies from their university's recruitment and retention efforts.

In Chapter 13, Susan T. Gooden of Virginia Commonwealth University and Brandi Blessett of the University of Cincinnati discuss the importance of cultural competency and social equity when educating public servants. The authors discuss examples and models of how the concepts can be promoted in public affairs programs and how these efforts can be evaluated.

Last, in Chapter 14, Hunter Bacot of the University of North Carolina at Greensboro covers how MPA programs build the governing capacity of their communities. Many programs achieve this goal by being involved in community outreach and by operating applied research centers. The applied research provides community partners with information to help the organizations make evidence-based decisions. This chapter provides an overview of community outreach work offered by MPA programs, evaluates the work, and discusses examples of programs that are successful at building community partnerships.

In the book's conclusion, we connect the themes running through the book's chapters, and additional resources to help manage public affairs programs. It is our hope that this book and the strategies within it will encourage faculty to assume positions of leadership in their programs and manage those programs in an effective, efficient, and fair manner.

Note

1. President Reagan made this remark during his inaugural address, and President Clinton discussed the end of big government during his 1996 State of the Union address.

References

Brainard, L. A. & Infeld, D. L. (2017). The challenges and rewards of service: Job satisfaction among public affairs program directors. *Journal of Public Affairs Education*, *23*(3), 811–824.

Breihan, A. W. (2007). Attracting and retaining a diverse student body: Proven, practical strategies. *Journal of Public Affairs Education*, *13*(1), 87–101.

Chen, C. A. & Bozeman, B. (2014). Am I a public servant or am I a pathogen? Public manager's sector comparison of worker abilities. *Public Administration*, *92*(3), 549–564.

Chetkovich, C. (2003). What's in a sector? The shifting career plans of public policy students. *Public Administration Review*, *63*(6), 660–674.

Edwards, L. H., Holmes, M. H., & Sowa, J. E. (2019). Including women in public affairs departments: Diversity is not enough. *Journal of Public Affairs Education*, *25*(2), 163–184.

Evans, A. M., Morrison, J. K., & Auer, M. R. (2019). The crisis of policy education in turbulent times: Are schools of public affairs in danger of becoming irrelevant? *Journal of Public Affairs Education*, *25*(3), 285–295.

Garrett, R. S., Thurber, J. A., Fritschler, A. L., & Rosenbloom, D. H. (2006). Assessing the impact of bureaucracy bashing by electoral campaigns. *Public Administration Review*, *66*(2), 228–240.

Hatcher, W., Meares, W. L., & Gordon, V. (2017). The capacity and constraints of small MPA programs: A survey of program directors. *Journal of Public Affairs Education*, *23*(3), 855–868.

Johnson, J. M. & Ng, E. S. (2016). Money talks or millennials walk: The effect of compensation on nonprofit millennial workers' sector-switching intentions. *Review of Public Personnel Administration*, *36*(3), 283–305.

Katz, E. (2017). Trump uses major foreign address to bash bureaucracy. *Government Executive*. Retrieved September 25, 2019, from www.govexec.com/federal-news/2017/07/trump-uses-major-foreign-address-bash-bureaucracy/139232/.

Kerrigan, H. (2011, August). Fighting to save the MPA. *Governing*. Retrieved September 25, 2019, from www.governing.com/fighting-save-MPA.html.

Kettl, D. F. (2018). Earning trust in government. *Journal of Public Affairs Education*, *24*(3), 295–299.

Kettl, D. F. (2019). From policy to practice: From ideas to results, from results to trust. *Public Administration Review*, *79*(5), 763–767.

Killian, J. & Wenning, M. (2017). Are we having fun yet? Exploring the motivations of MPA and MPP program directors in the United States. *Journal of Public Affairs Education*, *23*(3), 799–810.

Kim, J. (2015). What increases public employees' turnover intention? *Public Personnel Management*, *44*(4), 496–519.

Maciag, M. (2013, December). The public employee 'silver tsunami' looms for governments. *Governing*. Retrieved September 25, 2019, from www.governing.com/topics/mgmt/gov-governments-silver-tsunami.html.

Meek, J. W. (2018). Making a difference: Good governance in disrupted states. *Journal of Public Affairs Education*, *24*(2), 135–151.

Network of Schools of Public Policy, Affairs, and Administration (2017). *2016–17 Accreditation data report*. Retrieved September 25, 2019, from www.naspaa.org/accreditation/data-accredited-programs.

Sorkin, A. (Writer), Mottola, G. (Director) (2012, June 24). We just decided to. [Television series episode] In A. Sorkin, S. Rudin, & A. Poul (Executive Producers), *The Newsroom*. Burbank, CA: Home Box Office.

Vicino, T. J. (2017). Navigating the multiple roles of the MPA director: Perspectives and lessons. *Journal of Public Affairs Education*, *23*(3), 785–798.

Williams, D. G., Plein, L. C., & Lilly, R. (1998). Professional and career development: The MPA portfolio approach. *Journal of Public Affairs Education*, *4*(4), 277–285.

World Health Organization (2019). *QD85 burn-out. ICD-11 for mortality and morbidity statistics*. Retrieved September 25, 2019, from https://icd.who.int/browse11/l-m/en#/http://id.who.int/icd/entity/129180281.

2

UNDERSTANDING THE DEGREES

MPA, MPP, versus MNM

Thomas J. Barth and Justin D. Hamel

Whether you are taking on responsibility for an existing graduate program or exploring the creation of a new program, the understanding of the differences and similarities between different types of public affairs programs is fundamental to the clear identity and focus necessary for a sustainable, effective program. The nature of your program will drive faculty and student recruitment, as well as how you brand it to key stakeholders like employers. Indeed, the nature of your program will influence every other topic covered in this book.

This chapter is both descriptive and suggestive. Based on a review of the field, the basic differences between the Master of Public Administration (MPA), Master of Public Affairs (MPAffairs), Master of Public Policy (MPP), and Master of Nonprofit Management (MNP) qualifications are provided, as well as significant differences in other less commonly seen but related degrees with titles including public management, public service, etc. The focus on MPA, MPP, MPAffairs and MNP reflects what is arguably the most commonly discussed and overlapping degrees in the public affairs arena. Then, based on a review of the literature, 28 years of experience directing MPA programs at three institutions, and the fresh eyes of a new MPA student, a set of key competing but more subtle concepts are raised that are important to address in further differentiating a program beyond just program title and course names.

The Landscape

To provide an overview of the landscape of public affairs graduate education, Table 2.1 shows an inventory of degree titles for NASPAA member institutions. These data demonstrate that the MPA title is the most common by a wide margin, followed by MPP and the MPAffairs.

TABLE 2.1 Inventory of Degree Titles for NASPAA Member Institutions

Graduate Programs	Number	Graduate Programs	Number
Public Affairs		**Public Policy**	
Master of Public Affairs	19	Master of Public Policy	35
Master of International Affairs	1	Master of Public Policy and Administration	5
Master of International Public Affairs	1	Master of Public Policy Administration	2
Master of Public and International Affairs	1	Master of Science in Public Policy	2
		Master of Public Policy and Management	1
Public Administration		Master of Urban Policy and Leadership	1
Master of Public Administration	242	Master of Science in Public and Urban Policy	1
Master of Public Management	7	Master of Science in Public Policy and Human Development	1
Executive Master of Public Administration	4	Master of Arts in Public Policy and Management	1
Master of Public Administration: Health Administration	1	Master of Arts in Rural Public Policy and Planning	1
Master of Science in Public Administration	1		
		Other	
Public Service		Master of Science in Management	1
Master of Public Service	1	Master of Science in Administration	1
Master of Public Service and Administration	1	Master of Political Science	1
Master of Science in Public Service Management	1	Master of International Relations	1
		Master of International Development	1
		Master of Arts in Urban Studies	1
		Defense-Focused Master of Business Administration	1
		Master of Business Administration for Business, Government, and Nonprofit Management	1

Source: NASPAA (2019a)

MPA versus MPP

While it is very important to examine the websites of the programs with these various titles to drill down for the truly significant differences between them (see NASPAA website for a complete listing of program titles by university), the primary distinction in building a public affairs program is between the MPA and MPP degree. There is considerable discussion in the literature on this topic, and the following summarizes some of the salient points.

- MPA: The Master of Public Administration (MPA) degree is the professional degree for students seeking a career in public service or nonprofit management. MPA programs develop the skills and techniques used by managers to implement policies, projects, and programs that resolve important problems within their organization and in society (NASPAA, 2019b).
- MPP: The Master of Public Policy (MPP) degree is the professional degree for analyzing, evaluating, and solving all aspects of policy. As analysts and managers, MPP graduates work with quantitative and qualitative data to develop, assess, and evaluate alternative approaches to current and emerging issues (NASPAA, 2019b).

Boiled down, the generally understood distinction is that the MPA prepares public-sector managers while the MPP prepares public policy analysts. According to the NASPAA website, "The MPA is for people who want to run things and change things for the public good. The MPP is for students who want to analyze public problems and recommend improvements" (NASPAA, 2019b). Infeld and Adams (2011) note that the MPA has roots in the Progressive era and the attempt to separate professional administration from the sphere of politics, and cite the NASPAA characterization that MPA programs "develop the skills and techniques used by leaders and managers to implement policies, projects, and programs that resolve important societal problems while addressing organizational, human resource, and budgetary challenges" (p. 278). Rivlin's 1971 article (as cited in Infeld and Adams, 2011) explains that the MPP, in contrast, has its roots in the 1960s and 1970s, "amid widespread views that governments needed more sophisticated analysts with improved technical skills and that public programs needed to be evaluated more critically" (p. 278). Smith (2008) echoes this evolution:

> The roots of public administration programs are in state and local government administration. Indeed, many programs were initially focused on training city managers, and some programs still focus on this part of the public service community. As public administration grew, its mission broadened to include service in the national government and a variety of policy analysis positions in public organizations, research institutes,

consulting firms, and advocacy groups. The curriculum shifted to place more emphasis on policy analysis and less on the skills needed for working in state and local agencies, especially local municipal agencies.

(p. 116)

MPA directors should understand that there is a significant variation in the degree of distinctiveness between MPA and MPP programs across universities for a variety of reasons that are discussed later in this chapter. For example, Frederickson (2001) notes the tendency for preoccupation with US News and World Report rankings to make programs more similar. In contrast, Pal and Clark (2016) present an analysis of 99 MPA and MPP programs across five countries including the US. This study concludes that despite claims that there has been convergence among programs, they found there is in fact significant variation. Amidst this diversity of perspectives and approaches, the fundamental differences should be appreciated in building or shaping a program. In their analysis of differences and similarities between the two degrees, Infeld and Adams (2011) found the following:

> MPA and MPP students … differed to a nontrivial degree in the types of work they want to do. Compared to MPA students MPAs showed a markedly greater interest in managerial roles; and compared to MPA students, the MPPs evidenced consistently stronger motivations to master quantitative analytical techniques and to critique public policies.

(p. 300)

In his study of differences between MPA and MPA programs, Kretzschmar (2010) suggests that the programs differ in the faculty, their curricula, and how they train students. He notes that:

> the traditional MPA programs in his sample like Kansas, Florida State, and UNC Chapel Hill have mostly Public Administration doctorates on their faculty, with almost no Economists. The MPP programs (Michigan, Duke, Berkeley) all have a high number of Economists, and zero Public Administration PhDs.

(p. 54)

In terms of curricula, Hur and Hackbart (2009) conclude from their analysis that compared to MPP programs, MPA programs have lower percentages of economics and policy analysis classes and higher percentages of finance and budgeting and organization and human resource management. This difference in faculty and curricula reflects the different purposes of the programs: the MPA is about management and administration (program implementation), while the MPP is about the policies that guide the work of the managers and administrators (policy analysis). An illustration of these differences is seen in Table 2.2,

TABLE 2.2 Comparison of Core MPP and MPA Classes at George Washington University

MPP Core Classes	MPA Core Classes
Research Methods and Applied Statistics	Perspectives on Public Values
Economics for Policy Analysis I	Introduction to Public Service and Administration
Politics and Policy Analysis	Research Methods and Applied Statistics
Econometrics for Policy Research I	Economics for Public Decision-Making
Economics for Policy Analysis II	Leadership in Public Administration and Public Policy
	Public Budgeting, Revenue, and Expenditures
	Policy Analysis
	Capstone Seminar
	Public and Nonprofit Program Evaluation

Source: Trachtenberg School of Public Policy and Public Administration (2019).

which compares the core curriculum of the MPA and MPA programs offered by the Trachtenberg School of Public Policy and Public Administration at George Washington University.

Looking deeper into the descriptions of the two programs provides further distinctions to these areas of study. Note that the MPP core is all statistics, economics and policy analysis, reflecting the goal of providing students with "the ability to think clearly and analytically about social and economic problems and public policy" (Trachtenberg School of Public Policy and Public Administration, 2019). The George Washington University website also notes that the MPP prepares students for professional positions in all levels of government, but also in research institutes, think tanks, community advocacy organizations, and professional and trade associations. While the MPA core has a dose of statistics and economics, the preponderance of coursework is leadership, budgeting, program evaluation, and other management-related courses. These courses reflect the focus on management as well as policy issues in an intergovernmental and intersectoral context. In contrast to the MPP description, there is also a focus on developing sensitivity to "the ethical and value concerns that are central to the traditions of the field of public administration" (Trachtenberg School of Public Policy and Public Administration, 2019). The website notes that graduates are employed in government agencies at all levels, national associations, interest groups, and research and consulting firms. There is certainly some degree of overlap in the programs and employment targets that reflects the reality of blurred lines between policy and management in practice, but it is clear that if the career goal is a research institute or think tank, lean toward the MPP, while if the goal is management of an institution, lean toward the MPA.

MPAffairs

The third most common degree title is the MPAffairs. An examination of the several programs that use public affairs in their title can at times mean nothing more than a brand preference (i.e., they are in reality not very different from a public administration or public policy degree but want a different title to separate themselves), but this connotation in some cases carries significance as a broader or umbrella degree that provides many options and draws on multiple disciplines. An illustration is Washington State University, which states that it "draws on a variety of academic disciplines, such as political science, business administration, economics, sociology, health policy administration, environmental science/regional planning, law and criminal justice" (College of Arts and Sciences, 2019). This "big tent" approach is seen in concentrations that go beyond generalist public administration and public policy studies to include health policy and public service, justice studies, and environmental policy (College of Arts and Sciences, 2019). Another example of this broad spectrum is the MPAffairs offered by the Humphrey School at the University of Minnesota, which states that it provides "curriculum and experiential learning expertise" in six key areas: global policy; leadership and management; politics and governance; science, technology, and the environment; social policy and policy analysis; and urban and regional planning. Therefore, it is useful to think of a broad, multi-disciplinary program when you see the title Master of Public Affairs.

The summary below provides a useful way of broadly conceptualizing between these three degrees.

- MPA: Management focus – organization theory, budgeting, human resource management, data analysis for managers with traditional concentrations such as local government, budgeting, planning.
- MPP: Policy focus – policy analysis, economics, advanced statistics and quantitative methods with policy area concentrations.
- MPAffairs: Interdisciplinary focus – blend of policy and management, with broader concentration offerings such as international, environmental, energy, and justice studies.

Other Public Affairs Degrees

There is an array of other public affairs degrees providing distinct approaches to the education of public managers that merit consideration.

Master of Public Policy and Administration. There are five programs that combine administration and policy in their title, connoting that they serve both areas with one degree. An example is the University of Tennessee at Knoxville, which "aspires to produce graduates who are literate in the field of public administration, have the skills to be effective managers of organizational resources, and possess the analytical abilities to be creative problem solvers."[1] They provide a required core curriculum covering a blend of quantitative methods, general public and financial administration, economics, and public service ethics/ values. Students then can choose either public management or public policy options or tracks. In other cases, such as Mississippi State University, having administration and policy in the title reflected a very strong public policy concentration. It should be noted that Mississippi State University has subsequently dropped this concentration, although the title remains (E. French, personal communication, May 18, 2019). This example demonstrates that one needs to drill down to get a true picture of a program beyond a particular title. The point here is not to pass judgment on what is the best approach, but to make the reader aware of the different approaches to graduate education in public affairs, particularly when it comes to administration (implementation) versus policy (analysis). The recommendation is that program leadership and their faculty be clear and intentional about the purpose and focus of their degree to lessen ambiguity and confusion for students, employers, and other stakeholders.

Master of Public Management. Yet another distinct set of seven programs has a decidedly business orientation with a focus on management skills that are transferable across all sectors. An illustration is the Master of Public Management at Carnegie Mellon University, which states that it "prepares experienced professionals to manage in highly regulated industries such as healthcare, banking, and local government" (Heinz College, 2019). An examination of the core curriculum reveals a distinctly generic organization/business flavor with courses like organizational management, database management, management science, business writing for leaders, and strategic presentation skills. Students can pick up government-oriented classes through electives, but it is clear that the calling card for an MPM is generic management skills and tools versus a focus on the public administration or public policy context; this is the perspective that "government and nonprofit agencies can/should be run like a business." Furthermore, MPM programs like that offered by Johns Hopkins University are more likely to market that their program can place students in the private sector as well as the government and nonprofit sectors, and have core courses like essentials of public and private management, US tax policy, trade and security, and negotiation (Krieger School of Arts and Science, 2019).

Executive MPA. A final set of distinct programs worth noting are those known as "Executive MPA" programs (four are listed in the NASPAA database), designed for experienced managers and delivered in a manner that accommodates high levels of responsibility and less flexible work schedules (e.g., weekend, intensive, or online). Programs may require a minimum number of years of management experience, and classes are often taken lockstep for ease of longer-term planning and scheduling. An example is the Executive MPA in the Hatfield School of Government at Portland State University, where students take a lockstep set of courses on Saturdays that in some cases will look quite similar to regular MPA courses, but the program also features courses like leading public organizations, advanced budgeting concepts and techniques, and leadership development in the public sector. The audience for such executive programs should drive a different focus than a traditional MPA for pre-service or employees earlier in their career, with an emphasis on the primary challenges at the higher levels of an agency such as leadership and organizational development, agency culture, and values and ethics. Also noted are the field immersion experiences in Washington, DC and overseas, with the purpose of broadening the perspective and experiences of the executive (Hatfield School of Government, 2019). Program directors need to consider the target audience for their program and whether there is a sufficient market of mid-career, higher-level managers or executives in the government and nonprofit sectors to sustain an executive program.

Graduate Programs in Nonprofit Management

Another major development in graduate public affairs education is the emergence of nonprofit management as a focus of study. The treatment of graduate nonprofit management education merits attention in a chapter on understanding the public affairs degrees, as an MPA program director will likely need to consider how to address the nonprofit sector in their program. The following array of nonprofit management education programs in Table 2.3 demonstrate the emergence of nonprofit management as a concentration within MPA and MPP programs, but also the significant presence of nonprofit management within Master of Business Administration (MBA) and Master of Social Work (MSW) programs as well as stand-alone nonprofit management graduate degrees (Nonprofit Sector Resource Institute, 2016).

According to the Nonprofit Academic Centers Council, 157 schools nationwide offer at least one class in nonprofit management within a graduate department (Nonprofit Academic Centers Council, 2018). We count 125 MPA programs and 20 MPP programs with a formal concentration in nonprofit management. Mirabella (2015) notes that the number of universities with three or more graduate courses in nonprofit management increased from 82 in 1996 to 227 in 2014, and the number of universities with a graduate concentration increased from 105 in 2006 to 152 in 2014. The rise in the presence of nonprofit management graduate education is seen with NASPAA developing a separate set of accreditation standards for such programs and NASPAA having its own section on Nonprofit Management Education. Mirabella (2015) notes:

> This growth reflects … the continued expansion of the nonprofit sector itself, particularly as governmental retrenchment and the hollowing out of the state have led to an increased policy preference for contracting out to

TABLE 2.3 Inventory of Nonprofit Management Graduate Programs

Graduate Programs in Nonprofit Management	Number	Graduate Programs with NP Concentrations	Number
Master of Arts in Nonprofit Management	10	Master of Public Administration	125
Graduate Certificate in Nonprofit Management	7	Master of Public Policy	20
Master of Nonprofit Management	6	Master of Business Administration	18
Master of Science in Nonprofit Management	5	Master of Social Work	18
Master of Nonprofit Leadership	3	Master of Public Affairs	10
Master of Nonprofit Administration	3	Master of Urban and Regional Planning	2
Master of Nonprofit Leadership and Management	2	Master of Arts in Social Entrepreneurship and Change	2
Master of Science in Nonprofit Leadership	2	Master of Government Administration	2
		Master of Science in Management	2
		Master of Science in Public Service Management	1
		Master of Science in International Public Service	1
		Master of Arts in Public Service	1
		Master of Arts in Sustainable International Development	1
		Master of Arts in Urban Affairs and Public Policy	1
		Master of Arts in Urban Studies	1
		Master of City and Regional Planning	1
		Master of Community and Regional Planning	1

Source: Seton Hall University (2019).

nonprofit organizations for delivery of services to the public. Additionally, a series of events beginning in the 1960s led to the development of academic research centers dedicated to the study of nonprofit institutions, many of which expanded their activities to include education for future leaders of the sector as well.

(p. 2207)

It is instructive to compare and contrast these different approaches to graduate nonprofit education as follows. As with the graduate public affairs programs, it is very important for program directors to carefully examine programs at particular universities to understand the distinctive flavor of each.

MPA with Nonprofit Management Concentration

This model requires a certain number of nonprofit-focused courses on top of the core courses required of all MPA students. For example, Indiana University has the top-rated nonprofit specialty according to the 2020 US News and World Report rankings of the best graduate schools (O'Neill School of Public and Environmental Affairs, 2019). It requires the following two nonprofit courses: The Nonprofit and Voluntary Sector, and Management in the Nonprofit Sector. The course descriptions are as follows.

> **The Nonprofit and Voluntary Sector**: The theory, size, scope, and functions of the nonprofit and voluntary sector are covered from multiple disciplinary perspectives, including historical, political, economic, and social.

> **Management in the Nonprofit Sector**: An examination of nonprofit organizations and their role in society. Management issues and public policy affecting these organizations are discussed. Primary emphasis is upon US organizations, but attention is given to the global nature of the sector.

Students must then choose roughly seven elective nonprofit-focused courses from a wide-ranging menu covering strategic management, development, financial management, strategic planning, human resources management, and program evaluation, among others.

This program is on the high end of nonprofit course requirements, but, generally speaking, nonprofit concentrations within a public affairs program will require about five courses, with two required courses that ground students in the unique context of the nonprofit sector and provide core skills like financial analysis. Then students are allowed to select from a menu of electives tailored to nonprofit management such as fundraising, grant writing, program evaluations, or social entrepreneurship. Young's 1999 article (as cited in Mirabella and Wish, 2000) argues that the nonprofit concentration within an MPA makes sense because of the "closer philosophical bond between public administration and nonprofit management ..." (p. 221). Salamon's 1999 study (as cited in Mirabella, 2015) suggests several other advantages of the nonprofit management concentration in MPA programs provided by Salamon, including:

> the desirability of educating managers of both the public and nonprofit sector together, particularly given the significant interactions between personnel in the two sectors. Next there is a tremendous amount of cross-over among managers, and education within an MPA program would provide the flexibility necessary to make these career shifts.
>
> *(p. 2211)*

Thus, it is appropriate for MPA programs with a concentration on nonprofit management to promote the advantages of such a degree for students who may not be sure about whether the government or nonprofit sectors are the best fit for them, or as the degree that will provide an understanding of the blurred boundaries between the sectors and the flexibility to move back and forth (Gelles, 2016). Furthermore, Pandey and Johnson (2019) argue that public administration, public policy, and nonprofit management are "intersectional domains of inquiry" and that "knowledge development in each of these domains requires that we bring deep and intimate knowledge from other domains" (p. 4).

MBA with Nonprofit Management Concentration

MPA directors should become familiar with the MBA programs offering a concentration on nonprofit management as they can have a distinctly different look; an example is Yale University's Program on Social Enterprise within its School of Management. This program is marketed as "harnessing business skills and markets to achieve social objectives." Courses include managing social enterprises, inclusive business models, urban poverty and economic development, managing sustainable operations, introduction to responsible business, and strategic management of nonprofit organizations (School of Management, 2019). Mirabella (2015) documents several advantages offered by the business school setting, including sheer number, quality, and "depth of management" among the faculty compared to other degree programs.

Mirabella suggests that these nonprofit-oriented programs with a business/entrepreneurial twist are very attractive to young adults coming out of undergraduate programs, and MPA programs with nonprofit concentrations would be wise to take notice (R. Mirabella, personal communication, March 26, 2019).

MSW with Nonprofit Management Concentration

Another major player in graduate nonprofit management education is the MSW program. A representative example is the MSW at the University of Michigan, the top-ranked program in the US News and World Report rankings. After taking a foundation curriculum that provides the fundamentals of social policy formulation and program implementation, direct practice methods at multiple system levels, social work research, theories of human behavior, and a fieldwork experience, students can choose a concentration in the Management of Human Services, where two advanced courses are selected from a variety of management topics including organizational change and management, budgeting, MIS, human resources, leadership and resource development, grantgetting, contracting, and fundraising (School of Social Work, 2019).

Mirabella (2015) notes how "Dennis Young has pointed that social work can claim 'historical jurisdiction' over the nonprofit field because of their connection to human service organizations" (p. 2211). She also cites advantages of the profession's emphasis on values and ethics, and promoting MSWs from within the agency brings a greater understanding of the inner workings of the organization and familiarity with policy areas.

Stand-Alone Graduate Programs in Nonprofit Management

There are also stand-alone graduate programs based on the philosophy that proper preparation for a nonprofit manager requires more coursework specifically focused on the nonprofit setting. An example is the Master of Nonprofit Management program at the University of Central Florida, which is the first nonprofit management master's accredited by NASPAA (although stand-alone graduate programs in nonprofit management have been following curricular guidelines for years, established by the Nonprofit Academic Centers Council) (School of Public Administration, 2019). The establishment of this program is significant as it reflects a decision by an MPA program that a nonprofit management concentration is not sufficient for its market.

The required core curriculum of eight courses covers volunteerism, resource development, grants and contract management, financial management, human resources, nonprofit organizations, program evaluation, and a capstone in nonprofit organizations. The stand-alone program does allow for more courses concentrated solely on the nonprofit setting than is feasible within the confines of a typical MPA or MBA program.

The question as to what is the ideal preparation for a nonprofit manager is best answered by in-depth conversations with employers and other key stakeholders in the nonprofit market being targeted by a public affairs program, as discussed further below in the treatment of generalist versus specialist approaches to graduate education. Mirabella (2015) does note that the presence of stand-alone nonprofit management programs reflects the "unique attributes of the nonprofit sector, particularly the complexity of its environment and the resource issues facing managers within the sector" (p. 2211).

Key Issues to Address in Differentiating Your Program

Matching Your Program to Your Market

A successful public affairs program should align with its defined market, whether that be regional, statewide, or national. This market consists primarily of the leaders of the organizations that will be hiring your students. At the end of the day, some of the most important measures of a graduate professional degree program are the employability of its students and the professional success of its alumni. A program should thus carefully consult these leaders to make the basic determination as to whether the best fit is an MPA, MPP, MNM, etc. However, in a recent study of public affairs master's programs in the US and Latin American region, Cid (2018) reminds us:

> The hosting department indicates the academic discipline of most faculty members … and the set of priorities for course offerings in terms of mandatory/elective and sequence. The existing program design usually follows internal arrangements among program directors and faculty in defining course priorities and course offerings. However, student preferences or employers' needs related to these general characteristics are usually neglected.
>
> *(p. 20)*

As a general guideline, an MPA producing managers will be the best fit if you are a regional university and your market is small to midsize local governments, with a nonprofit concentration if there is a sizable nonprofit sector. This describes our program at UNC Charlotte. As the size of the local government and nonprofit sectors increase, so will the demand for analysts (MPP) or specialty degrees such as the MNP. If the market is state or federal government, think tanks, or consulting firms, the MPP becomes more desirable as more higher-powered policy analysts are needed. Of course, state and federal agencies need managers as well, so this is where you might consider both degrees or more blended programs, of which the George Washington and American Universities programs are examples.

Beyond the structure of your master's degree program, there may be market-driven opportunities to consider supplementary options such as certificate programs, non-credit professional development programs, and dual-degree offerings. Smith (2018) suggests that the increased complexity of public service provision and the rapidly changing policy and organizational environment have created a demand for shorter-term programs for working professionals who need updated knowledge and tools. At UNC Charlotte, for example, we offer certificate programs in Nonprofit Management, Urban Management & Policy, Emergency Management, and Public Finance & Budgeting that have a five-course sequence. We also offer a non-credit Public and Nonprofit Management Academy that provides three full days of training pulled from our MPA curriculum that also features roundtables of community leaders on the topics. Both the certificates and the Academy are responses to a large urban market where experienced professionals are looking to augment or update their skills but do not desire a full MPA degree.

In a similar vein, Smith (2008) also notes "the diversification of policy tools and organizational forms has increased the complexity of public policy, creating a need for MPA graduates with a broader set of skills" (p. 125). He recommends exploring the potential for joint degrees, with social work, planning, and environmental policy as examples. Certificates can also fulfill this demand, as students enrolled in other master's programs like social work may wish to add the nonprofit management certificate to supplement their clinical degree. Given their sheer number of dual-degree options (14), a useful source to explore for dual-degree arrangements is the Master of Public Affairs program in the Lyndon B. Johnson School at the University of Texas at Austin (Lyndon B. Johnson School of Public Affairs, 2019).

Ultimately, a primary driver of the structure of your program should be the government and nonprofit managers who hire your students, provide internships and fellowships, and financially support your program. To this end, a best practice among many public affairs programs is the utilization of a community or practitioner advisory board comprised of managers and alumni from key government and nonprofit agencies in their region. Hatcher, Meares, and Gordon (2017) discuss the importance of these advisory boards to MPA programs, but also suggest that that the "lack of involvement from advisory boards is significant for the field of public administration" (p. 862). Investment in an active advisory board, however time-consuming, is a wise strategy for an MPA program for taking the pulse of its market on a regular basis.

This statement of how the University of Tennessee at Knoxville redesigned its MPA to a Master of Public Policy and Administration program provides an example of a market-driven decision-making process that is a useful approach for program directors to consider:

> The short answer is that we re-invented our MPA program in 2012 after extensive consultation with our alumni and employers and after many PA faculty meetings in which we analyzed the changing knowledge and skill sets needed for the 21st century public service. The fruit of that process was a revised mission and a program curriculum that we

believed better reflect what servant leaders in the public service need in order to be literate in public administration and equipped with the skills to be effective managers who have the analytical abilities to be creative and ethical problem solvers. We concluded that all graduates from our program need the knowledge and skills in our Foundation courses and that this provides a reasonably solid basis for them to understand the context and perspective needed to pursue more specialized training for careers focused on either policy analysis or advocacy, or management. Several of our students actually take courses in both specialized tracks to enhance their competitiveness for careers in both areas. We think we got this right since we have placed 100% of our grads since the first cohort matriculated in spring 2013.

(D. Folz, personal communication, May 30, 2019)

Aligning Your Program with the Institutional Setting

Although your market should be your primary driver for the type of program you offer, the institutional setting matters, especially if you are building the program with existing faculty who are retooling to teach in a public affairs program. As an experienced public affairs program administrator notes, often you just need to "deal with the hand you are dealt" (C. Stenberg, personal communication, March 9, 2019). For example, a traditional political science department setting is more likely to have faculty with methods and policy backgrounds, while a business school setting would have faculty more aligned with management classes, whether those be government or nonprofit. However, in their study of the MPA/MPP in several "Anglo-democracies," Pal and Clark (2016) note:

> Once established … programs do have incentives to diverge and distinguish themselves. Sometimes this differentiation is driven by internal university dynamics. MPA and MPPA programs often have to position and defend themselves vis-à-vis their particular sister business schools and political science departments. On the other hand, in more collaborative contexts, they can build on niche programming in those sister units.
>
> *(p. 311)*

Despite the well documented, entrenched disciplinary biases and pressures of parent departments that may constrain particularly smaller MPA programs (Hatcher, Meares, & Gordon, 2017), departments and faculty have a vested interest in healthy enrollments, so a shared understanding of the different models for public affairs programs and dialogue between faculty and prospective students and employers can lead to a program that is the best fit for a given university setting.

Generalist versus Specialist

Drilling down below the difference between the degree names without getting into specific curricula, which are covered in a separate chapter, another fundamental difference between programs is the degree to which you are focused on producing generalist versus specialist students. This decision will drive the size of your core curriculum and the number of concentrations offered, as well as the focus on generic skills like program evaluation or strategic planning, versus substantive areas such as transportation or emergency management. Figure 2.1 provides a list of the frequency of concentrations in public affairs programs, and the decision on the concentrations offered will have a major influence on the market niche for your program and the faculty recruited.

This distinction between a generalist versus a specialist orientation has been discussed for many years in the field. Medeiros (1974) notes competing "philosophical orientations" in public administration education between approaches that satisfy "intellectual curiosity and a general appreciation of administrative concepts and issues" (i.e., generalist), those that provide a "thorough grasp of typical organizational patterns in one of several institutional realms ... with the perspective of a particular discipline or interdisciplinary area and a set of technical tools" (i.e., specialist) (p. 256), and those that purport to do both. In the *Frequently Asked Questions* section of the MPP webpage at the University of California, Berkeley, there is a specific question on "Does the GSPP program train generalists or specialists?" The answer to the question is instructive.

> The School first aims to train generalists, in the sense of providing basic policy skills needed in a variety of policy positions and across a wide range of policy issues. Having learned and applied the basic skills in the School's

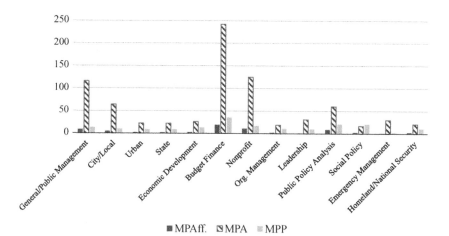

FIGURE 2.1   Frequency of Concentrations and Specializations

program, graduates are able to familiarize themselves rapidly with the details of a specific policy area relevant to their particular job. It would not be easy, however, for policy area specialists who lacked these technical skills to develop them once on the job. Feedback from alumni and employers confirms the soundness of providing an education for generalists.

The variety of positions reflects the multidisciplinary skills possessed by MPP graduates and the different types of policy roles sought by individual graduates.

(Goldman School of Public Policy, 2019)

At the end of the day, an MPA or MPP is a generalist degree compared to other more specialized graduate programs focused solely on areas like public health, urban planning, health administration, or nonprofit management. There are inherent advantages and disadvantages to such a degree, depending on the career goals of a student and needs expressed by employers. For example, in the case of planning, we would point out that our MPA students have had good success landing entry-level planning positions in local governments, because employers value their broader education and perspective; they can learn the technical planning pieces on the job. Regardless of where a program director stands philosophically on this issue, public affairs programs have an ethical obligation to explain the pros and cons of a more generalist degree, stressing that such an education does allow a student to gain entrance to a variety of organizational settings; this may be the best fit for a student unsure of their specific career goals other than a general interest in a public service career. However, the "best place" debate in graduate public affairs education will always be an issue for a program director; although this chapter focuses on the field of nonprofit management, similar questions can be raised about other fields, such as public finance and data analytics, where public affairs programs have converted concentrations into stand-alone degrees (see Martin School of Public Policy and Administration, 2019) or have plans underway (B. McDonald, personal communication, May 20, 2019; College of Urban Planning and Public Affairs, 2019). Gelles (2016) captures this tension well:

How much integration is enough for MPA generalists or students specializing in other areas? What might students need to understand if they specialize in other areas such as housing, municipal government, environmental management, or health, earning industry-specific degrees? Should sector discussions be made integral to an introductory institutions course and/or be part of all or most of the program's core? I am not suggesting that these things can or should be mandated, only that we should consider the questions.

(p. 421)

As discussed earlier in the case of nonprofit management, program leaders will need to decide if a concentration in nonprofit management within a public affairs program is adequate training or if a "stand-alone" program is necessary to properly prepare a nonprofit manager. Or, they may need to grapple with arguments on campus that nonprofit management education best rests in a social work, business, or interdisciplinary setting (Mirabella & Wish, 2000). Indeed, Mirabella has serious concerns that without strategic attention, MPA programs are in danger of losing claim over nonprofit management education to business schools (R. Mirabella, personal communication, March 26, 2019). This concern is warranted given the 18 MBA programs with a nonprofit management concentration.

Theory versus Application

Another useful distinction between programs to consider is a theory-driven versus applied program. This is evident in the courses, where the emphasis may be on grounding students in the classic and cutting-edge theory and literature, signified by intensive reading and research papers, versus classes that spend much more time on case studies, simulations, practitioner guest speakers and community-based projects. This emphasis can also drive the extent to which programs utilize practitioner instructors. This of course is not a mutually exclusive distinction, but the difference in emphasis is evident and can be a mark of distinction.

There is an extensive literature on this issue worth considering. For example, Dede (2002) discusses the tendency of public administration programs to be hyper-instrumentalized, and proposes a course to add some theoretical learning into the curriculum. Englehart (2001) argues that both theory and practice are necessary for effective public administrators, rejecting the idea that theory is irrelevant to the practice of public administration. Bushouse and Morrison (2001) use a case study of a service learning course to explore how service learning can be adapted for MPA programs.

Although not prevalent, a good example of the incorporation of service learning as a core part of its program is the Master of Public Service program at the University of Arkansas, which requires students to complete three courses where they engage in field projects: Practicum, International Public Service Project, and Capstone (see Clinton School of Public Service, 2019). This is a higher-than-normal emphasis on field projects, and reflects the program's focus on a "real-world" curriculum that embodies former President Clinton's "vision of building leadership in civic engagement and enhancing people's capacity to work across disciplinary, racial, ethnic and geographical boundaries." The core curriculum also looks very different from a traditional MPA or MPP:

- Program Planning and Development;
- Foundations of Public Service;
- Field Research in Public Service;

- Communication and Social (Ex)Change;
- Ethical and Legal Dimensions of Public Service;
- The Theory and Practice of Global Development;
- Seminar in Program Evaluation; and,
- Professionalism in Public Service.

Program directors should note how this distinction between theory and practice will impact the attractiveness of a program to practicing public administrators who want material relevant to their experience as well as pre-service students who want to be ready to apply classroom knowledge to the "real world." For example, Seton Hall's MPA program states that "we pride ourselves on bringing academic theory into practice" (Seton Hall University, 2019). The theory–practice balance may not be particularly evident in the course titles in a listed curriculum, but it will be imbedded in the course content. Denhardt, Lewis, Raffel, and Rich (1997) describe another example in the "Delaware Model," where the integration of theory and practice is embedded as a core guiding principle of the program:

> The Delaware model seeks to bring together theory and practice through the professional and psychological integration of full-time students into the implementation of the college's and the MPA program's applied research and service mission as a critical component of an experientially-based educational program.
>
> *(p. 160)*

This is an area that will also clearly be important in determining the type of faculty recruited by a program. Theory-driven faculty are interested in creating new knowledge with their research and leading students through an in-depth understanding of classic and cutting-edge concepts in the field. Application-driven faculty are interested in translating and testing theory in the field and helping students learn through the application of theory in the community. Again, there is no magic formula for how to balance theory and practice in a program, but these different approaches are meaningful to faculty and students and shape the identity of a public affairs program.

Parting Message from an MPA Student and Program Director: Truth in Advertising

From a student perspective, individuals pursuing a career in public service or the nonprofit sector often find themselves considering a graduate education without a great deal of knowledge of the field. Aside from graduation and alumni employment rates, students may not know what questions to ask or alternative means by which to judge how effectively a program may prepare them for the real-word opportunities they seek. Furthermore, the average

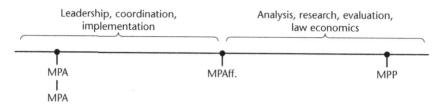

FIGURE 2.2 Public Affairs Education Spectrum

student is uninformed about things such as pedagogy and curriculum design. A simple internet search for "master of public service degree" provides a dizzying array of graduate degrees in public administration, public policy, public affairs, nonprofit management, and others. As a helpful starting point, a comparative analysis seems to suggest that the collection of degrees discussed in this chapter can be plotted along a spectrum illustrated in Figure 2.2, with the MPA and MNM at one end focusing on management skills, the MPP at the other end focusing on analytical skills, and the MPAffairs tending to be the umbrella program combining aspects of both and crossing multiple disciplines.

Ideally, the letters behind a graduate's name should clearly indicate where they fall on the spectrum and what skills they should be expected to possess. However, the reality is that these degrees may share many common elements and appear nearly indistinguishable on paper, so MPA directors should take care to assist prospective students in carefully choosing the degree that best corresponds to their strengths and professional goals and helps differentiate them from others in the job market.

Echoing this student perspective, from the lens of an MPA director a clear understanding of the differences between various public affairs programs and a shared understanding regarding the issues discussed in this chapter will help define your program and provide a clear understanding to both students and employers alike of the mix of knowledge and skills possessed by your graduates. Such a clear definition should drive the marketing of your program and recruitment of faculty, so that all stakeholders understand what your program is and what it is not. Otherwise, the pressures to increase or just maintain enrollments can create a misleading picture of your program by trying to be "all things to all people"; however, such false advertising is a lose-lose proposition, as you will have disgruntled students who discover that they are in a program that is not what they were really looking for, and you will have disappointed employers who find the students they hire from your program are not the right fit.

Note

1. The University of Tennessee at Knoxville's Department of Political Science website. https://polisci.utk.edu/mppa/index.php.

References

Bushouse, B. & Morrison, S. (2001). Applying service learning in Master of Public Affairs programs. *Journal of Public Affairs Education*, 7(1), 9–17.

Cid, G. P. (2018). A comparative analysis of public affairs master's programs in the United States and the Latin American region. *Journal of Public Affairs Education*. doi:10.1080/15236803.2018.1489094.

Clinton School of Public Service (2019). Clinton School of Public Affairs. *University of Arkansas*. Retrieved June 27, 2019, from https://clintonschool.uasys.edu/.

College of Arts and Sciences (2019). Master of Public Affairs. *Washington State University*. Retrieved June 27, 2019, from https://cas.vancouver.wsu.edu/master-public-affairs.

College of Urban Planning and Public Affairs (2019). Master of Public Administration. *University of Illinois at Chicago*. Retrieved June 27, 2019, from https://cuppa.uic.edu/academics/pa/pa-programs/master-public-administration/.

Dede, M. J. (2002). The praxis journal: Integrating theory and practice. *Journal of Public Affairs Education*, 8(4), 287–297.

Denhardt, R. B., Lewis, J. R., Raffel, J. R., & Rich, D. (1997). Integrating theory and practice in MPA education: The Delaware model. *Journal of Public Administration Education*, 3(2), 153–162.

Englehart, J. K. (2001). The marriage between theory and practice. *Public Administration Review*, 61(3), 371–374.

Frederickson, G. (2001). Reflections on ranking master's degrees in public affairs: The search for reputational capital. *Journal of Public Affairs Education*, 7(2), 65–71.

Gelles, E. (2016). Perhaps easier said than done: Is there a downside to integrating non-profit substance into the MPA core curriculum. *Journal of Public Affairs Education*, 22(3), 415–434.

Goldman School of Public Policy (2019). Master of Public Policy (MPP). *University of California, Berkeley*. Retrieved June 27, 2019, from https://gspp.berkeley.edu/programs/masters-of-public-policy-mpp.

Hatcher, W., Meares, W. L., & Gordon, V. (2017). The capacity and constraints of small MPA programs: A survey of program directors. *Journal of Public Affairs Education*, 23(3), 855–868.

Hatfield School of Government (2019). Executive Master of Public Administration program. *Portland State University*. Retrieved June 27, 2019, from www.pdx.edu/cps/executive-master-of-public-administration.

Heinz College (2019). Master of Public Management. *Carnegie Mellon University*. Retrieved June 27, 2019, from www.heinz.cmu.edu/programs/public-management-master/.

Hur, Y. & Hackbart, M. (2009). MPA vs. MPP: A distinction without a difference? *Journal of Public Affairs Education*, 15(4), 397–424.

Infeld, D. & Adams, W. (2011). MPA and MPP Students: Twins, siblings, or distant cousins? *Journal of Public Affairs Education*, 17(2), 277–303.

Kretzschmar, B. (2010). Differentiated degrees: Are MPA and MPP programs really that different? *Perspectives in Public Affairs*, 7(1), 42–67.

Krieger School of Arts and Science (2019). Public management. *Johns Hopkins University*. Retrieved June 27, 2019, from https://advanced.jhu.edu/academics/graduate-degree-programs/public-management/.

Lyndon B. Johnson School of Public Affairs (2019). Master of Public Affairs. *University of Texas*. Retrieved June 27, 2019, from https://lbj.utexas.edu/master-public-affairs.

Martin School of Public Policy and Administration (2019). Master of Public Financial Management (MPFM). *University of Kentucky*. Retrieved June 27, 2019, from martin. uky.edu/master-public-financial-management-mpfm.

Medeiros, J. (1974). The professional study of public administration. *Public Administration Review, 34*(3), 254–260.

Mirabella, R. (2015). Nonprofit management education. In Bearfield, D. A., Berman, E. M., & Dubnick, M. J. (eds), *Encyclopedia of public administration and public policy*, 3rd edn. (pp. 2207–2213). New York: Routledge.

Mirabella, R. M. & Wish, N. B. (2000). The "best place" debate: A comparison of graduate education programs for nonprofit managers. *Public Administration Review, 60*(3), 219–229.

Network of Schools of Public Policy, Affairs, and Administration (2019a). *Find your graduate degree for public service*. Retrieved June 27, 2019, from www.naspaa.org/schools-search.

Network of Schools of Public Policy, Affairs, and Administration (2019b). *MPA/MPP degrees*. Retrieved June 27, 2019, from www.naspaa.org/resources/why-public-service-degree/mpampp-degrees.

Nonprofit Academic Centers Council (2018). *Nonprofit Academic Centers Council*. Retrieved June 27, 2019, from www.nonprofit-academic-centers-council.org/.

Nonprofit Sector Resource Institute (2016). Nonprofit Sector Resource Institute. *Seton Hall University*. Retrieved June 27, 2019, from www13.shu.edu/academics/nsri/.

O'Neill School of Public and Environmental Affairs (2019). Master of Public Affairs (MPA). *Indiana University*. Retrieved June 27, 2019, from https://oneill.indiana.edu/masters/degrees-certificates/public-affairs/index.html.

Pal, L. A. & Clark, I. D. (2016). The MPA/MPP in the Anglo-democracies: Australia, Canada, New Zealand, the United Kingdom, and the United States. *Policy and Society, 35*(4), 299–313.

Pandey, S. & Johnson, J. (2019). Nonprofit management, public administration, and public policy: Separate, subset, or intersectional domains of inquiry? *Public Performance and Management Review, 42*(1), 1–10.

School of Management (2019). Program on social enterprise. *Yale University*. Retrieved June 27, 2019, from https://som.yale.edu/faculty-research/centers-initiatives/program-social-enterprise.

School of Public Administration (2019). Nonprofit Management, MNM. *University of Central Florida*. Retrieved June 27, 2019, from https://ccie.ucf.edu/public-administration/nonprofit-management/mnm/.

School of Social Work (2019). Management of human services. *University of Michigan*. Retrieved June 27, 2019, from https://ssw.umich.edu/programs/msw/overview/management-of-human-services.

Seton Hall University (2019). *Master of Public Administration*. Retrieved June 27, 2019, from www.shu.edu/arts-sciences/mpa-public-administration.cfm.

Smith, S. R. (2008). The increased complexity of public services: Curricular implications for schools of public affairs. *Journal of Public Affairs Education, 14*(2), 115–128.

Trachtenberg School of Public Policy and Public Administration (2019). Master of Public Policy (MPP). *George Washington University*. Retrieved June 27, 2019, from https://tspppa.gwu.edu/master-public-policy-mpp.

3

MODELS OF ACADEMIC GOVERNANCE

Myung H. Jin

What is an ideal governance model for MPA programs? The answer to this question is not made easy as governance models have always been discussed at the university level, not at the (public affairs) program level. However, this is a topic worthy of discussion because of the increasing complexity of how public affairs programs are structured and taught in the twenty-first century.

To introduce governance models for public affairs programs, one should start with what governance is in higher-education settings. The governance system in higher education refers to the legal distribution of decision-making power between various units within universities (e.g., faculty, academic committees, boards) and administrative structures (departments, programs, deans, and presidents) (Davidovitch & Iram, 2015). Others regard governance as the division of responsibility and accountability to reach decisions (e.g., Corcoran, 2004). Governance models can be distinguished between internal and external governance models. Internal governance refers to intra-institutional management dealing with determining procedures within institutions. Examples would include determining admission applications, hiring for new faculty positions, scholarships, program funding, and committee assignments. On the other hand, external governance deals primarily with institutional arrangements on the macro level, such as examining the sources of funding, governing rules by the school, and assessment of programs by the university (Boer & File, 2009).

Issues regarding governance systems at any level in higher education have been discussed perhaps mostly at the internal level (Rowlands, 2013), to empirically evaluate how to best manage the internal affairs of academic institutions. However, just as each program or department unit has its own set of bylaws and culture, most of which falls in the jurisdiction of internal governance, it very much affects the nature of external governance (Neave, 2003). Therefore, it is important that how to best govern at the internal level warrants further discussion, and this chapter focuses on discussing several models of shared governance, particularly with regards to public affairs programs.

The basic outline of this chapter starts with a brief history of the development of public affairs programs in general over the course of their 60-year history and a discussion of the changing needs for a fitting governance model for public affairs programs, followed by a literature review of the various models of governance in institutions of higher education. Each model of academic governance is, then, discussed for its compatibility with the Network of Schools of Public Policy, Affairs, and Administration (NASPAA) accreditation standards (NASPAA, 2014). Particular attention is given to the shared governance of faculty, and I provide justification for why public affairs programs require further expansion of the practice of such a governance model. I conclude with caveats that can occur depending on where public affairs programs are housed within a university.

Background

A proper discussion of, and search for, the right governance model for public affairs programs would not be complete without first understanding the history of how public affairs programs started and grew over time. The real impetus for professional training for public service came from municipal reform movements, particularly that of the New York Bureau of Municipal Research, which established the Training School for Public Service in 1911 (Ingraham & Zuck, 1996; McDonald, 2010). In 1924, the Training School was moved to Syracuse University and became what is now known as the Maxwell School of Citizenship and Public Affairs (Ingraham & Zuck, 1996). Although the voice for providing training for government jobs started to grow, particularly after a 1912 report by the American Political Science Association's Committee on Practical Training for the Public Service, the infrastructure to make the training services a reality was simply nonexistent (White, 1933). For example, according to a report by Roscoe Martin of Syracuse University in 1954, only 309 bachelor, 256 master, and 15 doctoral degrees were awarded in the academic year 1952–1953 (Ingraham & Zuck, 1996). Only 22 institutions reported awarding master and doctoral degrees, while 105 institutions reported only offering some courses in public administration (Henry, 1995).

Through the early 1960s, public administration still had not emerged as an identifiable program. This was partly because of the organizational location of public administration courses within universities. Of the 105 institutions reporting some courses in public administration, 68 were in departments of political science, 16 were in institutes or bureaus of research, and only 6 were in clearly identified schools of public administration. The remainder were in a variety of other organizational arrangements within the university (Henry, 1995).

Understandably so, the concept of governance at the time was viewed as an accessory at best.

Underlying the differing degree titles and organizational structures were major conceptual differences about what public administration was and what the components should be for a viable public administration curriculum. How should the program be defined and organized? Even among academics who supported the concept of professionalism in public administration, there were questions about the structure and content of course work, long before online and off-site coursework made it even more complicated to govern a public affairs program in modern times. Should public administration be a graduate or undergraduate-level program? This question was bedeviling faculty and directors of programs in the 1950s (Ingraham & Zuck, 1996). Today, the majority of public administration programs are offered at the master's level (NASPAA, 2018). Why? Is a certain level of maturity required of students wishing to register for public administration courses? Alternatively, is it because the field of public administration is too vast to be offered at the undergraduate level? If one is to argue that public administration programs provide training for those interested in pursuing careers in governmental agencies, there is likely the temptation to offer a sub-specialty track as careers in government agencies span many disciplines, including, but not limited to, public finance, financial planning, management, human resources, and city planning. Adding to the mixture, it is no secret that public administration draws from many other disciplines such as sociology, economics, political science, public policy, management, psychology, and criminal justice for its curriculum; it could, therefore, easily be a massive undertaking for any university considering a bachelor's degree in public administration. Clearly, there was a need for dialogue and discussion if reasonable consensus about the field of public administration and education for public service was to emerge.

Beginning in the 1970s, university programs in public policy, urban affairs, and public administration started to proliferate (Ingraham & Zuck, 1996). Programs serving full-time pre-service students expanded with the increased university enrollment of the baby-boomers; this was accompanied by growing demand from college-educated government employees for advanced professional training and skills. Part-time, in-service programs grew as a result. This time also saw the growth of programs with an urban policy focus; policy analysis emerged from the Johnson administration's emphasis on the Planning, Programming, and Budgeting System (PPBS) and schools responded with courses in systems theory, methodologies of quantitative and economic analysis, and program evaluation.

These environmental changes motivated many programs and universities to "reach out" and to better understand and provide for the world of government and public service (Ingraham & Zuck, 1996). Some established off-campus programs in government buildings; others went to military facilities for the same purpose. The role of practitioners as teachers and advisors increased markedly. Concern about course content, hours required for a degree, quality of faculty, and adequacy of resources created new issues.

The problem that followed, then, was the establishment of grounding standards to serve and help guide public service education programs and departments. Not surprisingly, the first attempt at developing standards was mainly "structural." The first eligibility criteria for what was called a "sustaining member" included a defined administration unit with a single administrative head, an identifiable faculty, a minimum number of faculty and students, and appropriate dedicated budgetary resources. The problem was, however, that only 20 institutions would have qualified under the criteria (Henry, 1995).

In the 1970s, governing or thinking about how to govern public affairs programs grew more complicated due to the proliferation of off-campus programs and the potential threats they posed to established programs. Moreover, the adoption of revised bylaws, which later became the NASPAA's first Constitution in 1977, required that the field of public affairs and administration encompass (1) public administration, public policy, and public management, and (2) such disciplines as criminal justice, economic affairs, environmental affairs, health, international affairs, social welfare, transportation, and urban affairs, going above and beyond public-sector organizations (Ingraham & Zuck, 1996). During the 1974 NASPAA Annual Conference, the "Guidelines and Standards for Professional Master's Degree Programs in Public Administration" were widely shared among the members who dealt not only with the matrix of competencies to be built into the curriculum, but also minimum program length, faculty, control of the program by a designated faculty, and adequate financial resources (Ingraham & Zuck, 1996). This proposal was unanimously adopted at the meeting.

Fast-forward to 2018, and 197 public affairs programs were accredited from 179 schools, totaling 23,359 enrollments nationwide (NASPAA, 2018). The explosion of technology and its impact on all levels of education, communication, and the real world of work have undoubtedly contributed to the proliferation of this unprecedented growth, not to mention the more than 20 specializations, such as nonprofit, environment, criminal justice, national security, education, and emergency, which led to the complexity of governing public affairs programs. Is there a one-size-fits-all model of governance suitable for all public affairs programs? In the next section, I review the various models of academic governance used in institutions of higher education and discuss their compatibility with NASPAA standards.

In Search of a Public Affairs Governance Model

Community-building within academic departments is perhaps not an easy task, as it is not widely practiced. In addition, public administration faculties are likely to include members with fairly diverse disciplinary backgrounds, including political science, economics, philosophy, law, environmental science, nonprofit, urban planning, and finance, for example, which makes the task of community-building even trickier than it would be in more homogeneous departments (Newcomer, 2003). What helps faculty work effectively with each other and with staff and students to provide an environment characterized by mutual respect and commitment to mutually agreed-upon goals when there is such disciplinary diversity in faculty backgrounds? What intellectual puzzles help stimulate our communities to thrive (Newcomer, 2003)?

While there is no one-size-fits-all model of governance, as there can be as many models as the number of public affairs programs that exist, they can be categorized broadly into two types of governance – one that is bureaucratic and the other collegial. In a nutshell, bureaucratic governance models thrive in an environment where there is a dominant leader and others being viewed more as subordinates than as colleagues. A collegial model, on the other hand, is one in which all members of the organization (or community) are viewed as being equal, with the sharing of responsibilities.

Some administrations favor a top-down, business-model form of governance where decisions made by the upper administration (e.g., the dean or other forms of chief administrator) are then handed down to lower-level administrators as well as to faculty members who are expected to accept and implement the decisions – often without question – in a traditional hierarchical fashion. This type of governance uses the bureaucratic structure as hierarchical and is tied together by formal chains of command and systems of communication. Is bureaucracy bad? Bureaucracy is referred to as the "networks of social groups dedicated to limited goals while at the same time pursuing maximum efficiency and regulations according to the principle of legal-rationality" (Baldridge, 1971, p. 2). While this definition may appear to limit bureaucratic governance model in its applicability for university administration, a number of scholars have used Weber's bureaucratic paradigm to describe the nature of bureaucracy that exists in higher education (e.g., Murphy, 2009; Samier, 2002; Stroup, 1966). For example, Stroup has listed the eight characteristics in higher education that are indicative of the bureaucratic model (Stroup, 1966, p. 2).

1. Competence is the criterion used for appointment.
2. Officials are appointed, not elected.
3. Salaries are fixed and paid directly by the organization rather than determined in "free-fee" style.
4. Rank is recognized and respected.
5. The career is exclusive; no other work is done.
6. The style of life is centered around the organization.
7. Security is present in a tenure system.
8. Personal and organizational property are separated.

Can bureaucracy maintain its place in higher education? Because most public affairs programs now reside within a more extensive network of the public affairs school (e.g., School of Public Administration) or college (e.g., College of Public Affairs), it is best to examine the governance decisions and features at the school level. In public affairs schools that exercise bureaucratic governance models, there are formal channels of communication that must be respected. In terms of the bureaucratic elements in the "people-processing" activities, it is surprising that faculty are not involved because such activities as record keeping, course scheduling, and many other routine activities that are designed to help the programs handle the masses of students should be handled by program faculty. This type of governance model can often be featured in for-profit schools, and schools whose instructions are mainly online and rely on part-time instructors for a large chunk of their courses (Schultz, 2013). In this environment, even the decisions of who teaches select courses are handled by a career administrator, not by the instructional faculty.

It is important to acknowledge, however, the merits argued by the supporters of the bureaucratic governance model, which they argue operates best when governed by those who had the training and thus the credentials for leading corporate policy and planning efficiently (Collis, 2002; Trakman, 2008). From a structural standpoint, this model may seem more than capable of meeting several NASPAA Standards. For example, due to the transparent formal chains of command and systems of communication, schools using a business-like, bureaucratic governance model, also known as corporate governance, can adapt more quickly to the changing nature of public service education. This was an important observation made back in the early 1980s by the Ad Hoc Committee on the Future of Public Service Education (Ingraham & Zuck, 1996). Because the clear ownership of tasks and rules is the gold standard for achieving maximum efficiency in bureaucracies, programs practicing this governance model may claim to have the advantage of being more efficiently able to collect the information they need relative to their performance and operating procedures. Will that information successfully guide the evolution of a program's mission and help the program be efficient? That remains to be seen.

Achieving effective governance, however, requires more than having just sound channels of communication. Schools based on the bureaucratic, business-like model often, if not always, rely on career administrators to make decisions on establishing degree requirements, making and implementing recommendations regarding the admission of students, or even advising students. This type of administration can pose a problem as it does not sit well from the perspective of NASPAA Standard 2, according to which full-time faculty members or their equivalent are to have substantial decision-making authority concerning all aspects – governance and implementation – of the program. Because in bureaucratic governance models a single charismatic leader tends to dominate the discussions involving all decision-making, faculty members will have substantially less influence over how programs are implemented and governed. Whether the task is to review the holistic admissions process so as to not give one criterion (e.g., GRE scores) the dominant weight in admission decisions, to require more core courses while reducing electives, to raise or lower minimum academic performance, to increase the number of courses offered online while reducing on-campus courses, or to decide what new research expertise (via a new hire) will help the program or the school the most, they all require the full dedication of faculty.

There are broadly two types of schools that lean closer to operating based on a bureaucratic governance model: For-profit schools, and those that adopt an online program designed by a specialist and rely on adjuncts to be the primary deliverers of the canned class (Schultz, 2013). From a business standpoint, the costs of offering a class are reduced, and at the same time the potential class size is maximized. Traditional schools, seeing this model flourish, began emulating it and expanded their online programs, often with minimal investments in faculty (Schutz, 2013). Because the focus is on cost efficiency, investments on such intangible items as increasing student learning outcomes are hard to come by.

Moreover, because of extensive reliance on adjuncts providing courses, ensuring the integrity of a public affairs program is harder to achieve for several reasons. First, most often there is no consistent communication between full-time faculty members and adjuncts. Because faculty meetings are usually held among full-time faculty members, for programs where adjuncts teach more than 70 percent of the curriculum, a question arises as to what percentage of the faculty members are aware of what the end game is.

Second, adjuncts' performances are not evaluated as rigorously as those serving on full-time capacity. Most often, adjuncts are entitled to teaching alone, which is in stark contrast to NASPAA's standard of faculty governance. NASPAA defines a program faculty member as one who participates in governing the rules and operations of the public affairs program and in the delivery of course instructions equivalent to that of a full-time faculty member, 9-month and 12-month contract combined, in the program, commensurate with the rank of his or her appointment. While we lack data on faculty serving in these types of institutions, one study notes that the normal expectations, such as research, public service, and institutional obligations, put on full-time public affairs faculty in traditional schools do not apply to adjuncts, whose professional autonomy is limited (Tierney & Hentschke, 2007). Because most who teach as adjuncts do not have deep knowledge of their program and a commitment to a participatory processes, it is difficult for them to play any significant role in the governance and execution of the program.

How are programs operating on a bureaucratic governance model performing with regards to serving their students? While not all schools based on this governance model are the same, they are often synonymous with for-profit schools. According to a 2012 US Senate committee report, many for-profit schools do not provide clear information on the cost of the program, the time to complete the program, the completion rates of their students, the job placement rate, and the transferability of the credit (US Senate, 2012). Given that the heart of NASPAA standards centers on serving students, which includes but is not limited to internships and career counseling, supervision of course scheduling, and job placement assistance to enable students to progress in careers in public affairs, administration, and policy, it is not surprising that the majority of schools operating on a business-like governance model are not NASPAA-accredited (NASPAA, 2014). While schools in this governance model may appear successful in terms of the sheer number of students being recruited, admitted students should also show good potential for success in professional graduate study in public affairs programs.

Moving Toward the Shared Governance Model: The NASPAA Way

What is a 'shared governance model?' Although institutions of higher education generally agree that shared governance model presents the optimal way to operate an educational program, the term shared-governance is often used interchangeably – wrongfully so – with others such as *collegial governance, shared leadership*, or *stakeholder governance* (Trakman, 2008). Before I define and discuss the shared governance model, it is essential to explain how these other names differ in concept, sometimes in stark contrast, from the characteristics of the shared governance model as featured in the NASPAA standards. Doing so will help clarify what a shared governance model will look like when implemented and practiced in the way that is intended.

The first point of clarification is with the collegial model (Moore, 1975; Trakman, 2008). In this model, the "community of scholars" (Baldridge, 1971, p. 4) would administer its own affairs, having few dealings with bureaucratic officials. This is a culture where all decisions are essentially carried out by group consensus. One classic example is when university decisions are made through a committee consisting of not just academic faculty, but also student representatives. The argument in support of this collegial model is that the ability to make the right and relevant decision is not limited to academic faculty; rather, everyone involved, regardless of whether he or she is on the giving or receiving end of the service, has the ability to make his or her own decisions for the betterment of the organization. The literature gives the argument for adopting a collegial model of governance strong support on the basis of professionalism, which emphasizes the professional's ability to make his or her own decisions and their need for freedom from organizational restraints. Understandably so, as online technology has made enrolling even hundreds of students in a course possible, critics of the bureaucratic model have called for a return to the "academic community" with all the accompanying images of personal attention, human education, and relevant confrontation with life. This collegial, academic community is now widely thought of as one answer to the impersonality of programs and departments growing in size and number.

Although few would oppose the notion that faculty members ordinarily are best equipped to understand the academic goals and aspirations of a program and how to achieve them (Pfnister, 1970), there is a misleading simplicity about the concept of the collegial model of governance. For one, the collegial model fails to deal adequately with conflict. In this model, very often consensus occurs only after a prolonged battle, and many decisions are not consensual at all but are the result of one group having prevailed over another. In this model, it is often not clear what the policy is·in any given situation. Second, in a collegial governance model, academic staff often lack governance skill or interest. For example, for a nine-month full-time faculty member whose performance is evaluated on research, teaching, and service, it is often not in his or her best interest to spend a substantial amount of time on drafting and determining governance policy, relating to stakeholders who are not directly involved in teaching or research, or taking responsibility for complex fiscal or personnel issues (Lewis, 2000).

Evidently, from a philosophical perspective, the collegial model is associated with academic democracy (Dewey, 1966; Hall & Symes, 2005). However, of concern is the issue that faculty members will accord disproportionately greater stress to respecting the program or department's independent academic mission, accompanied with less emphasis on improving its corporate capabilities (Coaldrake, Stedman, & Little, 2003). Programs operating on this model are believed to meet most of the requirements in the NASPAA Standards, particularly in relation to faculty members being able to exercise substantial determining influence over the governance and implementation of their program, ranging from making recommendations regarding the admission of students to defining and assuring faculty performance.

Some studies (e.g., Plante & Collier, 1989) have shown that collegiate models appear to be effective in terms of showing support and building trust with their student body. However, whether the academic staff have the requisite skills and lead in financial management and accountability, to what extent their increased administrative responsibilities will do more harm than good in terms of not being able to dedicate a substantial amount of time on serving students (e.g., internship placement and supervision, career counseling, job placement assistance), remains unanswered.

Another model of governance that is often confused with a shared governance model is a stakeholder governance model. Identified variously with collegial and representative governance, a stakeholder model of governance occurs when governance is vested in a wide array of stakeholders, ranging from students and alumni to corporate partners and the public at large (Baldridge, 1982; Longin, 2002). The stakeholder model exemplifies shared governance (Schick,

1992) in some way. Distinguishable from the collegial model, it vests governance in multiple representatives, not limited to academic staff (Trakman, 2008).

At its most inclusive, stakeholder governance provides for broad participation by internal and external stakeholders in decision-making beyond the appointment of representatives of a range of stakeholder groups (Alfred, 1985; Lapworth, 2004). Envisioning this model at the program level is not easy as programs lack separate boards of community groups that do not include the program faculty. The likely occurrence would be a school that has not only an MPA but also several other programs, such as in political science, criminal justice, and urban planning, where a faculty member from each program may have the voting right on governing decisions. The biggest question lies in determining which stakeholders ought to be represented on governing bodies. For example, if there is a curriculum committee at the school level to which each program would submit requests for changes to its own curriculum, it would be a disservice to reject or overturn the requests made by each program's faculty.

Last but not least, shared leadership is another governance model that can be adopted at the program level. Kezar and Holcombe (2017) define shared leadership as moving away from the leader/follower binary, focusing instead on the importance of leaders throughout the organization, not just those in positions of authority. The basic tenet behind shared leadership is that infrastructure can be created for the leadership of multiple people (Kezar & Holcombe, 2017). As organizations fight to innovate and learn new technologies, react to changing demographics, and adapt to external challenges such as higher financial accountability pressures, shared leadership appears to meet all of these demands.

It is important, however, to acknowledge the differences between shared governance and shared leadership. While shared governance is based on the principles of faculty and administration having distinct areas of delegated authority and decision-making, shared leadership, on the other hand, is more flexible and is characterized mostly for its focus on identifying those with the most relevant expertise to lead in any given situation. The primary benefit is that it presents multiple perspectives stemming from multiple individuals believed to experts in the given decision-making situation. This type of governance grew out of the need for organizations to develop a capacity to learn and adapt to the ever-changing academic environment (Wheatley, 1999).

There are basically five common characteristics of shared leadership (Kezar & Holcombe, 2017): (1) More individuals taking on leadership roles than in traditional models (e.g., a bureaucratic governance model); (2) there is less emphasis on the leader/follower distinction; (3) leadership is based more on who has the expertise necessary to lead in the given situation, not based on position or authority; (4) multiple perspectives and expertise are capitalized for problem-solving, innovation, and change; and (5) collaboration across units is emphasized. Shared leadership does recognize the importance of leaders in positions of authority, to an extent. However, the focus lies on how those in positions of power can delegate authority to those with expertise in the given subject or situation that arises in the organization. Given that colleges have historically operated under principles of shared governance and collegial decision-making (Macfarlane, 2014), shared leadership can be a more natural alternative in higher education than models relying on more top-down structures, as mostly seen in businesses and corporations.

One drawback can be that even though shared leadership adheres to the principles of distributed decision-making and collective input to some degree, shared leadership is different from shared governance. The hallmark of shared governance, for example, is that faculty and administrators, while collegial, have clear areas of decision-making and delegated authority. Faculty members traditionally are in charge of their curriculum, while administrators oversee budgeting. According to NASPAA Standard 2, it is exactly this administrative capacity and faculty governance that are expected to be the central players. Shared leadership is different in that it identifies and uses various individuals on campus that might have expertise in budgeting or curriculum. For example, under shared leadership, someone with expertise in the online instructional system, but no knowledge of the program's mission or its contents, might be invited to be the lead person if a curriculum change heavily depends on responding to growing demands for online learning. This can potentially clash with program faculty. There are distinct advantages in shared leadership whose structures – in the form of task forces or cross-functional teams – are easily adaptable to address issues in real time.

However, problems may arise if those who were involved in solving problems are not available to tackle future challenges. Therefore, inconsistency in the membership of task forces may be an issue. As mentioned before, multiple perspectives are consulted, and decisions are often, if not always, made by a relatively large group of people with varied expertise. As conditions that promote and sustain shared leadership vary depending on the specific model of shared leadership, I review the three most commonly used shared forms of leadership: Co-leaders, teams, and distributed leadership (Kezar & Holcombe, 2017).

Under *co-leaders*, also known as the *pooled leadership* model of shared leadership, a small number of individuals share the leadership post, functioning, for example, as an executive leader. This role can be seen in organizations that serve multiple and interweaving purposes. An example would be schools of public affairs programs that also house other disciplines that can be categorized under professional and social science programs, such as urban planning, political science, public administration, and criminology (Greenwood, Raynard, Kodeih, Micelotta, & Lounsbury, 2011). Each co-leader brings specialized but complementary expertise to the table (Hodgson, Levinson, & Zaleznik, 1965). The leadership responsibilities (i.e., decision-making) are shared only among the few co-leaders at the top of the organizational hierarchy.

The second approach is *team leadership*. Mutual sharing of leadership functions exists among individuals in a team setting. According to Pearce and Conger

(2003), team leadership is very much relational in that it requires interactive influence process among individuals within the leadership team where the objective is to help each other achieve organizational goals. Team leadership acquires both top-down influence and horizontal peer influence where the broad distribution of decision-making authority is bestowed upon a set of individuals instead of relying on a central unit or a person who acts in the role of superior (Pearce & Conger, 2003).

Fletcher and Kaufer (2003) postulate that team leadership often occurs through social interactions as a result of network relationships. This allows team leadership to be relational or interdependent as members of the leadership team can depend on each other to take charge of a given task. Fittingly, team leadership is contextual in that configurations of the leadership team can change depending on the nature of the issue at hand. While this flexibility can ensure that people with the most relevant expertise will assume leadership roles at the given moment, it may not be the ideal setting as finding the right personnel frequently can be a daunting task.

Distributed leadership is the third type of shared leadership. The distributed form of shared leadership is different from the co-leaders model, which relies heavily on executive director roles. Distributed leadership does not limit its candidates to its immediate team or organization as it is often dispersed across multiple organizational boundaries (Spillane, Halverson, & Diamond, 2001).

The models described above define shared leadership in different ways and at different levels, focusing on individuals, teams, organizations, or relationships within organizations. While all three models can be seen at the school level, where the dean (and associate dean) oversees the administration of the school, two of the models – co-leaders and team leadership – are more fitting to the governance standard set forth by the NASPAA at the program level. For example, both co-leaders and team leadership are based on the premise that leadership functions are shared among key team members, which would be referred to as an "adequate faculty nuclear" in NASPAA's governance terms, exercising substantial determining influence for the governance and implementation of the program. The key feature here is that leadership is stable over a specified time period. Distributed leadership may present a conflict for the faculty nuclear of MPA programs if leadership is dispersed across multiple organizational boundaries. People without the knowledge and understanding of the mission and the history of the MPA program may assume leadership in distributed leadership.

Making Shared Governance Work: Final Thoughts

Despite the emphasis put on shared governance by NASPAA, for schools of public affairs dealing with enrollment issues, the business model of top-down governance appears to be the preferred governance choice, over a shared governance model. It may be that evaluation is more transparent, particularly when the program is not going in the right direction. Another reason that shared governance may be ideal only in theory but not carried out in practice in higher education, in general, could be that there is simply not enough time for faculty to devote themselves to the administration and management of personnel. There is a reason why administrators do not teach, or teach very little (e.g., one course per academic year). Teaching takes a substantial amount of preparation, both before and during the semester. Administrators have a strict schedule (or try to follow a strict schedule) in their day-to-day operations, but that schedule often gets delayed when faculty are involved. For faculty involved in research and teaching, this can be demanding for at least several weeks in advance. In fact, getting faculty input can often take significant time and slows down the process of decision-making. Putting the blame on anyone is not easy for faculty, who are dedicated to their students and thus may be reluctant to give up their time for preparing to attend a committee meeting. Another primary reason that the shared governance model is not as successful as expected is that achieving consensus is often difficult in an environment where the task of attaining a diversity of opinions, rather than a lack thereof, receives considerable attention.

Conclusion

Is shared governance in trouble? Despite its problems and obstacles, shared governance may be the best choice for managing public affairs programs. For the shared governance of faculty to work efficiently and effectively, honestly held respect for differences in disciplinary and epistemological perspectives seems to be essential to creating a community inside university departments (Newcomer, 2003). That is, faculty must be willing to acknowledge the merits of multiple theoretical and practical approaches and tools. Repeated exposure to others' views on what constitutes knowledge and on the appropriate means for building knowledge is essential. Proximity and frequent exposure help to break down preconceived prejudices, for example, toward economists who prefer rational models or toward theorists who prefer post-structural orientations (Newcomer, 2003). Exposure to fellow faculty members' research, such as through faculty seminars or symposia, and the opportunity to work together on specific intellectual problems, such as through joint service on doctoral dissertation committees, are especially helpful in opening the dialogue about the relative advantages and disadvantages of different research approaches and techniques. "Good" governance does not merely happen. It is usually the product of painstaking effort to arrive at suitable governance structures, protocols, and processes. "Good" governance is also about timing and judgment (Trakman, 2008).

References

Alfred, R. L. (1985). Organizing for renewal through participative governance. *New Directions for Higher Education, 49*, 57–63.

Baldridge, J. V. (1971). Models of university governance: Bureaucratic, collegial, and political. In Baldridge, J. V. (ed.) *Academic governance* (pp. 1–20). Richmond, CA: McCutchan.

Baldridge, J. V. (1982). Shared governance: A fable about the lost magic kingdom. *Academe, 68*(1), 12–15.

Boer, H. & File, J. (2009). *Higher education governance reforms across Europe*. Brussels, Belgium: European Centre for Strategic Management of Universities.

Coaldrake, P., Stedman, L., & Little, P. (2003). *Issues in Australian university governance*. Brisbane, Australia: QUT.

Collis, D. (2002). New business models for higher education. In Brint, S. (ed.), *The future of the city of intellect: The changing American university* (pp. 181–202). Palo Alto, CA: Stanford University Press.

Corcoran, S. (2004). Duty, discretion and conflict: University governance and the legal obligations of university boards. *Australian Universities' Review, 46*(2), 30–37.

Davidovitch, N. & Iram, Y. (2015). Models of higher education governance: A comparison of Israel and other countries. *Global Journal of Educational Studies, 1*(1), 16–44.

Dewey, J. (1966). *Democracy and education*. New York: The Free Press.

Fletcher, J. K. & Kaufer, K. (2003). Shared leadership paradox and possibility. In Pearce, C. L. & Conger, J. C. (eds), *Shared leadership: Reframing the hows and whys of leadership* (pp. 21–47). Thousand Oaks, CA: Sage.

Greenwood, R., Raynard, M., Kodeih, F., Micelotta, E. R., & Lounsbury, M. (2011). Institutional complexity and organizational responses. *The Academy of Management Annals, 5*(1): 317–371.

Hall, M. & Symes, A. (2005). South African higher education in the first decade of democracy: From cooperative governance to conditional autonomy. *Studies in Higher Education, 30*(2), 199–212.

Henry, L. L. (1995). *Early NASPAA history*. Washington, DC: National Association of Schools of Public Affairs and Administration.

Hill, B., Green, M., & Eckel, P. (2001). *On change IV – What governing boards need to know and do about institutional change*. Washington, DC: American Council on Education.

Hodgson, R. C., Levinson, D., & Zaleznik, A. (1965). *The executive role constellation*. Boston, MA: Harvard Business School Press.

Ingraham, P. W. & Zuck, A. (1996). Public affairs and administration education: An overview and look ahead from the NASPAA perspective. *Journal of Public Administration Education, 2*(2), 161–174.

Kezar, A. J. & Holcombe, E. M. (2017). *Shared leadership in higher education: Important lessons from research and practice*. Washington, DC: American Council on Education.

Lapworth, S. (2004). Arresting decline in shared governance: Towards a flexible model for academic participation. *Higher Education Quarterly, 58*(5), 299–314.

Lewis, L. S. (2000). *When power corrupts: Academic governing boards in the shadows of the Adelphi case*. New Brunswick, NJ: Transaction Publishers.

Longin, T. C. (2002). Institutional governance: A call for collaborative decision-making in American higher education. In Berberet, W. G. & McMillin, L. A. (eds), *A new academic compact* (pp. 211–221). Boston, MA: Anker Publishing Co.

Macfarlane, B. (2014). Challenging leaderism. *Higher Education Research and Development, 33*(1), 1–4.

McDonald, B. D. (2010). The Bureau of Municipal Research and the development of a professional public service. *Administration and Society, 42*(7), 815–835.

Moore, M. (1975). An experiment in governance: The Ohio faculty senate. *Journal of Higher Education, 46*(4), 365–379.

Murphy, M. (2009). Bureaucracy and its limits: Accountability and rationality in higher education. *British Journal of Sociology of Education, 30*(6), 683–695.

National Association of Schools of Public Affairs and Administration (NASPAA) (2001). *Standards for professional master's degree programs in public affairs, policy and administration.* Retrieved July 31, 2019, from www.naspaa.org/copra/standards.htm.

Network of Schools of Public Policy, Affairs, and Administration (NASPAA) (2018). *NASPAA data and trends.* Retrieved July 31, 2019, from www.naspaa.org/sites/default/files/docs/2018-11/2016-2017%20Annual%20Data%20Report%20Luncheon%20Presentation.pdf.

Neave, G. (2003). The Bologna declaration: Some of the historic dilemmas posed by the reconstruction of the community in Europe's systems of higher education. *Educational Policy, 17*(1), 141–164.

Newcomer, K. (2003). Sustaining and invigorating MPA program communities. *Journal of Public Affairs Education, 9*(1), 35–38.

Pearce, C. L. & Conger, J. A. (2003). *Shared leadership: Reframing the hows and whys of leadership.* Thousand Oaks, CA: Sage.

Pfnister, A. O. (1970). The role of faculty in university governance. *Journal of Higher Education, 41*(6), 430–449.

Plante, P. & Collier, K. (1989). The role of faculty in campus governance. In Shuster, J. (ed.), *Governing tomorrow's campus: Perspectives and agendas* (pp. 116–129). New York: Macmillan.

Rowlands, J. (2013). Academic boards: Less intellectual and more academic capital in higher education governance? *Studies in Higher Education, 38*(9), 1274–1289.

Samier, E. (2002). Weber on education and its administration: Prospects for leadership in a rationalized world. *Educational Management Administration and Leadership, 30*(1), 27–45.

Schick, E. B. (1992). *Shared visions of public higher education governance: Structures and leadership styles that work.* Washington, DC: American Association of State Colleges and Universities.

Schultz, D. (2013). Public affairs education and the failed business model of higher education. *Journal of Public Affairs Education, 19*(2), ii–vii.

Spillane, J. P., Halverson, R., & Diamond, J. B. (2001). Investigating school leadership practice: A distributed perspective. *Educational Researcher, 30*(3): 23–29.

Stroup, H. H. (1966). *Bureaucracy in higher education.* New York: Free Press.

Tierney, W. & Hentschke, G. C. (2007). *New players, different game: Understanding the rise of for-profit colleges and universities.* Baltimore, MD: Johns Hopkins University Press.

Trakman, L. (2008). Modelling university governance. *Higher Education Quarterly, 62*(1/2), 63–83.

US Senate (2012). For-profit higher education: The failure to safeguard the federal investment and ensure student success. *Committee on Health, Education, Labor, and Pensions, 112.*

Wheatley, M. J. (1999). *Leadership and the new science: Discovering order in a chaotic world.* San Francisco, CA: Berrett-Koehler Press.

White, L. (1933). *Trends in public administration.* New York: McGraw Hill.

4

ADMINISTRATIVE ROLES

Directors, Chairs, and Deans

Robert W. Smith

Introduction

It is perhaps a given that scholars of public administration, public policy, and public affairs generally begin their careers in the academy seeking to make a difference in public life and practice whether through advancing knowledge in the field (conducting research and publishing) or by otherwise training and inspiring the next generation of public servants (by teaching and mentoring their students). Engaging in cutting-edge research that leads to new public policies or approaches that solve/address society's problems is equally a noble goal. Few newly minted Ph.D.s in public affairs disciplines start their careers by saying they want to go into higher education to purse an administrative track to reach the level of program director, department chair, or at some point dean.

Moreover, even seasoned academics who have risen through the professorial ranks from assistant to associate to full professor seem to steer clear of these roles for a variety of reasons. However, some junior and senior faculty in the field are lured into administrative roles by the promise of the opportunity to set the course of the program/department/college, the challenge of managing a complex organization, increased compensation, a stepping stone to future administrative appointments in the academy (at the provost level or higher), or, quite frankly, because no one else on the faculty was willing to serve in the role. This chapter explores the pathways to administrative roles in the discipline but primarily tries to offer observations and reflections on what you do when you get there, what the roles and responsibilities entail, and why it is important to think strategically about these administrative roles in the context of one's academic career and whether or not they are right for you.

Most scholars and professors in public affairs find themselves working in the context of a hierarchical structure within their college or university. The overarching organizational structure where the academic locus is grounded may be in the college or sometimes school (of public affairs). Within that structure the basic organizational unit where the courses are delivered and research is advanced is typically the department or program level. Most faculty are hired into the department or program as either an assistant or associate professor. Hence the department or program is often their primary academic home and where their tenure resides. However, it should be noted that there is a range of organizational variation depending on the college or university. For the purpose of the discussion in this chapter, we will advance the following organizational hierarchy for advancement: College/school (dean) – department (chair) – program (director). Within the department the MPA or MPP may be just one of several programs corresponding to the particular academic degrees that are being delivered.

The Elephant in the Room ("No One Trained Me for This Job")

It is perhaps appropriate to cut right to the chase of the matter and acknowledge that most scholars and professors in the field are not trained to be administrators in higher education. Despite the in-depth training in organization theory, human resources management, budgeting, and information systems, to name a few sub-disciplines, for the most part scholars in public administration/affairs are not trained to administer academic programs.

Ph.D. students are not typically enrolled in a professional development seminar or noncredit course entitled "Navigating Administrative Roles in Higher Education" or something similar. For the most part, Ph.D. students and newly minted colleagues are largely expected to learn the academic ropes, including the roles of administrators, by experience. And, to be fair, the academy should be singularly focused on preparing the next set of scholars and professors in their disciplines and unencumbered by yet another external constraint or mandate (administrative training). Yet, if the field cares about the future and not only about preparing frontline researchers and scholars, imparting some grounding in how the academy operates may inspire the next set of budding administrators to enthusiastically embrace the role with the goal of improving academic leadership and responsiveness and collegiality. For example, perhaps the inclusion of an annual three-part one-hour seminar or free-standing roundtable on collegiality in the academy would be appropriate to highlight that responsibility and authority is shared equally by, among, and across colleagues.

Clearly many professional associations provide important workshops, webinars, executive retreats, and seminars to provide some guidance and training in leadership of academic units (e.g., NASPAA). Colleges and universities equally offer in-house training and guidance for newly minted administrators.

Colleagues at all levels should be encouraged to seek out these opportunities either to explore whether an administrative career path is appropriate for you or whether you need to immerse yourself in such programs just to survive in a role you recently inherited. This chapter is intended to offer an overview and perhaps some insights into some of the roles and responsibilities you may find yourself in as a program director, department chair, or dean of a college. The chapter will also offer some perspectives on the influence of the university and college as they impact these administrative roles in connection with shared governance, allocation of resources, and other elements of the higher-education administrative environment.

The Journey from Faculty to Program Director

After you are hired into your first position in the academy there is excitement and pride about making a contribution to the discipline that defines you and/or that you believe strongly in, to dedicate a career to teaching research and service in the field of public affairs. As a newly minted Ph.D., you are excited about jumping into the classroom and immersing yourself in scholarship and perhaps blazing a trail of significant research, grant-funded projects, and making a long-standing contribution to the field. Some professors enter the academy after significant work experience, which adds a dimension to their ability to connect with students in the classroom and offer a vantage point of applied research.

Once in the department it is often a blur as time quickly advances and your tenure clock begins ticking. Six years go faster than you might imagine. First up for you as a new faculty member coming in as an assistant professor is the two-year or three-year review, where the critical assessment of your teaching, research, and service begins by colleagues and administrators. The review often focuses on the following questions: Are you on the right path? How are your student evaluations? Have you started to turn your dissertation into a book or several articles? Where are you on several research projects, or have you submitted articles for publication? If you find yourself in an MPA program, as you look around the department you will see junior colleagues, senior colleagues, graduate assistants, and students. But as you survey the department landscape several important colleagues stand out as significant (beyond the department secretary or fiscal/budget officer). Those significant colleagues in a department would of course be the department chair and the MPA program director. In addition to your colleagues on the search committee that hired you, these two faculty have probably played a very significant role in bringing you to the department. It is important to forge good and ongoing relations with these administrators and perhaps observe how they accomplish their respective roles and responsibilities.

There will likely be constants as you move ahead in the tenure process. Soon you will face the four-year review and eventually enter your penultimate year.

Presuming your record is stellar, your colleagues will recommend you for tenure and promotion, and you will be supported by the program director and the chair. Each typically will have input or more into advancing your portfolio forward with a positive decision. Being exposed to these two department-based administrative positions will likely reveal to you whether or not pursuing a path toward academic leadership is for you. Many times (sometimes even before tenure) the opportunity to take over as program director may be presented to you or you might actively seek that role. If this happens, it may be a situation of "throwing caution to the wind." Seeking any administrative post before you secure tenure is not recommended. Any administrative role will distract a junior faculty member from the imperative of research and publications, which are central to most tenure decisions. Not only will this role take up precious time and energy that should be devoted to scholarship, but any administrative role often requires making decisions that affect senior colleagues who may, in turn, be in a position to decide whether or not the administrator (MPA director) receives tenure. Nonetheless, it is a logical pathway from faculty member to administrator by assuming such roles as undergraduate coordinator or graduate coordinator, or in the more formalized role of program director. These "stepping-stone" administrative roles do prepare faculty members for an administrative track. In this chapter, we consider the next logical step from public affairs faculty member into administration, and that is the jump from faculty to MPA director. Hence before you know it, the job of MPA program director is presented to you or falls into your lap. What do you do? Do you eagerly accept the position, respectfully decline the opportunity, or perhaps "pull the last straw" amongst colleagues (meaning no one else wants to serve as program director)? Whatever the circumstance, you may have closely examined the role of the MPA director or only partially paid attention to the administrative roles played by the program director. Therefore, it would be useful to dissect the role of program director.

Becoming MPA Program Director

There are several responsibilities inherent in the role of a program director. Some of those duties and expectations are highlighted below. Table 4.1 offers a summary of the many roles chairs are expected to fulfill.

Perhaps the definitive work on the role of MPA director was presented by Vicino (2017) in his examination of the multiple roles of the MPA director. Vicino concludes that the MPA director is a manager, advocate, liaison, and entrepreneur, and plays an essential role in the implementation of these plans. "In an age of rapid change, leaders of public affairs programs will need to adapt their programs to respond to institutional and societal changes" (Vicino, 2017, p. 795). In most cases, the MPA director is not the unit head but is given substantial administrative responsibilities within the department or school. Caught

TABLE 4.1 Typical Duties and Responsibilities of MPA Directors

---

1 Create and maintain course schedules and teaching assignments and provide curriculum oversight
2 Manage department activities, administration, and budgets
3 Advise graduate and undergraduate students (award-manage financial aid packages/ assistantships)
4 Brand and market the program and promote graduates (for career and doctoral study)
5 Mentor and develop faculty and staff
6 Supervise part-time faculty
7 Pursue program and institutional accreditation and maintain related metrics
8 Manage the program's web/social media presence and overall public relations efforts
9 Build and maintain engagement with alumni, stakeholders, and related constituencies
10 Maintain excellent relations across the university (dean, provost, president, etc.)
11 Attend various leadership functions/meetings
12 Teach as may be negotiated

---

in between the unit and college level in the organizational structure, this middle manager reports to many stakeholders (Buller, 2012; Ginsberg, 2011). Directors of MPA programs have even further challenges to confront, including maintaining NASPAA accreditation, ensuring autonomous governance and decision-making, and engaging the public affairs community. An understanding of how to navigate these administrative roles is essential to an MPA director's success. Vicino (2017) identifies those roles as manager (administering operations), advocate (representing stakeholders), liaison (fostering relationships), and entrepreneur (in terms of strategic or innovative leadership).

Yet the fundamental attraction to the role of MPA director primarily rests on the aspiring administrator's altruistic sense of the imperative of public service, teaching, and research. Even if a professor volunteers to assume the role of MPA director (whether by persuasion or inherent generosity), the professor assuming that role must be focused on fulfilling an assignment that he/she believes is advancing the profession, the institution, and the students. Some professors may seek the role because there is a salary, course reductions, access to graduate assistants, and the prestige associated with the title of director. Although not the ideal motivation, it is clear that inducements or incentives for service are appropriate and must be considered in the calculus of accepting the position. Another rationale for accepting the position is because professors in public affairs fields have a proclivity for administrative roles or activities and may have prior administrative experience. Therefore, administering an MPA program is just another function or role that they are familiar and comfortable with. Likely the motivation for seeking the position is some combination of these factors.

There are also career, professional, organizational, and personal factors that must weigh on a decision to assume directorship of an MPA program. Although many colleagues have successfully gone down this route, it is advisable not to pursue the MPA director role if you are an assistant professor and not tenured. The responsibilities and pressures of serving as director can be overwhelming at times but at best are distractions from pursuing your academic career trajectory.

Between year one and year three, with a critical fourth-year review forthcoming, the focus for an assistant professor seeking tenure and promotion should be excellence in teaching, an active research agenda, publications under their belt, forthcoming, or in the cue, and a reasonable service component both within the department and college/university. This presumes an administrative role will deflect and distract the professor from the most important point in their career, achieving tenure and promotion.

Professors who might be attracted to a role as MPA director should also evaluate where they want to position themselves in the field. Some professors may calculate that assuming the post of MPA director will advantage their career by both positioning themselves with other directors and affording networking opportunities to pursue other roles or positions in those other institutions, or will be a credentialing element in their portfolio and experience that distinguishes their value in the discipline and knowledge of the field. Neither motivation is inherently wrong nor questionable but speaks to the reality of motivations and thought processes for pursuing the role of program director.

Professional considerations are related but can be manifest as the balancing of scholarship and research with the distractions of administrative life. Academics pursue a career in the academy because they enjoy teaching, are zealous in research, seek to push boundaries in the field, and want to make a difference in the world. Managing an MPA program is not necessarily conducive to the pursuit of that professional trajectory. Hence many prospective and strong candidates for the MPA director post choose to not pursue the position. And it must equally be noted that neither of these perspectives are mutually exclusive. Many MPA directors are well established and productive scholars in the field and have the capacity to undertake multiple roles at the same time. Some perhaps even benefited by pursuing an administrative track while advancing research or scholarship because it helped those professors wisely apportion time and energy and efforts to scholarship while pursuing administrative responsibilities. Organizational factors must also be considered in assuming the MPA post. Politics within the department, college, and university is real and must be anticipated and navigated. We can assume, of course, that the MPA director position may "step on toes" by forcing decisions about personnel, course selection, scheduling, finances, office space, or the assignment of graduate assistants. Saying no to colleagues can carry consequences when the director eventually returns to the faculty. Issues of the director's relationship with the chair and the dean must also be considered. Will those relationships be positive and personable, or will they be tense and frigid? Moreover, the longer-term consequences of decisions made as MPA director may weigh heavily on the director when he/she returns to the faculty. At a broader level, being an MPA director also opens the pathway to other administrative roles within the college and university. The prospective director must ask if that is the environment in which they want to operate. In essence will the benefits of the post outweigh the costs?

Finally, personal considerations of health, family, relationships, and finances must all be considered in deciding whether to take on the role of MPA director. The role of MPA director can be time-consuming, all-absorbing, difficult, contentious, political, and overwhelming. Those elements should be evaluated in any decision to take over as director. They will obviously affect your personal life and situation. But the benefits from serving as director and gaining invaluable experience, having an impact on the program and the discipline, and exposure to higher levels of academic administration are equally dimensions that can outweigh any negatives associated with the role.

When will you know it is time to pursue or take on the MPA director role? You may never know if there is a "best" time. The opportunity may fall into your lap, it may be forced upon you, it may be awarded to you, and the timing in life and career have everything to do with it as well. However, if you are relatively confident in where you may be with respect to tenure and promotion, have a sense that you are good at administrative duties, get along well with colleagues across the board, have your personal circumstances reasonably sorted out and stable, and have a desire to improve or advance the discipline, the time may be right to throw your hat into the ring. And, of course, making the move to the MPA director role need not occur as a sequential progression in your current institution. You may be recruited to apply somewhere else, you may see an opportunity at another institution, or colleagues may point you to an opening. But whether advancing within your current institution or securing the position in another university, the calculus and considerations are still the same. And after you have served a term or two, which are likely contracted for either three years or five years, you must then decide whether or not to continue in the role. Here considerations of time, commitment, energy, departmental or institutional politics, goal attainment, career progression, and personal factors must again be weighed.

Against this backdrop, it is important to emphasize that the field has clearly recognized the need to better understand and operationalize the role of the MPA director. Hence, before deciding to take on the role of MPA director, consulting some of the relevant literature would be advisable. While the literature is not extensive, it resonates with many of the themes raised in this chapter. For example, researchers have examined the motivations of MPA and MPP (Master of Public Policy) directors by applying relevant theories to examine the intrinsic and extrinsic values displayed by MPA/MPP directors (Killian & Wenning, 2017). In an extensive survey, Killian and Wenning (2017) found a variety of factors that motivate directors, from stipends to course releases to professional growth and networking to promoting the mission and core values of the program. Additional research along these lines seems prudent and highlights the need for faculty considering a move to MPA director to carefully assess and process their own motivational queues and underlying commitment to the discipline.

But, in addition to following one's "internal compass" to move toward an administrative role in the academy, having the external support mechanisms and environment in place to cultivate the necessary leadership and managerial skills and aptitude is equally important. This is highlighted by Brainard's (2017) work examining the need for an institutional support structure to train prospective program directors in the field. Her research emphasizes that most MPA directors generally lack management training and experience and essentially learn on the job. And while she applauds professional organizations like NASPAA for including panels or "New Director's" Institutes or half-day programs aimed at providing the knowledge, skills, and abilities necessary to succeed as an MPA program director, there is a need to expand both practical training and also address the gap in the public affairs literature, which does not offer much about directing programs.

Finally, Hatcher, Meares, and Gordon (2017), in a seminal study of small MPA program directors, confirmed the lack of both scholarship on and training for MPA directors. This gap in many respects almost appears to be pervasive across the nation and globe, and across both small and large MPA programs. They call for more extensive and consistent training of MPA directors. Again they recognize the important efforts of NASPAA and other organizations to offer and provide this training, but lament the limited availability and logistical issues (e.g., costs) of accessing this training, especially for small programs.

Overall, it seems clear that there is a need for increased formalized training of MPA directors and prospective MPA directors. Although outlining a definitive solution for this dilemma is beyond the scope of this present chapter, there are nonetheless some important steps and directions the discipline and the academy can take to address this leadership gap. First, this can be envisioned as both a supply and demand problem. The supply dimension can be addressed in a rather straightforward manner. Increasing the number of formal training experiences and opportunities for directors or prospective directors can be offered in a variety of professional settings (e.g., NASPAA) or by universities or colleges themselves. These training venues can take many forms: on-site or single-site training workshops for directors, virtual training sessions (stand-alone or as part of a series), an ongoing series of training modules for new or continuing directors, imbedded programs in conference programs or regional conferences, development of a seminal guide for MPA directors (online), refresher series for long-standing directors, or a decentralized consultant service to assist or guide program directors, to name a few.

The demand problem addresses a more fundamental issue inherent in the academy itself and not just public administration as a discipline. This internal dimension refers to the demand by the field itself (researchers, professors, students, administrators, etc.) to acknowledge that there is a dimension of academic training that must by necessity include preparing the next generation of students and scholars to assume the administrative reins of the field. Providing this grounding will help future academics navigate the nuances of academic life and administration but equally offers a defining opportunity to provide newly minted professors with the vision and skills to consider a pathway to administrative leadership in their respective fields. This can be accomplished by either fine-tuning the current doctoral curriculum and training provided to include roundtables, workshops, noncredit courses, mentorships, or even internship-like experiences in administrative capacities in the respective programs. If public administration pursues a strategy of addressing both the supply and demand side of this administrative dilemma the field will be better served in the long term by preparing future academics for positions of leadership in the academy but also by providing a framework for new academics to better understand the administrative hierarchy and leadership roles they will experience in their first job and for the balance of their university careers.

Assuming the Role of Department Chair

The department chair is typically elected by peers to manage department matters and otherwise provide overall leadership and guidance to the unit. However, the selection of the chair (in most instances) is ultimately approved by the dean. The power or scope of authority of a chair varies according the college or university and structure of faculty governance and prevailing personnel policies at the institution. The precise roles and duties are stipulated in either department bylaws, college guidelines, or university faculty personnel policies or statutes. In addition, many departments have an executive committee or a personnel committee that also works closely with the chair on a variety of personnel, tenure and promotion, or other administrative decisions. Whether this role is advisory or formal, active involvement by the chair in these matters is expected. Typical duties will fall into five broad categories: leadership, personnel, budgetary, curriculum/scheduling, and day-to-day management.

Overall, chairs provide effective academic leadership by facilitating the department in visioning and strategic planning, execution of the department/college strategic plan, and actively engaging with other units. Chairs also assume responsibility for follow-through on decisions assigned to the department by the college and university administration by communicating with faculty and staff, and conveying feedback from the unit to the dean. Chairs lead and work with faculty in the development of department curriculum, educational philosophy, academic standards, and the department's long-term planning efforts. They forward departmental recommendations concerning such matters as curriculum development, budgetary requests, position requests, multi-year schedules, and faculty development activities to the dean. Chairs communicate information to and from the dean and appropriate governance bodies, and report the results of department actions and deliberations.

Chairs coordinate with and assist the dean in advancing college priorities and imperatives that affect all college departments/divisions. They explore outreach to various stakeholders and help the dean and/or department establish rapport and dialogue with those constituents. Chairs also adhere to or exceed agreed upon/assigned timelines and deadlines. They also oversee searches, receive and review department search committee recommendations for hiring full-time faculty and staff, and make departmental recommendations to the dean. Moreover, chairs coordinate with the dean on the selection and negotiation of positions for full-time and part-time faculty and staff.

Equally, chairs mentor faculty (especially new faculty) and provide annual performance development plans. They also direct the work of support staff and student workers. They perform annual evaluations of faculty and staff; receive department personnel committee recommendations for reappointment, tenure, and promotion; and provide a separate and independent review to other committees, the dean, and administrators. The chairs develop and monitor professional development plans as noted in second, fourth, and annual reviews. Chairs are expected to enforce compliance with all university and system policies.

They lead the department in developing budget requests, priorities, and approving expenditures. Chairs ensure department budgets are managed appropriately and department personnel are compliant with all procedures. They develop multi-year course schedules and staffing plans for curricular delivery that are consistent with institutional priorities and student needs. Chairs assign faculty to courses and prepare schedules to meet student needs. Chairs work with faculty to prioritize and make recommendations about faculty workload to the dean for approval. Chairs typically oversee preparation of documents for follow-up and accreditation review, and prepare documents for curricular changes, catalog revisions, and other documents necessary to convey the department's curricular plans.

They develop and coordinate student recruitment, retention, advising, and service activities of the unit with relevant support offices; implement and monitor admissions, student progress, and closure requirements of the department's degree(s) as well as professional certification or registration of students. Chairs also coordinate academic assessment exercises. They prepare reports and analyses, and fulfill data requests from the dean and other university administrators. Chairs represent the department(s) to external organizations and groups, inter-institutional activities, and accrediting agencies.

Under this broad rubric of responsibilities and roles, chairs play a crucial role in the interface between the administration and the faculty. The chair is first and foremost a member of the faculty in one of the disciplines represented in the department or academic area. This role is often convoluted by the fact the chair is, in most cases, recommended by the faculty department to serve in that role. However, the appointment to the position of chair is made by the dean of the college or school. Hence the chair serves at the pleasure of the dean and must enforce or promulgate polices handed down by the administration. This responsibility often conflicts with the wishes of the department faculty about substantive or procedural matters in the department. An effective chair must be collegial, diplomatic, a sound administrator, an effective spokesperson, and an accomplished scholar/teacher. Each of these qualities is important for establishing the validity and respect required of faculty in the department. Typically, the chair assigned to the position holds the rank of associate or full professor. This fact underscores the fundamental connectivity between the discipline, curriculum, faculty, and chair/administration. Many faculty think only in terms of an administrative relationship rather than an academic context to the role of chair.

Indeed, one's role in the department changes when assuming the chair position. Overall the power of the chair is significant but not unlimited. At many levels the power of the chair is tempered by the fact that the department faculty tend to rotate through the position. But there are also some distinctive roles generally expected of a department chair. For example, a department chair is charged with looking at the department as a whole and at the department's relationship to the college or school. Many times the perspective on the role of chair is seen through a narrow lens. The job carries a significant administrative component, whether it is approving course substitutions, turning in the year's schedule, or advising new majors. Yet a significant component to the job is linked to the larger view of the academy and the responsibility to cultivate young colleagues through the probationary years, conducting a successful search, or re-thinking the department's curriculum. And so, the chair often struggles with a balance between ensuring smooth operations of an academic unit, juxtaposed against the department's position in the college and of the needs of students. What that means is that the chair must consistently weigh the needs of individual faculty members with the larger perspective for the rest of the department and college.

In reflecting on some key elements of the role, chairs must establish and cultivate a collegial environment, value colleagues, recognize that faculty have a stake in outcomes, foster a climate where faculty are part of a team, and ensure that faculty are co-owners of the department's programs. Practically speaking, a chair must be prepared to have the department develop its goals and an assessment of whether or not those goals are being achieved (ideally every three to five years). Also an inherent part of the role of the chair is to facilitate the sharing of service load within the department. Balancing the wide variety of factors that go into what courses are taught, when and by whom (including an assessment of the faculty's ability to teach from their strengths) is challenging. First and foremost, the needs of the program must supersede preferences for teaching slots, formats, and locations.

The chair plays a decisive role in onboarding new hires to the department. Although chairs are often just one component to the overall hiring of new faculty or staff to the department (e.g., they participate in interviews), they may play a role in the final decision-making about financial and logistical considerations for bringing on a faculty member. Although the final offer of a salary, course load, and research funds may be the ultimate call of the dean, the chair is closely involved in that process and sets the parameters of the hiring with direction from the dean and input from the faculty.

In addition to the joy of hiring new faculty, many times chairs must recommend to the dean or convey directly to a faculty member that a professor's contract will not be renewed because of underperformance on some or several elements of teaching, research, or service. Although this decision may have been reached by a department- or college-level committee, oftentimes the chair must break the news to the faculty member. It is rewarding to bring in new colleagues; it is very difficult to let them go. Whether an adjunct position or tenure-track position, not being reappointed can be devastating to the faculty member and their family. While there is no easy way to do this, being encouraging about future prospects, highlighting the faculty member's strengths, and pointing out other institutions or programs that might be a better fit may help lessen the bad news. But for the chair, whether recommending or initiating this personnel decision, the focus must be on what is best for the program, department, college, or university.

A significant role that often falls to the chair is the assignment of course releases or professional development funds. On an ongoing basis, as research and scholarship are essential ingredients to future academic success, the chair has an active role in the allocation of these research or professional development funds. In this context considerations of tenure or promotion milestones, the trajectory of the faculty member's focus on research/scholarship, and rank and years of service are factors to consider in such allocations. The same logic equally applies to the assignment of offices, graduate assistants, staff support, or other logistics. Overall it is fair to say that size matters, and the level of responsibility and scope of administrative duties is a direct function of the size of the department. A small department of, say, 5 or 6 faculty members will be much different from one of 18–25 faculty. Resources and the support infrastructure (e.g., an assistant/associate chair) will be related to how large the department is. In this arrangement chairs may be less accessible to rank-and-file faculty as they would be in a smaller department. However, the basic dimensions and responsibilities are essentially the same.

Of the many dimensions to the role of chair one of the most important is mentorship of faculty. The obvious role is of being the first resource for the vast array of questions any new person has; the most important thing a chair can do for the new person is to make them feel welcome as an integral member of the department and to convey to them that the chair's job is to help them succeed.

Whether in the form of reasonable course assignments, minimum course preparations, lower service expectations, and support for research and scholarship these are welcoming strategies to help new faculty feel acclimated and part of the team.

The other key dimension to discuss or highlight is the liaison role between the department and the dean. This is a key function of the chair. The dean turns to the chair for any issues facing the department, and is the person who will go to the dean with concerns initiated by the department. Hence, the chair must serve as the representative of the department, as a spokesperson, and as an advocate for the department. The chair must also convey to the department the perspective and concerns of the dean. Depending upon the nature of the responsibilities of chair and expectations of the institution, the chair may be largely a "manager," simply implementing policy made from above. When there is a conflict between what the department collectively agrees are its needs and directions and what is expected by the dean as the college's needs, the chair serves as the intermediary, conveying the department's perspective to the dean, and the dean's perspective to the department. If an issue is particularly contentious, the dean may meet with the whole department. But inherent elements or tasks that are common to most chairs include helping define positions in the department, leading searches (including various aspects, from approval of the search through to candidate choice), significant curriculum changes, course logistics (e.g., over- or under-enrollment, course caps, etc.), and gatekeeper and first-in-line resource person or the face of the department.

Moreover, there's a lot of unscheduled activity that comes to the chair − from students, staff, and faculty − and chairs need to be accessible. By default, this means that chairs have a more defined work life than rank-and-file faculty face (e.g., a relatively flexible schedule and the ability to do some of one's work away from the office). For a chair it's important to be in the office, with the door open, especially during certain times of the year (e.g., during summer for orientation activities, in August or January at the hectic start of a semester, or during department program reviews). Chairs must also expect endless emails from students, parents, faculty, staff, administrators, and external stakeholders. Much of this communication stems from the chair's role as point person for communication whether from the registrar's office, the office of academic affairs, or other departments. Another role worth highlighting that often seems to not be as widely recognized is the expectation that a chair attends all or most department and college events and social functions. Being "seen" and involved is an important component to the job.

Coping with these duties and responsibilities on a regular basis is a defining feature in the role of chair. Departmental cultures vary on how much is done by the chair and how much is delegated to others. Yet sharing key responsibilities among the faculty is crucial. Seeking advice and counsel is an imperative as chair. When faced with a difficult issue, don't hesitate to seek help. Sources for advice might be a former chair in the department, other chairs, and even the dean (who may be able to draw on past experience as a chair as well as current experience as dean). Also do not discount turning to colleagues for input and feedback.

It's Good to be the Dean… Maybe

There may be several academic deans at the institution typically leading any number of colleges or schools. Deans are the focal point for academic authority, next only to the president or chancellor and the provost or chief academic officer. Academic deans may preside over colleges, schools, or divisions comprised of several disciplines (e.g., arts and sciences, engineering, business, and public affairs). Most deans report to vice presidents or provosts. Deans' roles frequently vary according to academic field, institution type, and institutional context. In institutions marked by higher levels of disciplinary specialization, such as research and doctoral institutions, the number of academic deans is larger in order to accommodate the unique leadership demands of the diverse disciplinary programs housed in the institution.

Drawn from the senior faculty ranks, academic deans must be viewed as serving a dual role – scholar and administrator. Terms of appointment are typically in the range of five to ten years. Deans answer to faculty, the central campus administration, students, and alumni, and must serve varying interests and conflicting goals. Deans serve both academic and administrative purposes when they hire department chairs, or provide oversight of the management of the college/school. Depending on size, deans may have associate and/or assistant deans to handle responsibilities associated with administrative functions like finances, facilities, personnel, and management of academic programs or curricula. Deans are somewhat unique because they regularly interact with the president or chancellor, the chief academic affairs officer, the chief financial officer, the faculty, students, external stakeholders (such as donors and corporate supporters), and in some cases the external boards that provide institutional oversight.

The unique position occupied by academic deans situates them as linchpins for institutional change. Responsibilities of academic deans encompass areas such as: (a) Educational programs/curriculum; (b) faculty selection, promotion, and development; (c) student affairs/admissions; (d) budget/finance; (e) facilities development; and (f) public and alumni relations. Resources under their control vary but can easily involve hundreds of millions of dollars at large research institutions. With diminishing financial support of higher education and increased operational costs, the need to identify new sources of revenue has increased considerably. Soliciting/cultivating such support has become a primary function of academic deans in most institutions. These additional responsibilities associated with fundraising, the often complex financial environment, issues of student access and equity, and the focus on performance and outcomes has made the role of the academic dean ever more complex.

Academic deans are not only required to be scholars of highest repute but also to possess some measure of leadership talent. Communication with faculty is a central activity to the deanship and one that often provokes disagreement, if not conflict. Faculty interactions often involve sensitive issues, such as tenure decisions and salary concerns, demanding an acute sensitivity to faculty needs and skills in problem-solving and conflict management. The most effective deans are skilled in building consensus, influencing outcomes in support of academic programs in a context of disparate goals, and in negotiating for resources in an increasingly scarce resource environment. On a university-wide level, many of the rivalries among academic units are resolved in the relationship between the dean and the central administration. Thus, persuasiveness and ability to navigate the political environment are essential. Effective deans also possess skills in collaboration and integration that facilitate development and implementation of new academic programs and cultivation of new opportunities for research and student learning.

A significant challenge academic deans face is providing leadership where those being led do not believe they need to be led, or are immune to administrative policy and procedural dictates. This is the dynamic in play with many faculty. Moreover, faculty believe teaching and research do not require an extensive administrative apparatus that the dean presides over. Therefore, deans must operate in an environment where their authority is subject to ongoing challenge, ridicule, or disbelief.

Typically, deans ascend to their administrative post through the academic ranks, with some degree of success as a scholar and professor. Their career pathway often includes previous administrative roles such as department chair or maybe assistant or associate dean. For deans in public affairs colleges or schools, their backgrounds and training in institutional management, organization behavior, or finance may be important qualifying experiences. Another route may include previous leadership roles in public agencies or nonprofit organizations.

The dean is of course responsible for the overall leadership of the college/school, including its research, teaching, and service mission. The dean must help recruit and retain a diverse and talented faculty and staff, manage day-to-day operations of the college/school, balance the college budget, lead the school's advancement efforts, engage alumni, corporate, and philanthropic friends, and build and expand the school's engagement, impact, and visibility locally, nationally, and internationally. At the same time the dean must support and sustain scholarly and research excellence, drive curriculum renewal, pedagogy, and academic rigor, connect students to exciting career opportunities, encourage faculty and students to conduct active scholarship in applied arenas, secure additional resources for research and scholarship and professional development, offer leadership to a large and highly complex enterprise, build and cultivate consensus, and create and support a diverse and inclusive community while fostering a climate of collegiality and mutual respect.

At a broader level the dean must be viewed as an intellectual leader, whether a practitioner, teacher, or scholar, a visionary who brings a passion for students, research, and service; an experienced administrator with a track record of success in a large unit, school, or similarly complex environment; a leader with an astute understanding of finances and the relationship between academic priorities and budgets; an open and consultative leader; a proven collaborator who can partner with and motivate faculty, staff, and students; a skilled communicator who can inspire and cultivate key external constituencies and partners, and raise funds; a leader with a track record of supporting diversity and inclusion at all levels, who displays integrity, honesty, and enthusiasm, and a collegiality. At a strategic level, deans must set a vision and goals, develop paths for academic program growth, build consensus, manage and lead through change, empower and engage faculty and staff, and identify and resolve daily issues and conflicts. Some additional specific qualities are attributable to the successful dean, including expertise with budgetary matters, experience in administration, and supervision, which are essential (since the dean is the individual that hires and evaluates the faculty). However, this litany of attributes, skills, or qualifications is not meant to be an exhaustive list of responsibilities and roles for a dean. Moreover, these duties are not always very clear. The individual institution, college, and school dictate the scope and magnitude of these responsibilities.

The academic literature offers important guideposts to better understand the role of a dean. Studies suggest six core knowledge areas that are essential for a dean. These include: (1) Knowledge of the mission, philosophy, and history of the institution; (2) a learner-centered orientation; (3) instructional leadership; (4) information and educational technologies; (5) assessment and accountability; and, (6) administrative preparation (Bragg, 2000). In addition, the dean as a leader must be equipped to handle change. Change within the institution can encompass not only the institution itself but change in faculty, staff, and the student body (Walker, 2000). Bragg (2000) also states that deans should "possess democratic leadership, creative management, and finely tuned human relationship skills" (p. 75). It is evident that deans need to be multi-skilled as well as possess a range of knowledge in many areas. As such, it would be seemingly impossible to identify all the ingredients essential to be a successful dean. Equally stated, deans cannot know everything. For example, they cannot be experts on legal issues as wide-ranging as student rights and the Family Education Rights and Privacy Act, education access and the Americans with Disabilities Act, management's rights and the Fair Labor Standards Act, Title IX, sexual harassment and Title VII of the Civil Rights Act, which guide their actions on a daily basis. Nor can they be experts on topics as wide-ranging as academic freedom, financial aid, and housing, not to mention what constitutes teaching excellence and how to evaluate it (Findlen, 2000). Yet, deans are expected to find solutions to the difficult and varied situations that arise each day. They need to keep current with the world of higher education and the changes that are occurring not only at their own institution but at other colleges and universities as well. Keeping in touch with deans at similar institutions and developing a network of peers is a prudent strategy (e.g., public affairs and policy deans at other institutions).

Deans also find themselves playing conflicting roles on a regular basis. One fundamental challenge for any dean is no longer truly being a professor, yet not being solely an administrator (e.g., like the provost or president). Hence a dean is prone to role conflict and ambiguity. While it differs from one university to another, the dean's position generally involves managing students and faculty on the one side, and liaising with senior management on the other. Deans must be the communicators of the vision of the university for senior leadership, and meet the needs of the faculty on the other end at the same time. And, in a practical sense, deans must constantly put out little fires all the time. Dealing with emergencies or mini fires is an inherent part of the job and those situations are difficult to plan for.

And in the midst of the day-to-day activity associated with putting out fires, deans must have their sights on the longer-term strategy. Shifting gears from one issue or problem to the next is par for the course. It may come into play in a decision about how an admissions policy is developed, what subfield the next faculty hire should be in, or where to allocate scarce resources. As dean, you may have to think creatively about how to devise a new type of scholarship fund or how to restructure existing courses into an exciting program that will attract students from across the campus. The job is about moving a wide range of highly complex puzzle pieces around in real time with a foreknowledge that the implications could resonate for years or even decades. On top of it all, the dean is often the face of the school or college to the outside world at a time when external relationships are even more crucial. In this environment a dean must be ready navigate day-to-day operations, take on the role of spokesperson, and still think in terms of a strategic plan.

As dean, it may be normal to expect 15-hour days and a constant series of meetings with many units requiring quick decisions. There are also less defined aspects to the role, like walking into a meeting more or less knowing who will be there, what the issues are, and what desired outcomes are expected. Yet, often that same meeting requires a dean to pivot because a new person might show up, or new information about budgets might be mentioned, or a different idea might emerge. Is this new development important? Should there be more discussion? Do you stick to the original plan or refocus? Even though many decisions may be well thought out, a dean must consider how actions are perceived by, and affect, the president, provost, department chairs, faculty, administrative staff, students, their parents, community partners, and key donors. How would the decision play out on social media or in the local press?

For a dean compromise is an everyday event, especially when a policy is vague on whether a student should be expelled, or when the marketing department rephrases an academic program. You must be prepared to compromise when the provost asks you to reconsider a cap on our class sizes, or when you can't pay adjuncts what they deserve. Deans compromise because it is part and parcel of the job.

Despite these constraints or obstacles, there are some strategies for success. The quickest and surest way to pursue success is to be in control of the budget for your school or college. Also, systems and processes are how institutions operate and will continue to function long after your role as dean has ended. Embracing change is also an overarching construct of the job, whether negotiating, collaborating, mentoring, counseling, brainstorming, hiring, or firing. And the big-picture reality is that you are "just" the leader. Your success is absolutely and fundamentally linked to, and determined by, the people you work with. At many levels, the academy is about ideas, and a dean is the embodiment of a vision. Deans should never see their job as only making the system run smoothly. Deans are in place to teach and prepare students to become thoughtful and engaged citizens of a complex and pluralistic democracy. The academy is about producing and disseminating knowledge and the dean must embrace a vision for what that means and how it looks in their field (e.g., public affairs). Yet, the ultimate leadership challenge is how to activate and lead change to meet the stark realities of a new market and the reality of higher education in the twenty-first century. To be clear, leadership at the dean level must be always centered on the well-being and aspirations of the students. Data-driven decisions must drive initiatives and processes. Deans must be aware of their students, their faculty, the market, higher education, disciplinary fields, and the political environment. Being dean requires the expenditure of political and personal capital and the ability to rally people around innovation and change.

For prospective public affairs deans, the question arises about definitive guidance to follow. A dean must embrace conceptual and creative thinking, advocate for responsibility-centered management systems, and secure the resources needed to succeed. Deans must be both more cooperative and less conforming than their counterparts. At the same time, they must involve others in decision-making, minimize conflict, accept different views, and see participation as more important than winning. In addition, they must follow their own agenda, see deadlines as flexible, and be less restricted by rules and procedures. This combination is particularly key for the academic entrepreneur, who must drive consensus and generate buy-in while at the same time being willing to buck convention and innovate within existing models. This is what higher education and the college or school of public affairs requires today.

It is important to point out that the academic deanship is the least studied and most misunderstood position in the academy. As this chapter has highlighted, the work of administration and the pursuit of scholarly endeavors is not necessarily an inherent fit. Deans' academic interests turn them firmly toward the departments in their colleges, but their leadership of the colleges and schools depends largely on directions from the provost and university administrators. The resulting paradoxical situation causes many academic leaders to burn out from the strain of trying to be effective administrators on the one hand, and attempting to protect the academic autonomy and independence of faculty on the other (Gmelch & Miskin, 1993, 1995). Many academic leaders, such as deans, end their administrative careers fatigued and suffering from excessive levels of stress (Gmelch & Chan, 1994).

One empirical study examined a sample of 210 academic deans in research and doctoral institutions in the United States to investigate the relationship between academic discipline and the preparation of deans for their leadership role. Respondents reported relying on experience in past administrative posts and past relationships with faculty leaders as the most highly valued approaches to learning what the dean's job entails. Findings also suggested that how deans understand their role is very much related to the unique experiences they have accumulated as faculty members. Despite the low reliance overall on trial-and-error as a learning approach, deans in pure fields reported relying more on trial-and-error than deans from applied fields (like public affairs). This finding suggests that academic discipline cannot be discounted in considering the preparation of faculty for leadership roles (Del Favero, 2006). Perhaps the discipline of public affairs may afford better foundational training for the role of dean. Other research suggests the dean will play one of three roles: Initiator of conflict; defendant in a conflict situation; or conciliator in a conflict situation. Implicit in these descriptors is the proposition that it will be helpful for the dean to be aware of certain ground rules, or tactics, which can lead to a successful confrontation (Feltner & Goodsell, 1972).

Although even less research exists on the impact of gender or race in leadership in academic administration, some gender-oriented studies have focused on deans in public affairs programs. Although the number of female faculty members has risen in public administration and policy programs throughout the nation, few studies have analyzed the advances made in leadership roles at universities and colleges. The most commonly used method of examining success in academic settings is by analyzing the research productivity patterns of faculty members. However, evaluation should not be limited to measuring publication productivity alone, but also through measuring gender equity in leadership positions.

One important study analyzed the scholarly output and leadership patterns of faculty members in fields of public administration and policy by gender. The study used data from doctorate recipients to examine career trajectories at 241 schools offering degrees in public administration, affairs, policy, and management listed on the NASPAA website to examine leadership patterns by gender. The results suggest that female faculty members have lower productivity despite controlling for demographic, institutional, and career factors. However, when various interaction terms are introduced between female faculty, the productivity gap by gender disappears (Sabharwal, 2013).

Leadership patterns of female faculty in public administration and policy programs in the United States is clearly an understudied area. Overwhelming evidence suggests that women in local, state, and federal government jobs are less likely to be present in high-ranking positions (Guy & Newman, 2004). And to date there are few studies examining the role of female faculty members in positions of chairs or deans in public administration and related programs. An exception to this is Stabile, Terman and Kuerbitz (2017) who examine the role of gender in relation to director positions in MPA and MPP programs. They found that women served as program directors in direct proportion to their representation among the faculty – 35 percent. Their interview data suggested that although gender characterization of women in leadership roles still exist, both men and women program directors struggle to balance their director position with the expectations of teaching and research. And research and teaching suffer as a result. But some evidence suggests that female faculty members are indeed far less likely to be in senior-ranking positions. Specifically, female faculty members in public administration and policy are less likely to be in positions of chair or department or program heads when compared with male faculty. Overall, the studies suggest that while female representation in leadership roles in public affairs has certainly progressed over the years, much more needs to be done before women can achieve parity with men in leadership positions (Rubin, 2000).

And how does gender impact roles in the academy? Female faculty members in public service programs seem to take on a disproportionate amount of advising/mentoring responsibilities yet are less likely to be in leadership positions at universities (Rauhaus & Carr, 2019). This includes mentoring of students and colleagues, and otherwise undertaking social and gender equity causes in both service and teaching to the detriment of their career advancement. In addition, Elias and D'Agostino (2019) in their case study point out that of surveyed MPA students, many do not learn about gender competency through their MPA education. They emphasize the need for incorporating gender competency into MPA education to promote gender competency in public policy, administrative decision-making, and workplace culture. Their approach calls for greater gender competency in the MPA curricula, programming, and research and suggests the need to include MPA faculty and directors.

And, of course, gender is just one element relevant to the context of effective leadership in public administration and the academy at large. Issues of racism and discrimination in public administration must be addressed on a continuing basis, as should the promotion of diversity in graduate education, faculty employment, and leadership positions in the academy. The mixed results of successful and failed diversity-promotion practices in various academic programs must necessarily inform the field of public administration for both faculty ranks and leadership roles. A significant body of empirical research is uncovering patterns of action that have both intended and unintended effects of excluding candidates of color from recruitment pools, interview short-lists, and faculty hiring and advancement opportunities. The implications for public affairs education are clear in pushing for a new direction for diversity-related research, the articulation of diversity commitments, particularly by public administration departments and programs, and the resolve for meeting institutional commitments to racial equity with established practices and strategies (Rivera & Ward, 2008).

What's Right for You?

To make the decision about moving into administrative leadership in public administration and public affairs programs, departments, or colleges, conducting a self-assessment based upon the various characteristics, traits, skills, and experiences introduced in this chapter is a useful first step in contemplating such a move. As you assess your specific strengths, also ponder whether you like the big-picture view necessary in academic leadership. Perhaps most important is to consider your real or perceived connection to the field set apart from your narrow disciplinary focus/specialization interests coveted in academia. Part of this calculus is whether you're prepared to scale back significantly on your research and teaching. These activities necessarily take a backseat when faced with the scope of administrative duties. Especially for those considering appointments as program director, chair, or dean, prospective administrators must be sure they don't lie to themselves about how willing they are to put the classroom and research on the backburner. This is particularly the case when a professional sense of self is derived from the passion and dedication of years invested into being a scholar and teacher.

In other words, you have to think about whether you value service at least as much as research. Just what is your service mindset? Careful introspection should reveal your aptitude for helping colleagues achieve their professional goals and aspirations. Perhaps pursuing an interim appointment to a leadership role can help sort out whether administration is the right move. Also pursuing a scaffolded approach to ever-increasing tiers of leadership is another strategy to move forward in administration. Rising through the ranks from program director to chair to dean will allow you to evaluate your satisfaction derived from these roles.

Above all, those interested in these positions should honestly assess their own people skills and leadership abilities. A continual self-assessment to identify and cultivate skills fundamental to successful leadership is a key. Take advantage of mentorships, leadership training programs and executive seminars/workshops/courses. To make the move into academic leadership you should consider reflecting on the strengths you have, the experiences you've accumulated, and an understanding of the environment in which you will operate.

Any self-assessment should involve an ability to adjust to the shift in interpersonal dynamics that comes with leadership. Be prepared for the isolation that comes with being a leader. Equally, appreciate that the way a leader approaches issues plays a powerful role in terms of setting the tone for the faculty, staff and students you lead. The jump to administrator means you're going from someone who is friends with all of the faculty to an adversary of the faculty who you once considered colleagues.

That "isolation" highlights the need to really think about whether you're ready to make decisions that not everyone will like. And to prepare for that dynamic, take the time to talk to everyone who may be affected by your decision. Finally, immersing yourself in academic leadership requires that you "take care of yourself." It's easy to lose yourself in your work and not have time for anything else. Promise yourself you won't let administrative duties affect your health, time with my family, and long-term friendships.

In the end, most administrators want to emphasize how much the rewards outweigh the stresses in their jobs, especially knowing that many faculty are intimidated by administration. Oftentimes it is difficult or impossible to get faculty to think about stepping into administrative roles. And the reason is because we select faculty who are very passionate teachers and researchers, and we're not looking for faculty who are passionate administrators. But at the same time, the discipline is not necessarily encouraging faculty enough to think about administrative tracks. To help think about the positions and your interest in taking them on, Table 4.2 provides an overview of the roles that directors, chairs, and deans play.

Conclusions and Observations

In summary, the substantive and prescriptive literature on academic leadership reinforces several key takeaways implicit in this chapter. One treatment in particular warrants close consideration for positions on the pathway to academic leadership (Mabrouk, 2018). That treatment highlights the following.

1. Make sure you secure tenure. You don't want to enter academic leadership until you have achieved this goal. As an administrator, you may be able to continue some scholarly pursuits, but certainly not at the level or rate of productivity as would a full-time faculty member.
2. Seek out and engage in a strong support network. Identify a few individuals who have held or hold a similar position and whom you trust and respect. They don't need to be at your home institution – in fact, it is probably more helpful when they're not. Being somewhat detached should keep the focus on problem-solving rather than institution-specific machinations.
3. Obtain a contract, appointment letter, or other agreement outlining the terms of your administrative assignment. Line up resources and

TABLE 4.2 Summary (Snapshot) of Roles of Directors, Chairs, and Deans

Directors	Chairs	Deans
• Create and maintain course schedules and teaching assignments and provide curriculum oversight.	• Represent the department to other units in the college or school and report to the dean.	• Hire department chairs, associate and assistant deans, and other key college support positions.
• Manage department activities, administration, and budgets.	• Lead and work with faculty to develop department curriculum and academic standards.	• Provide oversight of the management of the college/school.
• Recruit students and manage admissions activities.	• Coordinate with and assist the dean in advancing college priorities and imperatives.	• Interact with the president or chancellor, the chief academic affairs officer, the chief financial officer, the faculty, students, external stakeholders, and external boards.
• Advise graduate and undergraduate students (award-manage financial aid packages/assistantships).	• Oversee searches, receive and review department search committee recommendations, and make departmental recommendations to the dean.	• Oversee faculty selection, promotion, and development.
• Brand and market the program and promote graduates (for career and doctoral study).	• Coordinate with the dean on the selection and negotiations of positions for full-time and part-time faculty and staff.	• Manage, maintain, and expand facilities.
• Recruit and retain faculty.	• Mentor faculty and provide annual performance development plans.	• Develop the budget and manage college expenditures and secure internal/external resources (fundraising).
• Mentor and develop faculty and staff.	• Handle student complaints or issues and maintain positive student communications.	• Engage in public and alumni relations.
• Supervise part-time faculty.	• Perform annual evaluations of faculty and staff; receive department personnel committee recommendations for reappointment, tenure, and promotion.	• Navigate central administration issues.
• Pursue program and institutional accreditation and maintain related metrics.	• Enforce compliance with all university and system policies.	• Develop new academic programs and identify areas for new research and innovation.
• Manage the program's web/social media presence and overall public relations efforts.		• Support and sustain scholarly and research excellence, drive curriculum renewal, pedagogy, and academic rigor.
• Build and maintain engagement with alumni, stakeholders, and related constituencies.		
• Maintain excellent relations across the university (dean, provost, president, etc.).		
• Attend various leadership functions/meetings.		

- Teach as may be negotiated.
- Maintain positive student relationships and communication

- Lead the department in developing budget requests, priorities, and approving expenditures. • Assign faculty to courses and prepare schedules to meet student needs.
- Oversee accreditation review, and prepare documents for curricular changes, catalog revisions, and other documents necessary to convey the department's curricular plans.
- Develop and coordinate student recruitment, retention, advising, and service activities with relevant support offices.
- Coordinate academic assessment exercises.
- Prepare reports and analyses, and fulfill data requests from the dean and other university administrators.
- Foster a collegial environment and open communications with faculty.
- Represent the department(s) to external organizations and groups, inter-institutional activities, and accrediting agencies.

- Create and support a diverse and inclusive community while fostering a climate of collegiality and mutual respect.
- Develop a vision and open communication across the college.

other support before you take the job. Because change happens frequently in administration, it is important to consider the term of appointment, administrative stipends, funding for professional development, and the basis on which merit will be evaluated. When leaving your administrative role, will you revert to your same tenure track line in the granting department? What are the details or parameters of your "return" to the faculty?

4. Participate in institutional and national professional development opportunities. Sign up for semester- or year-long professional development programs on or off campus, to meet and get to know other administrators at various levels across the university and on other campuses.

5. Always ask for feedback from those reporting to you to reveal where you need to grow as a leader and a manager.

6. Take the time to get to know your direct reports. Recognize that each unit has its own culture. Take the time and make an effort to learn the cultures of various units and don't assume that everyone agrees with the way you do things. Don't make assumptions based on your own culture, as they may turn out to be wrong. Listen, and don't be afraid to ask questions and truly hear the answers you receive.

7. Don't overstay your welcome. There is a shelf-life to academic leadership posts. One term or maybe two is appropriate. In this regard, look at your administrative role as a pivot point in your career. One level of administration is useful preparation and a proving ground for your next administrative appointment. And if you aspire to a future administrative post then pay careful attention to the demands of that next position.

8. Never assume that you will be promoted to an administrative post at your own institution. While you may be given the opportunity to serve on an interim basis, some institutions like to hire from similar outside institutions.

Faculty members interested in moving into these administrative roles assume there is some defined career path in academic administration. Oftentimes there is not. If you have already participated in the administrative life of your department, discipline, and professional association – or if you run an active research program – then you probably have more knowledge and experience than you probably realize to move into administrative roles.

The key question is whether or not you will find happiness and satisfaction in the role of an administrator, collegially working with and through all those around you. If, at the end of the day, you enjoy the challenge of grappling with complex problems of broad scope and significant impact – and that leverage the active, collegial participation of large teams or units of individuals – then maybe the job is for you.

TABLE 4.A1 Administrative Roles for Issue 1

Program Director	Department Chair	College Dean
The program director has worked carefully with her faculty to obtain consensus on the need for a new faculty member to be added for the program to be accredited. Course load and scheduling have been discussed, and there was agreement on adding an assistant professor rather than an associate. Because the department has an open line at present, funding should not be an issue. The stumbling block facing the director is that there is not any agreement on what sub-field the new faculty member should represent. There are two gaps in coverage in budgeting and finance and nonprofit organizations. Budgeting is a core class but many new students are from area nonprofits. How does the director balance these interests and then effectively approach the chair for support?	The chair heads up a 20-member department. There is a robust undergraduate political science program, which constitutes the largest enrollment in the department. There is also a struggling Master in International Studies program that has been approaching you for the past year or more to add a new faculty position to its program to balance out their coverage. A specialist in Middle Eastern Affairs is preferred. This program has three of the most senior tenured members of the department and they carry a lot of weight among their colleagues. However, the program only has 15 students and enrollments have steadily declined. As chair, your philosophy is if we have a program that can be accredited, it should be. You are leaning toward supporting the MPA program in its request. How do you approach your colleagues in international studies about their request for a new position in light of MPA program needs?	As the dean, your college has come under increasing pressures to better manage and control spending. The provost has noted that spending in your college was up for the past three years in a row when enrollments in the college have somewhat flattened. This is not just your college's problem and other colleges are in the same situation. You know that several of your departments have advanced requests to hire new faculty. They each make persuasive cases to fill these positions. There are pending requests from these departments to hire eight faculty members. The provost has informed you that only two will be filled next year. You happen to hold a Ph.D. in Public Affairs and would like to see the MPA accredited. But other departments have lost faculty due to attrition and retirements and there are some significant holes to fill in these departments. How might you approach this dilemma?

TABLE 4.A2 Administrative Roles for Issue 2

Program Director	Department Chair	College Dean
Your program has steadily been rising in the latest US News & World Reports rankings. You are convinced this is because of some very good recent hires. Also your program is known for excellence in teaching and is enjoying an increasing reputation for research and rigor in the field. Future growth and resources are dependent upon continuing to move in this direction. The decisions for promotion and tenure will be made by the personnel committees and the chair as recommendations to the dean. You happen to value each faculty member but for different reasons. As you look back over the past few years you reflect on what you might have done differently from your vantage point as director to better position these two candidates in their penultimate year. What do you contemplate?	In short order, the respective personnel committees will make their recommendations. At your institution you have a separate letter to add to the portfolios. This will be considered by the dean as part of his review of submitted materials. You reflect on the two faculty members and their role in the program and the department. For several years you have worked hard to build a collegial environment (that wasn't always that way). You have successfully steered the department toward a more student-centered experience and that is evident in recent surveys. Also, although there have been several Title IX issues on the campus, your department has been spared. You have strived to provide leadership that has balanced improving the academic reputation of the department against being an engaged department in the university and beyond. Do you take these views into account? Why or why not?	As dean you will receive several portfolios from your departments. This year 14 faculty members are up for tenure. You have made it a practice to heavily weight the decisions made by the respective personnel committees. The chairs' assessment is important, but it is just another factor. As dean you have done your best to get to know your faculty and their work and their contributions, but sometimes that is difficult to do. The parameters for tenure and promotion weight scholarship at 60 percent, teaching at 30 percent, and service at 10 percent. Prior to your arrival most candidates for tenure and promotion seemed to think the process was overall favorable to them. The contribution by faculty of course are varied and must be balanced and considered against the intangible factors that define faculty "worth." You view things a bit differently. How might you proceed in this matter? What would be your thought process or guideposts to help render a decision?

Appendix: Cross-Walk of Roles Across Selected Issues

Issue One

The MPA program wants to pursue NASPAA accreditation but lacks the required minimum of five designated faculty members dedicated to the MPA program. The program has four full-time faculty assigned to teach in the program (in the political science department). The program has seen an increase in students over the past three years and anticipates this growth to continue. The program needs to decide on a course of action to secure a new public affairs position, the department chair is facing conflicting pressures on which program area should receive a new position, and the dean of the college is facing funding constraints that will mean next year there will only be two new hires allowed. How might each administrator approach or handle this situation?

Issue Two

The successful and growing MPA program will have two faculty going up for tenure this year. One is a strong candidate who has several publications in top journals and a forthcoming book at a top press, and despite a reputation for being a "tough" teacher he has satisfactory student evaluations. However, this candidate is known for not getting along with colleagues and has been the subject of complaints from several students that are now being investigated by the university office of access and equity. The second candidate has three publications (two in minor venues and one in a notable journal). She has strong teaching evaluations and is well liked by students. Her service record in terms of department, college, university, and community is very strong. How do you approach these decisions from each distinctive role? Are your decisions somehow related? Should they be?

References

Bragg, D. D. (2000). Preparing community college deans to lead change. In Robillard, D. (ed.), *New directions for community colleges* (pp. 75–85). San Francisco, CA: Jossey-Bass.

Brainard, L. (2017). Directing public affairs programs. *Journal of Public Affairs Education, 23*(3), 779–784.

Buller, J. L. (2012). *The essential department chair: A comprehensive desk reference*, 2nd edn. San Francisco, CA: Jossey-Bass.

Del Favero, M. (2006) Disciplinary variation in preparation for the academic dean role. *Higher Education Research and Development, 25*(3), 277–292.

Elias, N. & D'Agostino, M. J. (2019). Gender competency in public administration education. *Teaching Public Administration, 37*(2), 218–233.

Feltner, B. & Goodsell, D. (1972). The academic dean and conflict management. *The Journal of Higher Education, 43*(9), 692–701.

Findlen, G. L. (2000). A dean's survival tool kit. In Robillard, D. (ed.), *New directions for community colleges* (pp. 87–94). San Francisco, CA: Jossey-Bass.

Ginsberg, B. (2011). *The fall of the faculty: The rise of the all-administrative university and why it matters.* New York: Oxford University Press.

Gmelch, W. H. & Miskin, V. D. (1993). *Strategic leadership skills for department chairs.* Bolton, MA: Anker Publishing Co.

Gmelch, W. H., & Miskin, V. D., (1995). *Chairing the academic department.* Thousand Oaks, CA: Sage Publications.

Gmelch, W. H. & Chan, W. (1994). *Thriving on stress for success.* Thousand Oaks, CA: Corwin Press.

Guy, M. E. & Newman, M. A. (2004). Women's jobs, men's jobs: Sex segregation and emotional labor. *Public Administration Review, 64*(3), 289–298.

Hatcher, W., Meares, W. L., & Gordon, V. (2017). The capacity and constraints of small MPA programs: A survey of program directors. *Journal of Public Affairs Education, 23*(3), 855–868.

Killian, J. & Wenning, M. (2017). Are we having fun yet? Exploring the motivations of MPA and MPP program directors in the United States. *Journal of Public Affairs Education, 23*(3), 799–810.

Mabrouk, P. (2018). The indispensable associate dean. *Inside Higher Ed.* Retrieved September 22, 2019, from www.insidehighered.com/advice/2018/02/21/why-associate-deanship-academic-position-worth-considering-opinion.

Rauhaus B. M. & Carr, I. A. S. (2019). The invisible challenges: Gender differences among public administration faculty. *Journal of Public Affairs Education.*

Rivera, M. A. & Ward, J. D. (2008). Employment equity and institutional commitments to diversity: Disciplinary perspectives from public administration and public affairs education. *Journal of Public Affairs Education, 14*(1), 9–20.

Rubin, M. M. (2000). Women in the American society for public administration: Another decade of progress but still a way to go. *Public Administration Review, 60*(1), 61–71.

Sabharwal, M. (2013). Productivity and leadership patterns of female faculty members in public administration. *Journal of Public Affairs Education, 19*(1), 73–96.

Stabile, B., Terman, J., & Kuerbitz, C. (2017). Gender and the role of directors of public administration and policy programs. *Journal of Public Affairs Education, 23*(3), 825–842.

Vicino, T. (2017). Navigating the multiple roles of the MPA director: Perspectives and lessons. *Journal of Public Affairs Education, 23*(3), 785–798.

Walker, K. L. (2000). Facing challenges: Identifying the role of the community college dean. United States Department of Education. Retrieved September 22, 2019, from www.ed.gov/databases.

5

STRATEGIC PLANNING FOR YOUR PROGRAM

Jerrell D. Coggburn and Jared J. Llorens

To say that these are turbulent times for higher education would be an understatement. Colleges and universities face a raft of challenges, including declining public resources, disruptive technological change, political pressure to perform from across the ideological spectrum, questions about the extent of student learning (Arum & Roska, 2011), and doubts about the return on investment for higher education (Blagg & Blom, 2018). Schultz's (2013) admonition that higher education's business model has collapsed succinctly captures this state of affairs. Further, higher education's challenges may be particularly pronounced for programs of public policy, affairs and administration (PA). As Rich (2013) notes, PA programs are under pressure to be relevant, improve time-to-degree and graduation rates, meet stakeholder needs, and generate more student credit hours. Performance on such measures is important, as evidenced by state governments' propensity to target PA programs for cuts and elimination during periods of fiscal stress (Kerrigan, 2011). Compounding these challenges, data from the US Department of Education show that fewer people are getting PA degrees, which may be attributable to growing anti-government rhetoric and fiscal uncertainty associated with public service careers (Maciag, 2017). Given this context, it would be understandable for PA programs to feel trepidation about their future.

In light of this turbulent landscape, it is imperative that PA programs adopt more strategic approaches to mission fulfillment and while not a panacea (Bryson, 2011; Gabris, 1992),[1] formal strategic planning efforts offer an approach for understanding and addressing the uncertainty facing PA programs. Bryson (2010) defines strategic planning as:

> a deliberative, disciplined effort to produce fundamental decisions and actions that shape and guide what an organization (or other entity) *is* (its

identity), what it *does* (its strategies and actions), and why it does it (mandates, mission, goals, and the creation of public value).

(pp. s256–s257)

Strategic planning has evolved from being a novelty for public service management (Eadie, 1983; Poister, Pitts, & Edwards, 2010) to the point where it is now a ubiquitous component of it (Bryson, 2010; Poister, 2010). Overall, the adoption and diffusion of strategic planning reflects its ability to produce a number of benefits, including promoting strategic thinking and action, improving decision-making, improving organizational effectiveness, and providing personal benefits (e.g., role fulfillment, improved morale) to those involved (Bryson, 2010, 2011).

Similar to its broader role in organizational management, strategic planning also has become an important and common managerial practice in higher education, be it at the institutional, department, or program level (Rowley & Sherman, 2001). The purpose of this chapter, therefore, is to offer PA program leaders practical guidance on strategic planning. It begins with a discussion of the Network of Schools of Public Policy, Affairs, and Administration (NASPAA) accreditation framework, which has created a strategic planning imperative for accredited PA programs and those aspiring for accreditation. Next, the chapter presents the major components of strategic planning, including analyzing stakeholder expectations, reviewing program mission, developing program strategies, and closing the loop through assessment and revision. Last, the chapter concludes with a summary of the role strategic planning plays in building and maintaining high-quality, impactful PA programs.

Strategic Planning for Public Policy, Affairs, and Administration Programs

The premise of this chapter is that strategic planning is an essential tool for academic programs seeking to maintain their mission-critical activities or expand into new areas of influence and programming. Simply stated, it is near impossible for an academic program to achieve sustained success without a clear understanding of such factors as its operational environment, core mission, and strategic goals. While universities often engage in strategic planning efforts that encompass a wide range of academic programming, it is imperative that individual academic programs do so as well.

NASPAA and the Strategic Planning Process

As a prelude to the discussion of strategic planning in practice, it is useful to acknowledge the considerable influence that the Network of Schools of Public Policy, Affairs, and Administration (NASPAA), an international accreditor for master's degree programs, holds in promoting strategic planning activities among

PA programs. Arguably, NASPAA, through its current accreditation standards, has made strategic planning an essential component of both accredited and member programs.

While NASPAA's pre-2009 accreditation standards focused primarily upon curriculum content across PA programs, NASPAA's current standards (adopted in 2009) seek to prioritize the unique context of PA programs as identified through individual strategic planning processes. With the adoption of its current standards, NASPAA endorsed a mission-centered approach to professional PA education. Though not without its critics (Guy & Stillman, 2016; Henry, Goodsell, Lynn, Stivers, & Wamsley, 2009; White, 2007), the mission-based focus has effectively broadened the scope of accreditation, making it available to programs whose mission diverged from the former prescriptive, curriculum-based standards (Raffel, Maser, & Calarusse, 2015).

Accredited programs are no longer mandated to address specific topical areas in their curriculum. Rather, they are now required to define and deliver NASPAA's five universal required competencies in a manner consistent with their overall program mission, as articulated in their strategic plan, and in accordance with NASPAA's seven accreditation standards.[2] Ultimately, the flexibility afforded to programs in the current standards mandates a corresponding strategic framework for ensuring that accredited programs are adequately preparing the next generation of public service professionals.

Highlighting the importance and centrality of strategic planning, NASPAA's first accreditation standard (Standard 1) is "Managing the Program Strategically" and accredited programs are held accountable to three sub-components within this broader standard (see Table 5.1). Explicit in these three sub-components of

TABLE 5.1 NASPAA Accreditation Standard 1: Managing the Program Strategically

1.1 Mission Statement: The Program will have a statement of mission that guides performance expectations and their evaluation, including:
  - Its purpose and public service values, given the program's particular emphasis on public affairs, administration, and policy;
  - The population of students, employers, and professionals the Program intends to serve; and
  - The contributions it intends to produce to advance the knowledge, research and practice of public affairs, administration, and policy.

1.2 Performance Expectations: The Program will establish observable program goals, objectives and outcomes, including expectations for student learning, consistent with its mission.

1.3 Program Evaluation: The Program will collect, apply and report information about its performance and its operations to guide the evolution of the Program's mission and the Program's design and continuous improvement with respect to standards two through seven.

Source: NASPAA (2015).

Standard 1 is the overarching expectation that professional public policy, affairs, and administration programs be strategically managed.

Mission. The first Standard 1 sub-component (1.1) requires programs to possess a mission statement "that guides performance expectations and their evaluation." In particular, a program's mission statement must address its "purpose and public service values," the "population of students, employers and professionals" served by the program, and the intended contributions of the program with regard to research and practice.

Goals, objectives, and outcomes. The second sub-component (1.2) of the strategic management standard holds that programs develop clear "goals, objectives, and outcomes" that are aligned with the overall mission of the program. The overarching goal of this component of the standard is to ensure that programs have a roadmap, in the form of objectives and outcomes, in place to fulfill their missions and that this roadmap is specific enough to provide a realistic assessment of a program's progress toward achieving its mission.

Evaluation and closing the loop. The third sub-component (1.3) relates directly to the evaluation of strategic programming efforts, with particular emphasis placed on continuous improvement (i.e., "closing the loop"). In other words, programs are expected to construct systematic processes to evaluate their progress in achieving program goals and to use the results of their evaluations to constantly improve upon their efforts. For example, if a program has identified the development of local government managers as one of its primary mission-driven goals, then it should also have a robust evaluation system in place to both assess its progress in meeting this goal and to identify areas of improvement. The evaluation of this goal could be achieved through numerous approaches, from local government job placement metrics to third-party reviews of student competencies in the area of local government management. An example of the latter could come in the form of performance assessments of program interns working in local government. Analyzing how local government supervisors assess the competency and performance of interns provides programs with the opportunity to identify programmatic shortcomings (e.g., systematically low assessments of, say, performance budgeting) that can, in turn, lead to curricular modification.

In sum, while there is little questioning the effect of the standards on the management practices of accredited programs, it is important to note that strategic planning is not something that is or should be confined to accredited programs and programs pursuing accreditation. Programs lacking budgetary and/or faculty resources (e.g., the need to have five faculty dedicated to the program or the so-called "five-faculty rule" for accreditation) or that simply are disinclined to pursue accreditation stand to benefit, nonetheless, by adopting strategic planning to build on strengths, mitigate weaknesses, exploit opportunities, address challenges and threats, satisfy stakeholders, and achieve the mission.

Strategic Planning in Practice

Given the emergence of strategic planning as a key component of public-sector and nonprofit management, a number of practical guides have been developed that speak directly to the field of PA (Bryson, 2011; Koteen, 1997; Mercer, 1991). Bryson's (2011) "strategy change cycle," in particular, has become one of the predominant models of strategic planning for public service organizations and has influenced the practice in higher-education settings as well (Dooris, Kelley, & Trainer, 2004). The following discussion draws upon these guides, adapting their lessons to the specific context of PA programs.

Initiating the Strategic Planning Process

The first step of strategic planning is deciding to do it. Such a decision may stem from a variety of sources (see Poister et al., 2010), which for PA programs might include a governmental mandate (e.g., a state law requiring strategic planning), a university strategic planning initiative, or a PA program-level decision that may or may not be accreditation-related. Accompanying the decision to undertake strategic planning are decisions about the program or department's readiness, who will lead the effort, who will be included on the planning team, and the timeline for completing the various aspects of the planning effort.

Within the context of PA programs, it is likely that the effort will be led by the program director or department chair and will include some, or for smaller programs all, program faculty as members of the planning team. The strategic planning timeline may often be dictated by the institutional calendar (e.g., a university's graduate school may require a strategic plan be submitted by a certain date as part of a campus-based program review and/or annual outcomes assessment process) or, perhaps, by external accreditation considerations (e.g., programs in NASPAA's accreditation process must have a plan in place in sufficient time to measure program outcomes and report them in a self-study report). The important thing to note is that programs need to clarify, upfront, who will lead and participate in the strategic planning process and the timeline for completing specific steps.

For programs considering strategic planning, the key planning questions to consider include the following.

- Is the program ready to proceed with strategic planning? Assuming yes…
- Who (e.g., department chair, PA program director, designated planning team leader) will lead the strategic planning effort?
- Who (e.g., program faculty, administrators, staff, stakeholder representatives) will be on the strategic planning team? In what capacity?
- What is the timeline for strategic plan completion?

Stakeholder Assessment

A critical aspect of strategic planning initiatives is the stakeholder analysis. A stakeholder "is any person, group, or organization that can place a claim on an organization's attention, resources, or output, or is affected by that output" (Bryson, 2011, p. 48). As Bryson (2011) notes, the most important aspect of strategic planning is likely the stakeholder analysis because an organization is unlikely to be successful if it does not understand who its stakeholders are, what those stakeholders expect, and how the organization is performing relative to those expectations (p. 132).

The exact mix of internal and external stakeholders and their relative importance to strategic planning will vary among PA programs. Generally, PA program stakeholders include: Prospective students (applicants), current students (further classified, as appropriate, including in-service and pre-service, traditional and nontraditional, online, etc.), alumni, faculty (full-time and part-time), and public service employers. Other institutional stakeholders might include those from the college (dean), university (provost, graduate school), and/or sister programs (e.g., an undergraduate program if there is an accelerated bachelor's/master's degree program; partner programs for joint master's degree programs like social work, law, natural resources, or engineering). Identifying these stakeholders is key to clarifying a program's thinking about the stakeholders (especially students and employers) its mission serves.

To illustrate the importance of stakeholders and their respective concerns, consider three key PA program stakeholders: Faculty, students, and public service employers. First, as generators and disseminators (i.e., through scholarly publication and teaching) of disciplinary knowledge, program faculty represent key program stakeholders. In most academic settings, program faculty have determining influence over curricular content, including the content and design of their respective courses, so a planning effort that fails to consider faculty stakes would be doomed from the outset. This underscores the importance of an inclusive strategic planning that embraces the notion that every faculty member is a leader (Pearce, Wood, & Wassenaar, 2018). At the same time, it is important to note that some faculty resistance related to turf, skills, and academic freedom can be expected (e.g., Peters, 2009).

Current students represent a second key stakeholder group. To be successful, PA programs must be able to attract, admit, educate, retain, graduate, and successfully place students in public service careers. This sets a premium on understanding the needs and expectations of students. As a result, programs should focus on student expectations in terms of advising support, career assistance, course offerings, and competency development (among others). Further, programs should explore how these expectations differ among various types of students (e.g., full- and part-time, in- and pre-service, traditional and nontraditional, historically underrepresented) the program serves. To be sure, students have expectations of their program. Identifying and understanding these expectations relative to how the program is performing represents fertile ground for identifying strategic issues (e.g., which students should be targeted for recruitment and how? how might the program's mode of delivery need to change relative to the students the program mission serves or intends to serve? what forms of advising, financial, social, and professional development support are needed to meet students' needs?).

Public service employers represent a third key external stakeholder group. The nexus between PA program curriculum and employer needs and expectations is one where stakeholder focus is critical; if programs are not developing students' knowledge, skills, and abilities (read "competencies") that match their natural public service markets' needs (Posner, 2009; McQuiston & Manoharan, 2017) then the performance of public service agencies and the credibility of PA programs both suffer. This underscores the importance of understanding what public service employers need from a PA program and how the program is performing relative to those needs and expectations.

In addition to identifying stakeholders and their respective stakes, a key consideration is determining how they are included in the strategic planning process (Bryson, 2004). Experts on public-sector strategic planning (Bryson, 2004, 2011; Poister, 2010) argue for more inclusive approaches to stakeholder involvement, be it through direct involvement (e.g., as planning team members) or greater efforts to gain their input through surveys and focus groups (see also Peters, 2009). For example, as part of the mission development and revision process, programs have choices about which stakeholders to involve and how. Some programs may present a new or revised mission statement to, say, current students and alumni and solicit their feedback about the statement (e.g., its clarity, relevance). Other programs may opt for a more inclusive process upfront, soliciting stakeholders' ideas about what should/should not be included in the mission statement before it is revised or drafted through surveys, focus groups, and/or participation as members of the strategic planning team.

In sum, the key considerations for stakeholder involvement include the following.

- Who are the key PA program stakeholders (both internal and external)?
- What do the various stakeholders expect from the program?
- How is the program currently meeting stakeholders' expectations?
- How can the program ensure the stakeholders' views are included in the planning process?

Reviewing, Revising, and Adopting a Program Mission

Owing to the mission-centric NASPAA program standards, and in line with general approaches to strategic planning in public and nonprofit organizations, developing the program mission statement is a key step for PA programs. The mission statement serves as the lodestar for programmatic decision-making. Many, if not most, PA programs will already have a mission statement. If so, then the mission development phase of strategic planning entails reviewing and either reaffirming or revising the mission statement. For new programs or those without an existing mission statement, this phase of strategic planning will entail developing and adopting an initial program mission statement. Regardless, the mission review (or development) and revision (or initial drafting) process should be inclusive, taking into consideration – either directly or indirectly – the perspectives and needs of key stakeholders including students, alumni, faculty, and public service employers.

Along with understanding stakeholders' expectations, an important consideration for PA programs is identifying those things that they are required to do. In other words, what are the formal and informal mandates of the program? As Bryson (2011) notes, such mandates may be found in laws (e.g., agency-enabling legislation), policies, organizational charters, or, for informal ones, in stakeholders' expectations that are nonetheless binding on the organization. Formal mandates might include a graduate school requirement for applicants to have a certain undergraduate grade point average or standardized exam score for program admission. Additionally, some campuses have requirements regarding faculty office hours, syllabus content (e.g., regarding grades, statements on student accommodation), and student contact hours for courses. For NASPAA-accredited programs, the standards and annual reporting requirements could be thought of as formal mandates (even if accreditation is voluntary). An example of an informal mandate might include a program's mode of delivery – a program serving primarily in-service students working full-time would be expected to offer courses at times (evenings, weekends) or modes (online) that allow students to make regular progress through the degree.

For illustration purposes, the current mission statement of the State University of New York (SUNY) at Albany provides a good example of how programs have crafted their missions to align with stakeholder expectations and NASPAA accreditation standards:

> The Rockefeller College MPA program develops leaders, managers, and advanced analysts who excel in public service within government and across sectors. We provide pre-service and mid-career students with a comprehensive core curriculum in public affairs and a diverse selection of electives to further tailor their training and prepare them to solve difficult administrative and policy problems in local, state, national and global communities. Our curriculum emphasizes the development of technical and managerial skills toward the responsible and ethical uses of discretion in the pursuit exemplary personal and organizational performance. Our academic and professional faculty (1) are accomplished researchers and practitioners, (2) draw on many years of experience,

(3) produce high quality academic and professional research, and (4) address significant issues in public management and policy.

(SUNY at Albany, 2019)

In contrast, Seton Hall University's mission statement for its MPA program highlights its efforts to prepare servant leaders with an added emphasis on ethics and theory.

The mission of the MPA program is to develop servant leaders for management positions in the public, private and nonprofit sectors. Within an interdisciplinary, collaborative and culturally diverse setting, we are dedicated to providing high quality graduate degree and graduate certificate programs that are intellectually stimulating, ethically oriented and have a theory-to-practice focus.

(Seton Hall University, 2019)

Last, American University's Master of Public Policy mission statement provides a great example of a program that has incorporated its international context and commitment to public values.

The mission of the AU Master of Public Policy (MPP) program is to prepare students to advance the quality of policy making in a variety of institutional settings in the U.S. and abroad by instilling a blend of analytical, contextual, ethical, and substantive skills and knowledge.

We will achieve our mission by preparing students to:

1. Formulate and evaluate public policy, and communicate analysis effectively to relevant stakeholders;
2. Address societal problems with policy analysis in the context of political/policy processes in the U.S. and abroad;
3. Improve the allocation of resources using sound, evidence-based evaluation of the costs and benefits of policy alternatives; and
4. Incorporate a range of values into policy analysis, including democratic/constitutional values, respect for the diversity of people and perspectives in the policy process, and ethical principles including commitment to upholding the public trust.

(School of Public Affairs, 2019).

A final point on program mission statements relates to academic setting. Since PA programs are nested within a larger institutional context, program leaders will need to ensure their program mission aligns with (or at least is not incompatible with) the broader department, school, college, and/or university mission. Doing so comports with the need to consider external (here, institutional) stakeholders in the mission review and development process. A program mission statement that complements the university's can help the program position itself strategically. For example, many urban and land grant universities have a mission that emphasizes community engagement and community-based research. A PA program that likewise incorporates practical, community-based problem-solving (be it through research, service learning, etc.) as a component of its mission would be in harmony with its institutional mission.

Assessing Programmatic Strengths, Weaknesses, and Opportunities for Improvement

Along with the establishment of a cohesive program mission, perhaps one of the most valuable components of the strategic planning process is the comprehensive assessment of program strengths, weaknesses, and opportunities for improvement. Two frameworks often employed in conducting such assessments are SWOT (strengths, weaknesses, opportunities, and threats) and PEST (political, economic, social, and technological).

SWOT analysis. Sometimes referred to as a SWOC/T (Bryson, 2011) or WOTS-UP (Koteen, 1997) analysis, the first framework provides a roadmap for conducting a systematic consideration of a program's internal strengths and weaknesses and its external opportunities and threats (SWOT). Overall, a SWOT analysis is helpful in providing a structure for academic programs to begin their strategic planning processes because once a program has identified its core mission, it can then undertake a realistic assessment of the factors that will influence or impact its mission fulfillment. Utilization of the SWOT framework is fairly straightforward and entails working sequentially through four questions: What are our program's (1) strengths, (2) weaknesses, (3) opportunities, and (4) challenges/threats?

The first step centers upon conducting a realistic assessment of the program's strengths and doing so from multiple perspectives. For example, a robust assessment of strengths might include and integrate feedback from faculty, students, alumni, and other related stakeholders. Further, the same process can also be applied to the second step of a SWOT analysis, weaknesses. While such assessments might identify multiple factors to build upon or in need of further attention, programs should pay particular attention to programmatic areas that directly influence mission fulfillment as identified in the early stages of the strategic planning process. For example, if a program's mission centers upon preparing students for public service careers both nationally and internationally, then these steps of the SWOT analysis should ultimately address such factors as the extent to which current students feel that they are receiving exposure to the necessary competencies to work in both contexts, the extent to which alumni believe that they were prepared for careers in both contexts, and the extent to which the employers of students and alumni believe that graduates of the program were prepared to function at a high level.

Identifying opportunities for programmatic growth and improvement, the third step of a SWOT analysis, is equally important but arguably much more dynamic than identifying strengths and weaknesses within a program. In practice, programmatic opportunities are often not readily apparent and may also be viewed differently by stakeholders with unique perspectives on a program's strengths and weaknesses. For example, there has been an exponential growth in online course and degree delivery formats across the higher-education landscape and the field of PA has not been immune to this growth. While the justifications used for launching online degree programs are as diverse as the programs currently in operation, they are commonly launched on the basis of perceived student demand, evolving market dynamics, and increased pressure for new revenue sources. For programs that have identified an inability to meet the instructional needs of their candidate pools due to traditional program delivery formats (i.e., in-person and daytime), exploring the feasibility of adding to or switching to an online delivery format may serve as a great opportunity for program improvement from the perspective of potential students. However, the opportunity might be viewed quite differently from the perspective of faculty if there are limited resources to aid faculty in switching to an online format.

The last step in a SWOT analysis, threat assessment, is equally dynamic and often less precise than the previous three steps. Threats, by their very nature, are probabilistic and as a result, programs must be comfortable with a degree of uncertainty in identifying and prioritizing potential threats to programmatic improvement. While not developed specifically for higher-education programming, the PEST model serves as a helpful framework in conducting a programmatic threat analysis.[3]

PEST analysis. The PEST model categorizes threats as being either political, economic, social, or technological (PEST) in nature, which can provide programs with a starting point from which to further refine their assessment of their unique threats. As Bryson (2011) notes, adding an "education" category to the PEST model makes sense when the focus is on higher education. Examples of economic threats for PA programs could be changing labor market conditions, such as a decline in public service employment in a local area, that could reduce the demand for graduate degrees in PA or, as is the case with many public institutions, reductions in state government support that can often result in higher tuition and fees for graduate students. A program might also be situated in a particularly competitive environment, with multiple (public, non-profit, for-profit) PA programs vying for students, internships and job placements, and other resources.

Likewise, technological threats might include the development of disruptive technologies that impact program delivery. Perhaps the greatest technological factor impacting contemporary graduate programs, across multiple disciplines, is the rapid growth and expansion of online degree programs and course offerings. As instructional technologies, particularly those framed around online access, have improved and become more prevalent across multiple learning platforms, degree programs in PA must now consider the potential impact of two dynamic trends. First, recent data suggest that, from a demand-side perspective, an increasing number of potential students will come to expect the availability of new or cutting-edge instructional technologies in the classroom (Lederman, 2018). Second, as the number of fully online degree programs grows, traditional programs will inevitably need to evaluate their relevant student market to determine the extent to which their candidate pools might be impacted by the presence of competitor programs.

While SWOT and PEST analysis should be tailored by program, there are a number of existing resources available to programs seeking to incorporate national or international trends into their analysis. A sample of resources is listed below.

NASPAA resources. NASPAA's (2019a) Data Center provides aggregate information on PA program applications, enrollments, student diversity, and degree completion along with various reports and presentations on PA program-related trends. For example, data from responding member schools show a decline in the number of annual fall enrollments (from almost 19,700 in 2014 down to 18,900 in 2018) and degrees awarded (from about 6,100 in 2014 to 5,800 in 2018). Such historical data offer context for programs as they gauge their own experiences relative to the discipline.

Further, NASPAA offers member PA programs the opportunity to participate in various surveys that provide baseline data and trend data. For example, NASPAA administers an annual alumni survey, data from which programs may use for both PEST and outcome assessments. Programs are only required to generate contact information (i.e., email addresses) for program alumni three years out from graduation and, in return, they receive valuable information regarding long-term outcomes of their degree and, when viewed over time, employment trends.

Higher-education outlets. Print and online publications focused on higher education provide insights on higher-education trends. Most prominent, *The Chronicle of Higher Education* provides information on faculty compensation, the composition of faculty (e.g., tenure-track, contingent), pedagogy, and legislation affecting higher education. Its 2019 Trends Report, for example, identifies five major higher-education trends, including the changing nature of higher education's public compact, evolving business models, and the student experience and success. Similar reports on the state of higher education can be found on online media outlets such as *Inside Higher Ed*.

Federal government agencies. Several federal agencies provide information related to higher education generally, and PA specifically. The US

Department of Education's National Center for Education Statistics collects and reports education data through its Integrated Postsecondary Education Data System (IPEDS). The annual Condition of Education report, for example, reports data on degree completion and economic outcomes. The College Scorecard likewise offers searchable online database of higher-education institutions, which will soon include program-level (as opposed to the current institution-level) performance data. More relevant to PA programs, the US Census Bureau publishes a number of relevant reports regarding the size of the public-sector workforce (i.e., federal, state, and local) and government finances. Similarly, the US Bureau of Labor Statistics reports data (employment, wages) for the nonprofit sector.

Academic journals. PA-focused teaching journals like the *Journal of Public Affairs and Education* (*JPAE*) and *Teaching Public Administration* (*TPA*) publish articles related to trends affecting PA programs. For example, Peters and Maatman (2017) identify certain political, economic, and financial trends that have long affected PA programs, signaling that the magnitude of challenges facing public service – not their nature – has changed in recent years. Similarly, Rich (2013) provides a broad (and troubling) assessment of the political economy of professional PA education while Smith (2008) considers the increased complexity of public services and the implications for PA curricula. Finally, *JPAE* publishes the annual NASPAA presidential address, which typically includes "big-picture" themes affecting public service education. These and other PA journals also publish articles related to curriculum innovation, assessment, and other aspects of PA program management.

Private services. PA programs may also have access, through their campus institutional research or career services offices, to tools like "Burning Glass," which provides customizable (local, regional, national) labor market data, including information on the number of public service jobs (by sector) and the critical competencies employers were searching for in applicants. Such information can help program faculty and leaders assess the match between their program curriculum and the needs of both students and public service employers.

As this admittedly incomplete list of potential resources demonstrates, there is a wealth of information from which programs can draw as they attempt to understand the external forces and trends impinging upon them. However, collecting, collating, and presenting this information in a manner that can be easily utilized by a strategic planning team is no small task. To be useful SWOT and PEST materials need to be prepared and provided to participants in advance of any strategic planning meeting or retreat. Doing so will facilitate the identification of strategic issues.

Information gleaned through SWOT and PEST analyses is critical to identifying and, in turn, prioritizing the key strategic issues the program will address in its strategic plan. Regarding the prioritization of strategic issues, a common criticism of strategic planning is that it often results in a lengthy list of issues that may be overwhelming and hence be likely to go unaddressed. To counter this, programs are well advised to prioritize certain strategic issues, focusing selectively on the most compelling issues identified during the preceding stages of strategic planning while continuing to monitor the internal and external environment for emergent issues (Poister, 2010).

After a program has generated a pool of strategic issues, it must consider which ones should be included in the strategic plan. That is, which of the identified items is truly "strategic" and, as such, warrants inclusion. To aid in such determinations, the planning team may find criteria-based decision tools, such as a payoff matrix (Leemhuis, 1985), to be valuable. Bryson and Alston (2011) offer another useful tool for sorting issues into strategic and non-strategic (i.e., operational) categories, according to several criteria related to timing, risk, breadth, scope, and implications for the organization's capacity.

Establishing Goals, Objectives, and Desired Outcomes

If carried out comprehensively, the preceding steps of the strategic planning process should provide programs with a clear sense of their programmatic mandates, strategic needs, and desired actions in pursuit of their mission. The next step is to establish a set of goals related to program mission. Such goals may be presented as a single set of program goals or, depending on the number of goals, subsumed under broad categories like faculty (e.g., teaching, research, service, engagement, diversity), students (recruitment, retention, degree completion, intern and placement, learning goals, diversity), and program (resources, administrative capacity, program rankings, accreditation, autonomy, alumni relations, and development). An example of the former comes from the University of North Carolina at Chapel Hill's (2019) 2016–2017 assessment plan, which outlines the following program goals.

- To attract diverse, high-quality students and prepare them to be successful public service leaders and problem-solvers.
- To ensure that students demonstrate an understanding of the program's competencies and public service values in preparation of becoming public service leaders.
- To ensure that students experience meaningful professional work experiences that allow them to confront the program's competencies and values within a public service setting.
- To facilitate a student's success through a co-curricular process of courses, supporting activities, and "high touch" culture, working as a program team with clear roles and responsibilities.
- To recruit and support a diverse faculty who are recognized as thought leaders of engaged scholarship, advancing both the theory and practice of public administration.

- To graduate students who become public service leaders, providing direction and vision for the organizations and communities in which they serve.

To facilitate goal achievement, programs also will need to develop strategies and objectives (milestones) to be achieved as the strategies are implemented (Bryson, 2011). For example, a program's diversity-related goals for student recruitment and retention might include specific strategies (e.g., recruiting at historically Black colleges and universities or hispanic-serving institutions; offering scholarships to students from underrepresented groups) to obtain measurable results in a certain timeframe (e.g., increase the number of underrepresented students by 10 percent per year for the next three years).

One important set of goals and objectives for PA programs comprises those related to program competencies and student learning outcomes (SLO).[4] Regional institutional accreditors and voluntary program accreditors like NASPAA have established standards requiring programs to develop and report on students' progress toward SLOs. For PA programs, SLOs are developed as part of the operational definition of NASPAA's five universal required competency domains (see note 2). As shown in the above example of program goals, PA programs normally have a broad goal (or goals) related to competencies, as defined by programs in accordance with their mission. Such goals are expanded upon with statements of specific learning outcomes for each competency, which set the program's expectations for what their students should know and be able to do.

Evaluation of Strategic Actions and Closing the Loop

Once programs have identified and established performance expectations that are grounded in their mission review, stakeholder feedback, and programmatic analyses (i.e., SWOT/PEST), attention should then be turned to the establishment of a robust system for evaluating progress in attaining strategic goals and incorporating the results of evaluation efforts into future program improvements (i.e., "closing the loop"). Program goals, objectives, and outcomes set the stage for program assessment and continuous improvement. This focus on strategic plan implementation, assessment, and revision is how strategic planning effects strategic management.

To facilitate the process of continuous program evaluation and improvement, NASPAA has encouraged programs going through the accreditation/reaccreditation process to utilize logic models to provide a concise 'roadmap' of how programs intend to achieve their strategic goals. While individual logical models can vary considerably, the core components consist of program inputs, activities, outputs, and short/long-term outcomes. Additionally, logic models can be helpful in identifying how progress in achieving targeted programmatic outcomes is measured through individual program measures.[5] For illustrative purposes, the program logic model for Indiana University's graduate PA program is shown in Figure 5.1.

The key programmatic benefit of constructing a logic model is that it provides clear links between the goals a program intends to accomplish and how it intends to accomplish those goals. Further, if the evaluation process identifies gaps in goal attainment, logic models can be useful in pinpointing those areas where programs might need to make strategic investments (e.g., faculty inputs) or recalibrate departmental activities (e.g., curriculum). And, consistent with the adage that "a picture is worth a thousand words," logic models are a dense form of communication, conveying a good deal of information about a program to internal and external stakeholders in a single, easily digested image.

Monitoring and assessing program outcomes may appear initially to be an onerous undertaking. Yet, closer inspection of the various inputs, activities, outputs, and outcomes embedded in the logic model highlighted above reveal that, in most instances, the requisite data are readily available. Program data are typically accessible – either through a program's own archival records or from a central university office like institutional research or graduate school – for applications, admission, enrollment, time to degree, and degree completion, including breakouts for demographic groups. Such data allow programs to chart progress toward student-related goals. Data related to faculty goals – for research (articles, citations, grants), teaching (course evaluations, teaching innovations), service and engagement (professional associations, editorial roles, board service, media, etc.) – are typically gathered as part of an annual faculty activity reporting and performance appraisal process. Program goals related to governance, diversity, capacity, and support services are typically assessed relative to the adequacy of financial, human, and infrastructure resources (inputs and activities).

For longer-term outcomes and impacts, programs typically use a mix of direct and indirect assessment tools. For example, student exit surveys, alumni surveys, and public service employer surveys are often used to assess perceptions of program quality, satisfaction, and importance to graduates' professional public service career. Social media (e.g., LinkedIn) provide means to maintain connections with program alumni and, for assessment purposes, track their professional accomplishments. And, finally, in the area of SLO, programs use a variety of assessment approaches (e.g., comprehensive exams, capstone projects, service-learning projects and evaluations, course-embedded assessment of signature projects) to assure success in developing students' professional public service competencies.

An important (and perhaps obvious) point related to assessment is the need to ensure that those responsible for collecting and analyzing assessment data are clearly identified along with a timeline for doing so. Such information is typically included in the strategic plan or, perhaps, in a separate assessment plan.[6] Using assessment data to monitor progress on achieving program goals and mission is integral to continuous performance improvement. When assessment suggests the

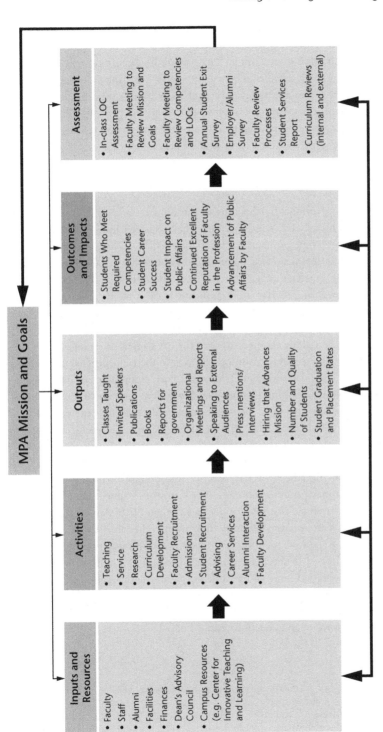

MPA Mission and Goals

Inputs and Resources
- Faculty
- Staff
- Alumni
- Facilities
- Finances
- Dean's Advisory Council
- Campus Resources (e.g. Center for Innovative Teaching and Learning)

Activities
- Teaching
- Service
- Research
- Curriculum Development
- Faculty Recruitment
- Admissions
- Student Recruitment
- Advising
- Career Services
- Alumni Interaction
- Faculty Development

Outputs
- Classes Taught
- Invited Speakers
- Publications
- Books
- Reports for government
- Organizational Meetings and Reports
- Speaking to External Audiences
- Press mentions/ Interviews
- Hiring that Advances Mission
- Number and Quality of Students
- Student Graduation and Placement Rates

Outcomes and Impacts
- Students Who Meet Required Competencies
- Student Career Success
- Student Impact on Public Affairs
- Continued Excellent Reputation of Faculty in the Profession
- Advancement of Public Affairs by Faculty

Assessment
- In-class LOC Assessment
- Faculty Meeting to Review Mission and Goals
- Faculty Meeting to Review Competencies and LOCs
- Annual Student Exit Survey
- Employer/Alumni Survey
- Faculty Review Processes
- Student Services Report
- Curriculum Reviews (internal and external)

FIGURE 5.1   Logic Model for Indiana University's MPA Program

Source: NASPAA (2019c).

program is not making sufficient progress toward attaining its goals, or the emergence of new issues, the program has an informed basis for making programmatic adjustments. Such adjustments might entail tweaking expectations (e.g., if goals were too high or low), establishing new strategies (e.g., for emerging issues or where existing strategies are falling short), or redoubling commitments to existing strategies that show promise. Doing so represents the proverbial "closing the loop" of strategic program management, with the assessment feeding back into the program's mission-based strategic planning process.

Conclusion

In sum, strategic planning has become commonplace in public and nonprofit organizations. This has occurred as more public service leaders and organizations have realized strategic planning's benefits, which include more systematic thought regarding organizational operating environments, promotion of organizational learning, greater dialogue on priorities and options, greater support for strategic initiatives, and better communication of strategy and priorities to internal and external stakeholders (Poister, 2010, p. s248). Strategic planning is also widely practiced across higher-education institutions, including at the academic program level. This is especially true for PA degree programs where curriculums often cover strategic planning and where the field primary accrediting body, NASPAA, has made strategic planning a core component of its accreditation standards. Moreover, the disruptive and turbulent context of higher education depicted in this chapter's introduction would seem to lend credence to Bryson's (2010) observation that "the need for strategic thinking, acting, and learning is only going to increase" (p. s260).

In light of strategic planning's importance to the field, this chapter has sought to offer practical guidance on the practice of strategic planning in the PA graduate professional program context. For program leaders and faculty who have undertaken strategic planning under in an initial NASPAA accreditation or reaccreditation effort, many will find that, upon reflection, the accreditation decision becomes almost secondary. Indeed, participants typically come to realize that the process of strategic planning is rewarding in and of itself. This is manifest in a heightened sense of esprit de corps among program faculty, a more holistic understanding of the individual degree programs, and, oftentimes, the process imbues program stakeholders – especially faculty and students – with a sense of shared purpose and commitment.

Notes

1. For critical assessments of strategic planning, see Halachmi (1986), Mintzberg (1994), Goldsmith (1997), and Roberts (2000).
2. NASPAA's Universal Required Competencies include the ability to: (1) Lead and manage in public governance, (2) participate in and contribute to the policy process,

(3) analyze, synthesize, think critically, solve problems, and make decisions, (4) articulate and apply a public service perspective, and (5) communicate and interact productively with a diverse and changing workforce and citizenry.

3. When conducting a SWOT analysis, a simple but powerful tool is the snow card technique (see Bryson, 2011, pp. 170–172). In a nutshell, participants work sequentially through the four SWOT prompts, brainstorming and recording ideas, selecting the best of those ideas (e.g., the greatest strengths), and recording them (one per card) on a snow card, affixing the snow cards to wall, clustering the cards into thematic categories (and subcategories), and recording the results.

4. Assessment of student learning outcomes (SLO) is a topic worthy of separate treatment, which is beyond the scope of this chapter. Readers interested in learning more about SLO assessment in the context of public service education are encouraged to review NASPAA's (2019b) online guidance for Standard 5.

5. Assessment measures can be either direct or indirect and often include such metrics as candidate applications, admissions, degree completion, time-to-degree, student demographics, internship and job placement, faculty research productivity, and teaching performance.

6. For a thorough treatment of developing a robust program assessment process, see Aristigueta & Gomes (2006). Numerous examples of PA program assessment plans are available at NASPAA's (2019d) online peer examples.

References

Aristigueta, M. & Gomes, K. M. B. (2006). Assessing performance in NASPAA graduate programs. *Journal of Public Affairs Education, 12*(1), 1–18.

Arum, R. & Roska, J. (2011). *Academically adrift: Limited learning on college campuses.* Chicago, IL: University of Chicago Press.

Blagg, K. & Blom, E. (2018). *Evaluating the return on investment in higher education: An assessment of individual- and state-level returns.* Washington, DC: Urban Institute.

Bryson, J. M. (2004). What to do when stakeholders matter: Stakeholder identification and analysis techniques. *Public Management Review, 6*(1), 21–53.

Bryson, J. M. (2010). The future of public and nonprofit strategic planning in the United States. *Public Administration Review, 70*(s1), s255–s267.

Bryson, J. M. (2011). *Strategic planning for public and nonprofit organizations,* 4th edn. San Francisco, CA: Jossey-Bass.

Bryson, J. M. & Alston, F. K. (2011). *Creating your strategic plan: A workbook for public and nonprofit organizations,* 3rd edn. San Francisco, CA: Jossey-Bass.

Dooris, M., Kelley, J., & Trainer, J. F. (eds) (2004). *Successful strategic planning: New directions for institutional research.* San Francisco, CA: Jossey-Bass.

Eadie, D. (1983). Putting a powerful tool to practical use: The application of strategic planning in the public sector. *Public Administration Review, 43*(5), 447–452.

Gabris, G. T. (1992). Strategic planning in municipal government: A tool for expanding cooperative decision making between elected and appointed officials. *Public Productivity and Management Review, 16*(1), 77–93.

Goldsmith, A. A. (1997). Private-sector experience with strategic management: Cautionary tales for public administration. *International Review of Administrative Sciences, 63*(1), 25–40.

Guy, M. E. & Stillman, R. (2016). On NASPAA accreditation: Fred was right… but for the wrong reason. *Journal of Public Affairs Education, 22*(2), 303–312.

Halachmi, A. (1986). Strategic planning and management? Not necessarily. *Public Productivity Review, 10*(2), 35–50.

Henry, N., Goodsell, C. T., Lynn, L. E., Stivers, C., & Wamsley, G. L. (2009). Understanding excellence in public administration: The report of the task force on educating for excellence in the Master of Public Administration degree of the American Society for Public Administration. *Journal of Public Affairs Education, 15*(2), 117–133.

Kerrigan, H. (2011). Fighting to save the MPA. *Governing, 24*(8), 36–39

Koteen, J. (1997). *Strategic management in public and nonprofit organizations,* 2nd edn. Westport, CT: Praeger.

Lederman, D. (2018, November 7). Online education ascends. *Inside Higher Ed.* Retrieved July 25, 2019 from www.insidehighered.com/digital-learning/article/2018/11/07/new-data-online-enrollments-grow-and-share-overall-enrollment.

Leemhuis, J. P. (1985). Using scenarios to develop strategies. *Long Range Planning, 18*(2), 30–37.

Maciag, M. (2017). Decline in diplomas: Students aren't seeking public service careers the way they used to. *Governing, 30*(8), 56–57.

McQuiston, J. M. & Manoharan, A. P. (2017). Developing e-government coursework through the NASPAA competencies framework. *Teaching Public Administration, 35*(2), 173–189.

Mercer, J. L. (1991). *Strategic planning for public managers.* New York: Quorum Books.

Mintzberg, H. (1994). The fall and rise of strategic planning. *Harvard Business Review, 71*(1), 107–114.

Network of Schools of Public Policy, Affairs, and Administration (2015). *Accreditation standards for master's degree programs.* Retrieved July 25, 2019 from https://accreditation.naspaa.org/wp-content/uploads/2015/02/naspaa-accreditation-standards.pdf.

Network of Schools of Public Policy, Affairs, and Administration (2019a). *Data center.* Retrieved July 25, 2019 from www.naspaa.org/data-center.

Network of Schools of Public Policy, Affairs, and Administration (2019b). *Standard 5: Matching operations with mission: Student learning.* Retrieved July 25, 2019 from https://accreditation.naspaa.org/standard-5/.

Network of Schools of Public Policy, Affairs, and Administration (2019c). *Peer examples: Logic models.* Retrieved July 25, 2019 from www.naspaa.org/sites/default/files/docs/2019-02/SPEA_LM.pdf.

Network of Schools of Public Policy, Affairs, and Administration (2019d). *Peer examples.* Retrieved July 25, 2019 from https://accreditation.naspaa.org/resources/peer-examples/.

Pearce, C. L., Wood, B. G., & Wassenaar, C. L. (2018). The future of leadership in public universities: Is shared leadership the answer? *Public Administration Review, 78*(4), 640–644.

Peters, R. A. (2009). Using focus groups and stakeholder surveys to revise the MPA curriculum. *Journal of Public Affairs Education, 15*(1), 1–16.

Peters, R. A. & Maatman, J. (2017). Long-term trends accentuate the import of creative and critical thinking skills developed by design thinking and ill-defined questions. *Teaching Public Administration, 35*(2), 190–208.

Poister, T. H. (2010). The future of strategic planning in the public sector: Strategic management and performance. *Public Administration Review, 70*(s1), s246–s254.

Poister, T. H., Pitts, D. W., & Edwards, L. H. (2010). Strategic management research in the public sector: A review, synthesis, and future directions. *American Review of Public Administration, 40*(5), 522–545.

Posner, P. L. (2009), The pracademic: An agenda for re engaging practitioners and academics. *Public Budgeting and Finance, 29*(1), 12–26.

Raffel, J. A., Maser, S. M., & Calarusse, C. (2015). Accreditation and competencies in education for leadership in public service. In Menzel, D. C. & White, H. L. (eds), *The state of public administration: Issues, challenges, and opportunities* (pp. 70–88). New York: Routledge.

Rich, D. (2013). Public affairs programs and the changing political economy of higher education. *Journal of Public Affairs Education, 19*(2), 263–283.

Roberts, N. (2000). The synoptic model of strategic planning and the GPRA: Lacking a good fit with the political context. *Public Productivity and Management Review, 23*(3), 297–311.

Rowley, D. J. & Sherman, H. (2001). *From strategy to change: Implementing the plan in higher education.* San Francisco, CA: Jossey-Bass.

School of Public Affairs (2019). Mission statement. *American University.* Retrieved July 10, 2019 from www.american.edu/spa/ma-ppol/mission.cfm.

Schultz, D. (2013). Public affairs education and the failed business model of higher education. *Journal of Public Affairs Education, 19*(2), ii–vii.

Seton Hall University (2019). *NASPAA self-study.* Retrieved July 25, 2019 from www.shu.edu/political-science-public-affairs/upload/Seton-Hall-University-NASPAA-Self-Study-8-8-2016.pdf.

Smith, S. R. (2008). The increased complexity of public services: Curricular implications for schools of public affairs. *Journal of Public Affairs Education, 14*(2), 115–128.

SUNY at Albany (2019). MPA program self-study report. *Network of Schools of Public Policy, Affairs, and Administration.* Retrieved July 25, 2019 from www.naspaa.org/sites/default/files/docs/2019-02/Albany%20SSR.pdf.

University of North Carolina at Chapel Hill (2019). MPA assessment plan. *Network of Schools of Public Policy, Affairs, and Administration.* Retrieved July 25, 2019 from www.naspaa.org/sites/default/files/docs/2019-02/UNC%20Assessment.pdf.

White, H. (2007). ASPA's legacy to public administration. *PA Times, 30*(10), 16–20.

6

THE ACCREDITATION PROCESS

Maja Husar Holmes

A critical component of the MPA director position is ensuring academic quality through systematic assessment to guide curricular and programmatic changes. A valuable approach to engaging in continuous programmatic assessment is the opportunity for MPA programs to voluntarily pursue accreditation. The Network of Schools of Public Policy, Affairs, and Administration (NASPAA) serves as the accreditor of master's degrees in public administration, public affairs, and public policy.

Accreditation is an external review process to assess the quality of colleges, universities, and educational degree programs. NASPAA accredits professional degree programs, focusing on measures of student learning and competence that are fundamental to the discipline and profession (Association of Specialized and Professional Accreditors, 2019). NASPAA does not accredit an entire school or institution. This means that departments or institutions with more than one master's degree relating to public service must seek accreditation for each distinct degree program. Not all NASPAA institutional members seek accreditation for their degree programs since accreditation is voluntary. Accreditation of MPA programs connects the public service profession to quality improvements in the educational preparation through a rigorous peer review process. Overall quality of the program is demonstrated through a mission-based application of accepted universal competencies for public service education and program standards (NASPAA, 2019a). For MPA directors, the decision to seek accreditation provides an occasion to engage in strategic assessment of the programmatic mission, goals, and curriculum through a defined self-study framework and external review and feedback.

Understanding the history and context of the NASPAA accreditation process is relevant for program directors as they develop master's programs that prepare graduates to contribute to public service. Since the accreditation process is voluntary, administrative leaders, faculty, and institutions must consider the value of accreditation. This chapter discusses why public affairs programs may seek accreditation, recognizing the significant commitment of resources and time to engage in accreditation. I offer specific strategies to prepare for and manage the accreditation process. The intent is to demystify the accreditation process. Specifically, I articulate the many resources available to graduate program administrators and faculty in participating in a quality improvement process to promote quality public service education.

The History of NASPAA Accreditation

NASPAA serves as the membership organization of graduate education programs in public policy, public affairs, and public administration. Today, NASPAA's twofold mission is to ensure excellence in education and training for public service and to promote the ideal of public service (NASPAA, 2019a). A signature component of the association has been the development and evolution of the accreditation process and standards for master's programs in public affairs. Initial interest in supporting the accreditation of public administration programs to advance careers in public service stemmed from deans of schools of public affairs and directors of public administration programs in the 1950s, which led to creation of the NASPAA in 1969. NASPAA membership doubled in its first decade of incorporation in the 1970s from 77 programs to over 200 programs by the 1980s. As the number of public administration and public affairs master's programs grew, a leading accrediting body for business schools, the Association to Advance Collegiate Schools of Business (AACSB), showed interest in incorporating the programs in its accreditation process (Guy & Stillman, 2016). With an interest in distinguishing the public administration graduate programs from business management and administration programs and to emphasize public service as a distinct form of educational orientation, NASPAA membership moved to cement its role as the chief accrediting body for MPA and similar degrees programs.

In the late 1970s, NASPAA began informal institutional reviews of public affairs programs. In 1980, NASPAA listed the first set of programs found to be in substantial conformity with the initial standards. In 1983, NASPAA converted the process to formal accreditation (Guy & Stillman, 2016). NASPAA committees review, revise, and seek input from institutional members on the accreditation standards on a decennial basis. Ultimately institutional members of NASPAA are responsible for approving the accreditation standards. The Council for Higher Education Accreditation (CHEA) recognizes NASPAA as the accreditor for graduate degree programs in public policy, administration, and affairs. As a CHEA-recognized accreditation body, NASPAA reflects the values and principles of the broader higher-education accreditation community to (1) promote academic quality and advance student achievement, (2) demonstrate public accountability for performance and transparency, and (3) sustain an effective accreditation structure and organization (CHEA, 2019). This also means that as CHEA changes its standards to keep up with the evolving higher-education environment, the NASPAA accreditation standards must adapt (Clark & Menifield, 2005; Guy & Stillman, 2016).

To ensure arms-length between NASPAA, the membership association, and the accreditation process, the peer review and accreditation decision-making is administered through the Commission on Peer Review and Accreditation (COPRA). COPRA as the body within NASPAA that issues accreditation decisions consists of 14 members, 13 of whom are academic professionals, with 1 current public service practitioner. It has a regularly rotating membership with overlapping three-year terms. The NASPAA Executive Committee selects COPRA members and the chair. The commission is responsible for reviewing self-study reports and site visit reports, issuing interim reports to articulate clarifications or additions to meet the standards, reviewing the totality of documentation for conformance to NASPAA accreditation standards (NASPAA, 2019b).

COPRA is supported by NASPAA staff that include the chief accreditation officer, the director of global accreditation, and an accreditation associate. Volunteer site visit teams that include two academics and one practitioner support the peer review process. The site visit team verifies and clarifies the description of the program as presented in the Self-Study Report. The site visit team gathers evidence to support that the program is describing itself accurately, information on the concerns (if any) cited by COPRA in the Interim Report, or how the program addresses the NASPAA accreditation standards (NASPAA, 2017). Additionally, the site visit is an opportunity to exchange information, discuss innovative developments, and respond to common issues among professional peers in advancing quality public service education.

Since NASPAA began accrediting master's programs that aim to uphold the education of the public service profession, the number and diversity of master's programs has evolved. One of the most significant changes adopted by NASPAA has been the transition from only accrediting programs in the US to becoming a global accreditor. Today, NASPAA has accredited programs in seven countries (the United States, Colombia, China, Egypt, New Zealand, South Korea, and Venezuela). However, the vast majority of the programs are still based in the US. In 2019, the NASPAA roster of accredited programs includes 202 degree programs at 183 member schools (NASPAA, 2019c).

The Value of Accreditation

Programs that choose to pursue accreditation recognize the value and commitment of dedicating the time and resources. The accreditation process for graduate programs that promote and support public service is voluntary and reflects a peer review ethos. Programs make the intentional choice to pursue accreditation for a variety of reasons, including (1) as an opportunity for participating in systematic programmatic improvement, (2) for internal and external recognition of a quality educational experience, and (3) for the support of broader community of graduate programs that collectively uphold public service values.

The accreditation process is an opportunity for programs to intentionally reflect on, revise, or reaffirm the current program mission, the program goals, to articulate student learning outcomes, and to assess if programmatic and curricular activities are achieving goals and learning outcomes. The strength of the NASPAA accreditation standards is that they provide guiding principles to frame programmatic and curricular assessment. Also, the process of soliciting both internal and external feedback on the assessment process and outcomes provides fruitful discussions to shape the implementation of mission-based program goals and curricular assignments. Programs recognize that the accreditation process is not just germane during the year programs apply for (re)accreditation, but a continuous practice. The accreditation process is an opportunity to generate a shared understanding of the program's mission among all programmatic stakeholders to guide changes in programmatic goals and curricular revisions (Rivenbark & Jacobson, 2014). Programs can implement strategic assessments without pursuing accreditation, but the interaction with external evaluation bodies provides an added layer of feedback and accountability to the key ethos in the field of preparing professionals for public service.

Programs also appreciate that obtaining accreditation is a mark of both internal and external recognition of a quality educational experience. Internally, within their respective institutions, public affairs graduate programs acknowledge that being accredited provides legitimacy for supporting the degree program with adequate resources. This is particularly important as universities explore the value of discrete graduate programs within their institutions. In era when program viability and legitimacy is being challenged within universities, accreditation provides validation for the impact of the program. Programs can also use the accreditation guidelines to advocate for faculty hiring, facilities that promote a professional learning environment, and resources that support student and faculty success. For example, the current accreditation standards require that programs identify a nucleus faculty that includes at least five full-time faculty or their equivalent who "exercise substantial determining influence for the governance and implementation of the program" (NASPAA, 2009, p. 5). Additionally, programs must demonstrate that nucleus faculty teach a substantial portion of the courses delivering core competencies. This requirement is a rationale for programs to advocate for faculty resources to directly support public service graduate programs.

Externally, accreditation is a mark of quality for prospective students, alumni who are active in public service professions, and potential employers who seek to hire graduates. More broadly, accreditation raises awareness and relevance of graduate programs for public service. The field of graduate programs is crowded and expanding. This makes it even more important as prospective students and employers recognize the particular applicability of public service graduate programs, especially as distinct from MBA and other specialized degree programs. Data collected through the accreditation process helps define this relevancy, by documenting where students work, the impact on their careers and influence in public service.

Participating in accreditation offers programs the support of a broader community of graduate programs that collectively uphold public service values. NASPAA accreditation started because public administration graduate programs wanted to distinguish themselves from business-oriented management and administration programs. Upholding and reaffirming public service values in the mission, goals, and curriculum is central to the NASPAA accreditation standards. These values include "pursuing the public interest with accountability and transparency; serving professionally with competence, efficiency, and objectivity; acting ethically to uphold the public trust; and demonstrating respect, equity, and fairness in dealings with citizens and fellow public servants" (NASPAA, 2009, p. 2). This emphasis on public service values explicitly differentiates graduate programs accredited by NASPAA from other professional graduate programs. The emphasis on public service generates a community of programs with complementary missions. The accreditation process provides a collective platform within the profession and discipline for reaffirming and defining public service values. Through the accreditation process, programs have an opportunity to actively reflect on their best practices and curricular innovations through the self-study report and site visit. Programs receive feedback on their mission-based approaches in the accreditation process through reports from the commission and site visits. The process provides a forum to explore emerging areas of curricular foci and adapt graduate programs to prepare the next generation of public service professionals.

The Accreditation Process

The guiding principle of the current NASPAA accreditation standards, which were adopted in 2009, emphasizes that master's programs are driven by public service values and contribute to the knowledge, research, and practice of public service. The accreditation standards reflect that graduate programs are mission-based, establish mission-relevant observable program goals and student learning outcomes, engage in systematic assessment, and use assessment information to guide program improvement. Additionally, the accreditation standards require programs to practice transparency in program goals, student learning outcomes, and program expectations to potential students and stakeholders (NASPAA, 2019c).

To be eligible for NASPAA accreditation, programs must meet four criteria (NASPAA, 2009).

- The institution offering the master's degree program should be accredited (or similarly approved) by a recognized regional, national, or international agency.
- The mission, governance, and curriculum of eligible master's degree programs shall demonstrably emphasize public service values. However, it is up to the degree program to define the boundaries of the public service values it emphasizes, be they procedural or substantive, as the basis for distinguishing itself from other professional degree programs.
- The degree program's primary focus shall be that of preparing students to be leaders, managers, and analysts in the professions of public affairs, public administration, and public policy.
- The normal expectation for students studying for professional degrees in public affairs, administration, and policy is equivalent to 36 to 48 semester credit hours of study.

As the variety and curricular emphases of master's programs have evolved, one of the key challenges for NASPAA is distinguishing if a graduate program distinctly applies public service values. The global growth of public administration master's programs has raised discussion about how public service is articulated to pursue the public interest with accountability and transparency, demonstrating respect, equity, and fairness in dealings with citizens and fellow public servants. Additionally, the emergence of new specialized degree programs, for example, nonprofit management, raises some important considerations for programs to accurately capture how the program emphasizes public service values.

Once programs are advised to proceed with accreditation, there are a couple of key steps to be aware of in the accreditation process, including the following.

- Programs complete a detailed self-study report. The self-study report allows programs to directly respond to how they are operationalizing and conforming to the NASPAA standards based on the program mission.
- COPRA reviews the self-study report and issues an interim report that identifies areas for additional clarification and information and recommendations for moving forward with a site visit. At this time, COPRA also assigns a COPRA member to serve as the COPRA liaison to the program. If COPRA identifies specific NASPAA standards for additional information or clarification, programs are encouraged to respond to the Interim Report before the site visit.
- COPRA assigns a site visit team in consultation with the program. Site visits are generally 2.5 days that include visits with program faculty,

students, alumni, the advisory board, and university officials. Site visit teams issue site visit reports that are reviewed by the programs, with the opportunity to respond.

- COPRA meets annually in June to review the complete documentation programs and site visit teams have provided, including the self-study report, the interim report, the program's response to the interim report, the site visit report, and the program's response to the site visit report. The accreditation decision is based on substantial conformance with accepted standards, demonstration of identification and assessment of student learning outcomes based on the NASPAA-defined competencies, and engagement in program evaluation. Based on the standards, COPRA also considers whether adequate resources exist to support the degree program. Additionally, all accredited programs must identify a minimum of five full-time nucleus faculty members, exhibit adequate institutional support, and define and assess other indicators of program quality.

COPRA has several options in determining accreditation decisions. Programs can be (re)accredited for a full seven-year term, accredited on a one-year term, or denied accreditation. The distinctions in the accreditation decisions are based on the degree of conformity to the NASPAA-defined accreditation standards. It is important to note that the accreditation process is meant to be formative, not punitive, reflecting the peer review ethos in supporting graduate programs that aim to prepare public service professionals. In that spirit, programs complete brief annual accreditation maintenance reports that encourage ongoing reflection and assessment on programmatic goals and curricular reforms. The annual reports are reviewed and approved by COPRA members to ensure continued conformance with accreditation standards.

Preparing For and Managing the Accreditation Process

The accreditation process can seem daunting, time-consuming, and resource-intensive. Based on perspectives provided by MPA directors, faculty who have participated in the accreditation process, and NASPAA staff, there are some valuable resources to make the accreditation process run smoothly and achieve the intended outcome of the accreditation process – to support continuous program assessment and improvement. The next section explores specific recommendations for preparing for and managing the accreditation process.

Make the Assessment Process Meaningful

One of greatest challenges and opportunities for programs engaging in accreditation is the assessment process. The NASPAA assessment process reflects a mission-based approach to defining program goals and student learning outcomes. The mission-based approach is a growing trend in higher education, allowing programs to define their strategic direction within the specific professional context. For NASPAA-accredited programs the program mission should define its purpose and public service values, given the program's particular emphasis on public affairs, administration, and policy, acknowledge the target population of students, employers, and professionals the program intends to serve, and articulate contributions it intends to produce to advance the knowledge, research, and practice of public affairs, administration, and policy (NASPAA, 2009). The mission then guides performance expectations and their evaluations. Degree programs are increasingly being asked by their home institutions to articulate and assess their goals and specific student learning outcomes. To secure resources internally, programs must assess student learning outcomes, demonstrate impact, and engage in curricular revisions to achieve mission-based student learning outcomes. The evolution toward competency-based assessment standards is an opportunity to articulate a true alignment between the program's mission, curriculum, and competencies, and to prevent the possibility of mission drift (Rivenbark & Jacobson, 2014. The key to developing and implementing a sustainable assessment process is to keep it simple and focused on the mission of the program. Increasingly universities are providing support to programs to create sustainable and meaningful assessment procedures.

Engage Faculty Early and Often

Pursuing accreditation is a group activity. The NASPAA accreditation process is formative and not credential-based. Key program stakeholders make an intentional decision to participate in the accreditation process. Program faculty members are critical to the process. Identifying program faculty is the first step. Public affairs and public policy master's programs are embedded in diverse organizational structures, including as stand-alone public administration departments, integrated in political science or other related departments, or part of a comprehensive school. A key step is identifying the nucleus faculty that exercise substantial determining influence for the governance and implementation of the degree program (NASPAA, 2009). On the ground, this means that faculty are actively involved in mission generation, defining and monitoring program evaluation goals, articulating student learning outcomes, and invested in bringing the program's mission to life. Effective strategies for faculty engagement in the accreditation process include the following.

Assign and compensate (course release or supplemental salary) a faculty member to coordinate accreditation process. Assigning a dedicated faculty member to the accreditation process provides consistency, a communication fulcrum, and accountability to the process. However, this does not mean that the faculty member completes the documentation on their own;

rather, they coordinate the accreditation process to make the process inclusive and participatory. With smaller programs, the MPA director is responsible for coordinating the accreditation process. In larger programs, MPA directors can assign dedicated faculty member(s) to coordinate the accreditation data collection, reports, and site visit.

Set aside faculty meetings to collectively review and reflect. Given that the intent of accreditation is a formative assessment, making time in the academic calendar to collectively review information about the current state of the program (enrollment, diversity, curricular approaches) is critical. Creating space for reflection on program goals and student learning outcomes, challenging existing assumptions, and organizing activities to meet the program mission creates a more integrative approach and actions steps to improve the program.

Share, listen, and report. Regardless of whether the program has 5 or 25 nucleus faculty members, adopting a norm of sharing program data, listening to faculty ideas, and reporting consensus activities demonstrates a robust faculty governance process. Embracing a learning organization culture allows for faculty flexibility and openness to make major adjustments to the curriculum and to change specific course content to accommodate the competencies, which includes teaching new materials and using the grading rubrics for data collection (Rivenbark & Jacobson, 2014.

Leverage Significant Stakeholders

Faculty, students, alumni, internship supervisors, prospective employers, and university collaborators both convey a valuable perspective, but also support the accreditation process. Specifically, faculty are an integral part of the program evaluation in identifying student learning outcomes, participating in assessment summaries, and drafting diversity and inclusion policies. Students can be part of the accreditation process. For example, some programs have used research methods courses or capstone classes to analyze the alumni survey data. The impact is that this is an applied research analysis that supports student engagement and builds their analysis skills. Alumni, internship supervisors, and prospective employers can serve on program advisory boards to offer consistent feedback and perspectives to programs. This includes responding to proposed program mission statements, generating ideas for student support, and identifying professional projects that reinforce curricular connections. External stakeholders, such as internship supervisors or capstone clients, can also contribute to the assessment process. Using established rubrics or evaluation templates, external stakeholders offer direct assessment of student learning outcomes. Increasingly, universities and colleges have dedicated assessment and evaluation offices, whose staff can provide student and faculty data and help programs craft assessment procedures. Across higher education, institutions are asked to document student learning outcomes; the assessment and evaluation units may offer tools and resources to help degree programs.

Compose the Self-Study Report

The most critical component of the NASPAA accreditation process is the self-study report. Use the narrative and appendices to tell your program's story. There are prescribed components to the self-study report. However, programs should take advantage of the appendices to document the nuances of the assessment process and outcomes. The intent of the accreditation process is for programs to demonstrate intentional connection between the program mission, programmatic goals, student and faculty support, institutional resources, and implementation of the universal competencies. Programs are unique, and that should be reflected in the narrative and documentation. The NASPAA accreditation resource website provides useful examples of complete self-study reports, program evaluation templates, frameworks, and rubrics for assessing student learning outcomes and diversity plans.

Embrace the Site Visit

One of the most rewarding parts of the accreditation process is the site visit. This is an opportunity to share your program with peers in the public administration community. The two-and-a-half day visit should include meetings with program students, faculty, and academic leaders (such as the dean and provost), provide access to additional documentation, allocate time for the site visit team to review documents and respond to COPRA Interim Report items. The most meaningful part of the site visit is the report at the end of the visit. It is critical that nucleus faculty participate in this session. This is an opportunity for the site visit team to reflect to the program what it observed and confirmed. Site visit teams do not provide evaluative judgment. That is the role of the COPRA Commission. However, the site visit team does serve as the eyes and ears of the Commission by verifying information and documenting additional information to ensure compliance with the standards.

Use the NASPAA and COPRA Resources

With the increasing number of programs seeking accreditation, NASPAA and COPRA have expanded the resources to guide programs through the accreditation process. In preparing for the accreditation process, NASPAA has provided several helpful resources for programs both online and during annual NASPAA meetings. NASPAA has a dedicated website with standards resources, documentation examples, and webinars for programs to access for the accreditation process. Additionally, at the annual conference, NASPAA provides more targeted initiatives to guide the accreditation process. The Accreditation Institute is a one-day workshop for programs seeking accreditation to prepare for both the eligibility application and/or self-study report. The day is designed to provide the tools to be successful in mission-driven, outcomes-oriented, evidence-based accreditation-earning program management. "Accreditation speed consulting" is a relatively new development aimed to support currently accredited programs. It connects programs with individuals who have experience in the accreditation process, including current and former COPRA members, and site visitors. It is an opportunity for programs to ask targeted questions in preparing for the accreditation process. It is important to note that consultants cannot speak for COPRA. Instead, they offer advice and context as individuals with COPRA experience. Support from COPRA continues during the accreditation process. When programs are under review, each program is assigned a COPRA liaison. The role of the liaison is to clarify areas of concern raised in the Interim Report, communicate expectations about the site visit, and communicate with the site visit team.

Challenges in the Accreditation Journey

Pursuing accreditation does impose some challenges for public administration programs. Accreditation takes both monetary and staffing resources. Initial accreditation fees are over $5,000, and reaccreditation fees are approaching $5,000. Additional costs related to accreditation include travel for the site visit team, hosting advisory groups, and compensating faculty and/or staff to assist in the accreditation process. Once accredited, programs pay an annual accreditation fee in the amount of between $500 and $800 depending on student enrollment (NASPAA, 2019d). This cost, in addition to the annual NASPAA membership, can be a significant barrier for smaller programs with fewer resources. Additionally, dedicating faculty and staff resources is critical to committing to program assessment and improvement through the accreditation process. Programs have to be creative and mindful in using existing resources to manage data collection, assessment materials, and curricular and program changes based on emerging needs and opportunities.

Conclusion

NASPAA accreditation is at a pivotal point as it approaches its fourth decade. Accreditation standards have evolved significantly over the past decades with greater thought of how to promote public service explicitly while maintaining flexibility and creativity to develop and implement mission-based public service master's programs that reflect unique contexts. The balance and evolution reflects a robust dialogue in the field about defining essential skills for public administration (Guy & Stillman, 2016) and providing students with "students with an adequate framework within which they can situate their public service orientation and weigh the consequences of their actions in different contexts" (Turner, 2015, p. 42). NASPAA accreditation as a means toward continual programmatic improvement encourages the articulation of the shared commitments across all public affairs programs and the application of possible unique program perspectives, characteristics, and innovations (Svara & Baizhanov, 2019). The enduring opportunity for public service degree programs is to engage in a systemic assessment that explicitly connects the program mission to program goals, curriculum, student learning experiences, and resources.

References

Association of Specialized and Professional Accreditors (2019). *ASPA info sheet.* Retrieved May 2, 2019 from www.aspa-usa.org/students/.

Clark, C. & Menifield, C. E. (2005). The dynamics of NASPAA accreditation: A challenge for organizational expansion? *Journal of Public Affairs Education, 11*(1), 35–43.

Council for Higher Education Accreditation (2019). *Recognition of accrediting organizations: Policy and procedures.* Washington, DC: Council of Higher Education Accreditation.

Guy, M. E. & Stillman, R. (2016). On NASPAA accreditation: Fred was right… but for the wrong reason. *Journal of Public Affairs Education, 22*(2), 303–312.

Network of Schools of Public Policy, Affairs, and Administration (2009). *NASPAA standards: Accreditation standards for master's degree programs.* Washington, DC: Network of Schools of Public Policy, Affairs, and Administration.

Network of Schools of Public Policy, Affairs, and Administration (2017). *Self-study instructions.* Washington, DC: Network of Schools of Public Policy, Affairs, and Administration.

Network of Schools of Public Policy, Affairs, and Administration (2019a). *NASPAA: Quality in public affairs education.* Retrieved May 20, 2019 from www.naspaa.org/about_naspaa/members/code/.

Network of Schools of Public Policy, Affairs, and Administration (2019b). *COPRA: Commission on peer review and accreditation.* Retrieved May 20, 2019 from https://accreditation.naspaa.org/about/the-commission-on-peer-review-and-accreditation/.

Network of Schools of Public Policy, Affairs, and Administration (2019c). *About accreditation.* Retrieved May 20, 2019 from https://accreditation.naspaa.org/about/.

Network of Schools of Public Policy, Affairs, and Administration (2019d). *Accreditation fees.* Retrieved May 20, 2019 from www.naspaa.org/accreditation/accreditation-step-step/accreditation-fees.

Rivenbark, W. C. & Jacobson, W. S. (2014). Three principles of competency-based learning: Mission, mission, mission. *Journal of Public Affairs Education, 20*(2), 181–192.

Svara, J. H. & Baizhanov, S. (2019). Public service values in NASPAA programs: Identification, integration, and activation. *Journal of Public Affairs Education, 25*(1), 73–92.

Turner, A. H. (2015). Instilling public service values and professionalism through information literacy. *Journal of Public Affairs Education, 21*(1), 41–45.

7

BUDGETING FOR DEPARTMENTAL NEEDS

John R. Bartle

This chapter discusses how to effectively manage a budget for an academic department, with a particular focus on a specific academic program, in this case the Master in Public Policy, Affairs, or Administration (hereafter referred to as the MPA). The chapter discusses both the details of budgeting and spending, as well as the strategies that can help an MPA director be successful. This chapter takes a contingency approach, which posits that the best strategy depends on the organization's environment (Morgan, 1986). The environments facing MPA programs vary significantly, so there is no one best approach. This chapter develops four major themes.

1. The importance of capitalizing on the organizational structure.
2. Developing an approach to advocacy and implementing it.
3. The importance of flexibility in spending.
4. The important limitations on spending and the budget process.

While the budget is by its nature a constraining factor, there usually are ways to get things done and make the budget work for the MPA program. This chapter endeavors to help an MPA director to improve the finances of the program.

The first section discusses the different governance and reporting structures of an academic program within the university organization. The second section identifies the fund structure of universities and expenditure categories. The third section identifies different budget formats that apply to program budgets. The fourth section discusses three key features of university budgeting, followed by a conclusion and some practical tips for MPA directors.

Program Structure

Governance Structure

Universities vary significantly in their governance structures. The most obvious difference is between public and private universities. Both types of universities receive revenue from tuition and fees, philanthropic donations, grants and contracts, and enterprise revenue (for operations such as dormitories, food services, and athletics). Public universities also receive state aid; however, in recent years some states have made large cuts in state aid, forcing universities to rely more on tuition and other sources. Thus, there is a spectrum of "publicness" among universities (Bozeman, 1987).

Many universities have multiple campuses with both an overarching governance structure and a campus structure. For example, most public university systems have multiple campuses, and they often exist alongside independent state college systems and community college systems. In other cases, they are integrated into one statewide system of higher education. While private universities are more often a single-campus operation, this is not always the case.

There are often other MPA programs in the same university system. This creates a different type of competition. Often, university governing bodies are reluctant to maintain two or more similar academic programs in the same system unless travel distances are prohibitive. Therefore, an MPA program may need to distinguish itself from existing programs in the same system by creating a different focus or set of specializations. It is critical that the MPA director make the value of the program clear to university leaders so they see it as a good investment opportunity and not a "money pit."

Reporting Structure

It is unusual for a single academic program such as an MPA to be its own department in a university. Typically, the MPA is one degree in a multiple degree-granting department, school, or college (hereafter referred to as "academic unit"). Therefore, the level of politics is similar to the models of bureaucratic politics we are familiar with in public administration. In that situation, the MPA director is one actor among others advocating for resources within the larger academic unit. In other cases, the MPA may be the only degree in a unit that receives its funds in the campus-wide allocation process. In that case, the MPA director is working with the campus budget officers and in competition with other department chairs and deans. In this chapter, we assume the first case is the typical one.

In either case, the MPA director is in the role as the advocate for the program. The director needs to know the needs of the program, and be ready to make requests and advocate for the program. They will be in competition with other program directors who are typically colleagues. There is a fine line to walk in advocating for more resources. If a program director is seen by fellow program directors as too greedy or "empire building," they can lose their effectiveness. On the other hand, if they are not assertive enough, they will miss opportunities to grow their program. While there are many political strategies for program advocates, typically the most effective is to have information ready, be able to show the importance of the program and hopefully be able to show that allocations to the program will be money well spent.

MPA programs may be in competition with other programs that have a lower per-student cost (such as large undergraduate programs), or with more expensive programs (such as doctoral programs; science or engineering programs that require expensive equipment; or programs where faculty are paid significantly more, such as business or law). In general, administrators compare MPA programs to other graduate programs. Because MPA programs typically do not require expensive buildings or equipment, and the salaries of MPA faculty are not especially high, the costs for the program are favorable. Further, MPA programs have the opportunity to operate on a larger scale than many graduate programs. This reduces the average cost per student, and leads to more enrollments, student credit hours, tuition revenue, and graduates, all of which are important to higher-level administrators.

External program advocates should also be developed to make the case for the program to university presidents and provosts. It is not uncommon for program alumni to be well-placed politically, either as elected or appointed officials or prominent nonprofit leaders, and the MPA director should engage them as advocates. External program supporters other than alumni can help make the case also. Part of an MPA director's job is to develop an advocacy network armed with talking points about the value and importance of the program. If you are in competition with other MPA programs, you should emphasize your comparative strengths. As issues shift, you may also need to pivot to recraft your message. Ideally, you want your program to be an important part of the solution to the challenges faced by the university and community.

Keep in mind that money is not the only resource; you may also want office space, the time of others, support from key advocates (internal or external), or publicity. Just as you will want to be effective in acquiring financial resources, you will also need other resources. Each of these resources have their own process for requesting and allocation, so learn what they are and develop relationships that can make you effective in acquiring them. The rules of advocacy and networking both apply.

Funds and Expenditures

Fund Categories

The governing body for the campus will have an accounting structure that creates a set of funds. Each fund will have designated revenues coming in and expenses going out. Usually, the *general fund* is the largest fund for the program. Typically, the general fund account receives revenue from tuition and state aid (for public institutions). The expenses paid from the general fund include permanent appropriations such as salaries, supplies and equipment, and travel. This base budget pays for regular operations; as such, it is the most important fund for the program. Without it, the program cannot operate.

The program may also have one or more *enterprise funds*. In the same way that governments finance toll roads, recreation facilities, and trash services with user fees and other specifically designated revenue sources, so too universities often have funds that allow programs to deposit revenues from fee-based services such as contracts, workshop fees, applied research, and alternate delivery of academic programs (such as distance education, international programs, or off-campus delivery). Given the applied nature of public policy and administration programs, these activities are common, and the program director should endeavor to put the revenues from these activities in an enterprise fund over which he or she (or the academic unit chair) has a high degree of control. These funds can be particularly important because the surplus of revenues over expenses may be a flexible source of funds with relatively few limitations. Therefore, it is important to capitalize upon opportunities to generate a profit from these kind of sources, and to grow new sources of revenue where possible. This can be very helpful to pay for new initiatives, cover unexpected deficits elsewhere, or to reward highly productive faculty or staff.

Another important set of funds comes from philanthropic donations to the program, usually through the university's charitable foundation. These *fiduciary funds* are held in trust by another party (usually the foundation) as instructed by the agreement that established the fund. For academic programs, these fiduciary funds often support scholarships, endowed professorships, or capital projects. There are three types of fiduciary funds: endowed, expendable, and quasi-endowed. *Endowed funds* have a permanent principal and the return from the principal then funds the activity. So, for example, an endowed fund of $1 million may support a scholarship. If the earnings from the investment are 5 percent, then there would be $50,000 annually for the scholarships in perpetuity. An *expendable fund* accepts deposits and then the money can be used immediately for the specified purposes. Unlike an endowed fund, it is not permanent, and the activity needs to be funded each year. A *quasi-endowed fund* is a hybrid between the two. Some portion of the fund goes into a permanent endowment, and the other portion can be used to fund the specified activity.

The MPA director's involvement in fundraising from donors is likely to be sporadic. When they are involved, it can be very important because it can provide very useful financial support outside of the base budget, sometimes on a permanent basis. It is important to know the funds you have and to make good use of them. It is also important to know the difference between the fund types and to work with your development staff to make new gifts as useful as possible to the program. While some donors may start out with specific ideas of how to steer their funds, they need to hear your advice about the most important needs of the program, and they may be willing to alter their giving plans to maximize program impact. Therefore, you need to know what your priorities are, and know the options in establishing any new donor fund. Afterwards, be responsive to the donor to let them know of the importance and impact of the funds. Simple "thank you" letters from students can be very gratifying and induce donors to give more in the future. In addition, donors talk to each other, so they may be willing to help you grow the fund by bringing in other donors.

Capital funds are also important for universities to support buildings, equipment, and other long-term assets. Program directors are less likely to be involved in these decisions, but they can be very important. For example, if capital funds are made available for an expansion or renovation in an existing building, this can provide more high-quality space that can be very attractive to future students and faculty. Capital funds usually come from campus central resources, so it can be a challenge to get your program on the list of priority capital improvements, but always be ready with ideas that can be shaped into a proposal. As John Kingdon (2011) taught us, windows of opportunity do not open very often, so when they do you need to be ready with your proposal and be able to make a case that it fits with the university's priorities.

The different funds are the different "pockets" administrators use to fund various priorities. While some funds can be used for a broad range of expenses, many are restricted and so an administrator may find themselves "resource poor" for some priorities and "resource rich" for others. It is critical to know what funds you have and how you can use them. While it is important to follow these limitations, you always want flexibility. When establishing funds, try to get the most flexibility possible and when working with university budget controllers, try to get them to give you as much flexibility in their interpretation of how to use funds.

Expenditures

Expenditures for MPA programs are generally similar among universities. The largest category is for personnel. MPA programs generally spend less on capital and equipment than science programs. This means that funding for the permanent budget for faculty and staff is the most important source of funding for MPA programs.

The different sub-categories of *personnel spending* include salaries for full-time faculty, part-time faculty (adjuncts), staff, graduate assistants, as well as the associated employee benefits such as health and life insurance. Institutional practices may vary as to who pays the cost of employee benefits: The academic unit or the university. It is important to keep that in mind, as the salary may not constitute the full costs of the employee.

Programs will also have costs for *equipment and capital*. These might include costs for copiers, computers, paper, furniture, and supplies. For most MPA programs these costs are much less than personnel costs. In some cases, programs may need to buy or rent vehicles, or lease office space, although these costs are less typical.

Travel costs are usually relatively small parts of the budget, but their discretionary nature makes these costs more visible. Deans or provosts are likely to cut or limit these costs in times of budget stringency, and they are an easy target for external critics who might characterize some travel as junkets. Travel costs are not homogeneous. For example, travel from one campus to another for faculty to teach classes in different locations is a necessary cost, while some conference travel may be less critical. International travel might be important but it can be expensive and certainly can be characterized by critics as an unnecessary luxury. Therefore, a program director should be careful in controlling their travel budget both to conserve funds and for public relations reasons.

Scholarships may or may not be under control of the program or the academic unit. Often, these come from endowed funds, which are more stable and less prone to budget cuts than other spending. At the same time, they are also less responsive to programmatic needs. The term of the scholarship can also be important; if a scholarship is granted for two or more years, this gives the program less flexibility than if it is a one-year term. Of course, the recipient would prefer to have the scholarship for the full time they are in the program, and this feature might affect whether they accept the scholarship and admission to the program. Often scholarships are distributed differently to other expenditures. This means that the politics may involve different actors and processes. Again, learn these processes to enhance your effectiveness.

In all cases, the MPA director needs to monitor carefully the spending for which they have responsibility. Monthly budget reports should be regularly reviewed, and any questionable expenditures should be examined. The rate of spending also needs to be monitored. If spending on a certain category is projected to exceed the budget, it should be slowed. If the spending is vital to continuing the operation, then the program director needs to seek permission from the appropriate superior for additional funding or to move funds from other sources to cover the projected deficit. The earlier you ask permission, the better.

Budget Formats

There is a variety of different budget formats used by public and private organizations, and the same is true of universities. The oldest and most common is the *line-item* format. Many universities follow this format, in either its pure form, or a hybrid form. In this format, the objects of expenditure are the focus of analysis (McKinney, 2015). Typical line items are salaries and wages, employee benefit costs, employee travel, supplies, equipment, and capital expenses. These categories are used for each department and then are aggregated across the organization. Appropriations may be binding for each item of expenditure. For example, spending on salaries and wages may be limited to the appropriated amount. Even if there is a surplus in the equipment appropriation, it may not be used for salaries that exceed the budgeted amount. In other cases, there is flexibility among the line items or it may even be the case that the individual line items do not matter as long as the total program budget is not exceeded. Program managers always prefer more flexibility, while budget office controllers may require that the program stick to the line items. This is a common tension in budget management.

Line-item budgeting facilitates budgetary control. If the dean or provost does not allow the program to use funds outside of the line items for which they were budgeted, this restricts the actions of the program in hiring, purchasing, or travel. The dean or provost might allow one program flexibility in certain cases, while not allowing other programs the same flexibility. This is a way to favor one program over another in an opaque way, which may serve their goals. While line-item budgeting provides effective expenditure control, it can also make it difficult to respond to legitimate needs.

Line-item budgeting is also consistent with incrementalism. This often makes sense for universities, as a large portion of the budget is in salaries, much of which are for tenured faculty or other faculty or staff who have stable positions. As a result, the budget often does not change much from one year to the next. Indeed, it may render unnecessary the process of requesting, allocation, and appropriation by the budget office and/or higher university authorities. The incremental approach makes the allocation process simple. An increment is added or subtracted, perhaps across the board, to meet the university's target spending total. This lends itself to a stable environment.

The stability and ease of line-item budgeting is also a disadvantage. Over time, programs with faster-growing enrollment may not be allocated much more than programs that are stagnant or declining as there may not even be a regular process of requesting budget allocations. This approach also does not facilitate strategic planning, so programs that need to grow to serve the goals of the university may not be allocated more in a line-item budgeting process. Line-item budgets also provide little guidance about the impact of spending on organizational goals.

Zero-based budgeting (ZBB) attempts to build the budget from zero by creating a process for an annual comprehensive budget review. Decision packages are identified in each unit, which are the basic building blocks of the unit. Different academic programs might be the decision package. The decision packages may have different levels, such as the number of cohorts of an academic program. The price tags associated with the levels of the decision packages approved then become the allocation to the unit. For universities ZBB is unlikely to be practical in a literal sense. Many costs are inflexible, such as salaries, utilities, and maintenance. One alternative might be to estimate the mandatory spending for next year and the levels of the associated decision packages, and then allocate the remaining funds among the decision packages that fund new or expanded programs.

A similar but more practical alternative is *target-based budgeting* (TBB), sometimes known as envelope budgeting. In this method, the budget office establishes limits on the first round of allocation. It might be a certain decrement, say a 10-percent cut, compared to last year's spending, which may or may not be the same for all programs. Then programs may make requests for additional allocations in a second round. This has the advantage of focusing the budgetary discussion on the increments and not the base budget, which may be uncontroversial in the short run. It can also be related to performance, as a program may have to specify how outputs and outcomes would be improved with the additional allocation.

Performance budgeting became more popular during the "reinventing government" movement in the 1990s. In this approach, budget allocations are tied to the outputs and outcomes of the programs rather than the inputs as with line-item budgeting. For example, if a program predicts it can increase enrollment with an additional allocation, the dean or provost may grant it, and then hold them accountable for the enrollment increase. If the goal is achieved, the program keeps the allocation; if not, it can be rescinded. Compared to line-item budgeting, performance budgeting shifts the focus away from inputs to outputs and outcomes. It is less control-oriented, and can stimulate growth in program quantity or quality. They key is that the performance encouraged by the organization must match with its strategic objectives. It also requires a robust set of performance measures upon which all agree and that create the right incentives. For example, if allocations were based on total enrollments, there would be an incentive to increase enrollments for the least expensive classes (large lecture classes) and a disincentive for expensive classes (such as doctoral classes). Many universities weight enrollments to avoid this problem.

A recent budget innovation is *responsibility-centered budgeting* (RCB). This has had a significant influence on some US universities. It has three key attributes.

1. Costs incurred and income generated are attributed to each academic unit, creating an incentive to generate a profit.
2. Units are given expanded authority to develop programs to increase profit.
3. The costs of support services (such as libraries and student counseling) are attributed to the academic units; and state subsidies, if any, are also allocated to the units (Whalen, 1991).

Clearly, the allocation of costs and profits to the academic units is an important part of the RCB process. You should take the time to understand this process and try to make sure your program is being treated fairly.

RCB creates a very different set of incentives for programs. MPA programs may benefit from this approach because of the relatively low costs and the potential for high enrollment. However, the capacity of MPA students to pay higher tuition is limited by their expectations for future incomes. The governance structure becomes especially important in this case. If MPA programs are in academic units where other programs generally run losses (such as doctoral programs), the MPA may be used as a "cash cow" and the profit used to subsidize the other programs. However, other programs (such as large undergraduate programs in political science) may produce significant profits, which can be used to subsidize the MPA program, or at least take the pressure off the MPA program to produce a profit.

As discussed, different budget formats emphasize different values. While the values of control (incrementalism), regular budget review (ZBB and TBB), improved outcomes (performance budgeting), cost control, and profit (RCB) are all important values in budgeting, the organization needs to decide which values are most important and structure its budgeting appropriately. Many budgets are hybrid formats, with some combination of two or more of these or other values. The different formats also create differing levels of competition among the actors, which in turn affect the outcomes (Rubin, 2000). When the scope of competition widens, the actors change, and the outcome of the decision-making process can change (Schattschneider, 1960). The different budget formats call for different strategies to be successful, as suggested by contingency management.

While many decisions are routine, you will want to put the program in a favorable setting. If the MPA program is in a pool of other programs it does not compare favorably with, it is more likely to suffer budget cuts than if it is compared to weaker programs. A savvy program director will learn the budget format, and figure out the steps to best position the program. To be successful, it is important to understand the power dynamics at work in the process. Often there are key actors who know how to get things done in the system. Getting their counsel, and learning the key leverage points in the process, will help increase the MPA director's effectiveness.

Key Features of University Budgeting

There are three key features an MPA director should keep in mind as they consider how to manage their budget: (1) Discretion and accountability, (2) variation and stability in resources, and (3) the ubiquity of politics in budgeting. These features are common across time and space.

Discretion and Accountability

As has been mentioned, program directors understandably want the most discretion possible over their budget. You may want to re-program funds during the budget year to respond to unexpected needs and opportunities. Doing so gives a greater feeling of efficacy and facilitates getting greater value for your money. At the same time, your chair or dean may be reluctant to grant a high degree of discretion as they may be under pressure to control spending. They also want to be perceived as fair in their treatment of all programs, so your request for greater discretion than others have may not be looked upon favorably.

A way to ease this tension is to establish a trusting relationship with your chair or dean. If you are honest with them and do what you say you will do, they are more likely to trust your management of program funds. In turn, they are likely to expect you to be accountable for the funds and to produce the results you promise. While there will be disruptions to any plan, a trusting relationship goes a long way to giving you a reasonable degree of discretion. Work to establish and maintain this trust.

The flip side of requesting discretion from higher-level authorities is whether or not you should grant authority or resources to faculty and staff who request it. How much the MPA director is responsible for this varies. If you are, then you will be asked for allocations for graduate assistants, travel, research funding, or other resources. You should have an open, transparent process that is perceived as fair and consistent with program goals. This will mean sometimes turning down requests from colleagues who are close friends. It is difficult, but an important aspect of program management. Keep in mind the program goals, resource availability, the incentives created by your decision, and how you will justify your decision to other colleagues. As Mark Twain said, "Do the right thing. It will gratify some people and astonish the rest."

Accountability is an important theme in public administration that we often teach in our classes. You will want to know your short-term and long-term goals and be able to show you are on the right path toward achieving them. You may be required to have formal or informal performance goals that you and other faculty and staff have agreed to. Monitor your progress, see what works, and learn from your mistakes. This will allow you to be more precise about your goals and, as Bing Crosby sang, "accentuate the positive and eliminate the negative."

Variation and Stability

Universities are in general more stable than many organizations. Revenues tend to be more stable than private for-profit and nonprofit organizations. Academic tenure creates a stable core of spending that can be a large part of your budget. It is easier to manage a more stable organization simply because change is less frequent and more contained to a small set of issues. However, when change happens it can be disruptive, in good or bad ways. These changes can come from either external or internal forces, and may be related to each other. In these times, a longer-term vision, ideally accompanied by a strategic plan, can guide the program. A program that is not prepared for change will struggle to articulate a good reason for continued funding to higher academic leadership, and make them vulnerable.

The theory of punctuated equilibrium offers some lessons for university budgeting as it seems descriptively accurate of many universities. True, Jones and Baumgartner (1999) use the theory to explain why there are periods of stability and episodic punctuations of major activity. The stable periods fit the incremental model while the punctuations are periods when issues are raised to the level of macropolitics. During the stable periods, there is not a major change in programs or budgets. When there are punctuations, a program grows or is cut in a significant way, re-shaping the future. During these punctuations, competing program images and issue framing may become critical in determining major, long-term decisions. This underscores the importance of establishing a good reputation, as well as effective internal and external advocacy.

Politics of Budgeting

As Rubin (2000) wrote, "public budgets are not merely technical managerial documents: they are intrinsically and irreducibly political" (p. 1). The politics of budgeting needs to be understood and embraced and MPA directors are very well trained to do it. The politics may be very small-scale or of a more mid-range level. It is rare, though possible, that the politics of MPA budgeting will be at the more macro level, involving university presidents, legislators, and others. As mentioned before, advocacy is an important part of the job. The MPA director needs to be comfortable in the micropolitics of persuasion, compromise, and coalition-building. It is important to keep the faculty and other internal decision-makers on-board as a cohesive group, ideally giving a similar message about the importance and value of the program. As the broader priorities of the university shift and evolve, so should the message and maybe even the curriculum of the program.

Budgets are indeed not only technical documents. They reflect values and priorities. Your job is to align program priorities with campus priorities and get higher-level administrators to agree with you.

Conclusion

MPA directors face many challenges, most of which require money. Managing your resources well is harder than it seems. It requires a detailed knowledge of the campus budget process, rules on spending, the ability to read a financial report, political savvy, and effective advocacy. Fortunately, you learned many of these skills in your own academic training. Putting this knowledge to work can get you a long way toward successful program management.

No one approach works everywhere. Effective management is dependent on the environment, circumstances, organizational structure, and political challenges and opportunities. Successful administrators benefit from their own experience and that of others. Seeking counsel of others and looking for opportunities is a well-founded strategy. Look for small successes early on and learn from your mistakes. As you get your bearings, you will learn the system and develop a reputation as an effective manager. Success breeds success, so forge ahead and show your students you actually *do* know something about management!

Appendix: Tips for Effective Budgeting

1. Know what information you have.

   a. Be able to read and understand a budget and know different fund types.
   b. Don't be afraid to ask questions.

2. Practice effective funds management.
   a. Establish a reliable flow of revenue to fund your core expenses.
   b. Manage your funds and use what flexibility you have to cover the most important costs.
   c. Control your spending and stay within budget.
   d. Prepare for budget reductions by holding some funds in reserve and prepare for increases by having proposals for program expansion ready.

3. Understand the incentives of the campus budget format.
4. Be patient but persistent. Several small increments can add up to a big change.
5. Inform your superiors about efficiencies you have achieved and address and explain any shortcomings.
6. Use alumni, government officials, and nonprofit executives as advocates (external support).
7. Befriend campus budget officers and work with your chair and dean (internal support).
8. Distinguish your program and persuade your superiors that the program is valuable for the campus and community.

References

Bozeman, B. (1987). *All organizations are Public: Bridging public and private organizational theories*. San Francisco, CA: Jossey-Bass.
Kingdon, J. (2011). *Agendas, alternatives, and public policies*, 2nd edn. Boston, MA: Longman Publishers.

McKinney, J. B. (2015). *Effective financial management in public and nonprofit agencies*, 4th edn. Santa Barbara, CA: Praeger.

Morgan, G. (1986). *Images of organization*. Newbury Park, CA: Sage Publications.

Rubin, I. (2000). *The politics of public budgeting: Getting and spending, borrowing and balancing*, 4th edn. New York: Seven Bridges Press.

Schattschneider, E. E. (1960). *The semi-sovereign people: A realist's view of democracy in America*. New York: Holt, Rinehart and Winston.

True, J. L., Jones, B. D., & Baumgartner, F. R. (1999). Punctuated equilibrium theory: Explaining stability and change in American policymaking. In Sabatier, P. A. (ed.), *Theories of the policy process* (pp. 97–115). Boulder, CO: Westview Press.

Whalen E. L. (1991). *Responsibility-centered budgeting: An approach to decentralized management for institutions of higher education*. Bloomington, IN: Indiana University Press.

8

EFFECTIVE FACULTY DEVELOPMENT

Kathryn Newcomer and Jasmine McGinnis Johnson

This chapter discusses what is entailed in effective faculty development. We envision faculty development as the provision of ongoing clear and consistent guidance and support to all faculty members to help them thrive and find joy in their work and to help them succeed in teaching, research, and service. Our scope covers all faculty members in public affairs programs, including junior and senior, tenure-track/tenured and contract, and full-time and part-time. And our audience is not limited to department chairs, for while university leaders play an important role, all more senior faculty members play critical roles in faculty development, as they model behaviors that may inspire faculty to succeed, and shape a culture that is conducive to acceptance of differences, inclusion, faculty success, and retention.

Faculty members are the most vital resources for university programs. They provide the engine that keeps programs going, and their continuing growth is essential for both their personal and their community's success. Performing many, and sometimes new, roles in a constantly changing higher-education environment is challenging. Unlike many other professions, university faculty members come to their jobs without sufficient preparation to play some roles, such as teaching and grant writing. And then they face new roles and responsibilities as they progress through their careers for which they may not be adequately prepared, like teaching online courses and managing degree programs.

Effectively developing faculty members is an increasingly complex challenge given the differences in needs across individual faculty members as well as across their careers, differing university and departmental cultures, and the changing nature of the student body that faculty members address (see Sorcinelli, Austin, Eddy, & Beach, 2006). Aligning resources, tools, and mentors appropriately to individual faculty members is more like diagnosing a disease than it is applying a band-aid to a cut knee. And some of the needs for growth our faculties face are likely to call for team-based development activities, e.g., diversity equity and inclusion training. Given the diversity in the interests and attitudes of faculty members, creating effective team-based professional development interventions is vital, yet also not straightforward (see Gast, Schildkamp, & van der Veen, 2017).

Developing faculty members effectively requires continually scanning the larger environment as it affects demands on our faculty, as well as keeping a close watch on our home departmental culture and individual faculty members. Thus, in this chapter, we start with an environmental scan, then move to offer more practical guidance. We first describe the landscape for faculty development within universities and colleges in the US and note some challenges especially pertinent to public affairs faculties. Second, we introduce a theory of change that outlines how faculty development should proceed when successful. Third, we describe fundamental activities and processes, including mentoring, that is needed to develop our faculty effectively. We also describe some local challenges that may impede effective faculty development, despite the best intentions and efforts of our faculty leaders. Throughout the chapter, we offer tips for action to help faculty leaders and junior faculty develop and thrive in a turbulent higher-education environment.

The Landscape Affecting Faculty Development

To set the stage for a discussion of faculty development, we first highlight the most important aspects of the higher-education landscape in the US that affect how faculty development operates. Most of these contextual conditions present challenges to effectively developing and retaining faculty. We characterize them here as they deserve attention by academic leaders in public affairs faculties, but we do not offer solutions to address them here.

Financial Pressures on Universities and Tenure

We are witnessing changes in the composition of faculties across American colleges and universities due to many trends, including reductions in tenure-track positions, and expansion of online programming with heavy reliance on part-time faculty. On fundamental driver is increasing financial pressures being placed on most colleges and universities to cut costs. State legislatures are reducing funding for public schools, and too many colleges compete for sometimes diminishing cohorts of college-age applicants. Aggressive marketing by for-profit colleges, and overly heavy reliance on tuition by private, nonprofit schools are leading them to take cost-saving measures. And boards of trustees and university administrators are quite aware that granting tenure imposes high, long-lasting personnel costs, thus pressures to cut tenure lines have been growing (Sorcinelli et al., 2006).

Pressures to maintain or reduce the number of tenure lines in programs has many types of consequences. With perceived, or real, scarcity, the road to tenure becomes more intimidating to pre-tenure faculty members, and even more emphasis may be placed on peer-reviewed research than the typical weighting of research, teaching, and service that is expressed in most tenure guidelines (The Volcker Alliance, 2017). And when tenure slots are becoming increasing dear, there are the additional effects of raising the angst surrounding the higher standards to be met to earn tenure, which can increase the anxiety among pre-tenure faculty, and intimidate our doctoral students who may be contemplating academic careers.

With fewer tenure lines and to save money, there is increasing use of non-tenure-track full-time faculty members by schools. There is likely to be less clarity regarding expectations for their development, and criteria for promotion decisions for them, as they bring quite different backgrounds and needs than the full-time faculty members. There are many different titles for the non-tenure-track full-time faculty members, including clinical faculty, professors of practice, and regular part-time faculty. And importantly, the routes taken to the academe by these non-tenure-track faculty members vary. For example, senior practitioners or politicians who have recently retired may be brought in. The different categories of faculty members present issues about the different sorts of development experiences they require (even when they think they do not!), and criteria for promotion as well, since the criteria for tenure are likely not appropriate.

Structural Racism and Faculty of Color

Persisting structural racism and bias affects virtually all public policy in the US, and touches universities in multiple ways that affect faculty recruitment, development, and retention. Centuries of oppression, legal discrimination, and sanctioned inequality have long tails that continue to shape where people live, what opportunities they are exposed to, and how people engage with one another (see Brown, Kijakazi, Runes, & Turner, 2019). We adopt here the definition of structural racism developed by the Aspen Institute Roundtable on Community Change, which defined structural racism as

> a system in which public policies, institutional practices, cultural representations, and other norms work in various, often reinforcing ways to perpetuate racial group inequity. It identifies dimensions of our history and culture that have allowed privileges associated with "whiteness" and disadvantages associated with "color" to endure and adapt over time.
>
> *(Lawrence, Sutton, Kubisch, Susi, & Fulbright-Anderson, 2004, p. 11)*

The ways that higher-education leaders are reacting to structural racism may help and/or hurt faculty development. On the positive side, there have been efforts to recognize both conscious bias and unconscious bias. For example, measuring and calling out unconscious bias has become more routine, e.g., *Blindspot: Hidden Biases of Good People* by Banaji and Greenwald (2013). Yet recognizing that biases exist does not help the faculty members of color who may experience differential treatment from students and colleagues, and faculty development processes are typically not tailored in ways that may be sufficient to help (Behari-Leak, 2017).

Across institutions of higher education, there is a recognized need to recruit and retain diverse faculties (for example, see Gasman, Samayoa, & Ginsberg, 2017), yet there are special challenges to developing and retaining faculty of color. While other chapters in this volume address issues of student recruitment and retention, as well as cultural competency and social equity, recruiting faculty of color is another topic deserving much more coverage. In this chapter, retention is the focus due to its link to effective faculty development. The reality is that there are additional challenges for diverse faculty members that affect their development and success – especially women of color.

Faculty of color face differential treatment that is not always visible. They are disproportionately burdened by demands made at the department and at the university level to provide demographic representation on committees and task forces. They are more prone to experience frustration and burnout when their universities are talking about diversity issues, which often, and most of the time, affect them more than other faculty members. In addition, they are expected to devote time to advise other faculty about diversity efforts, both formally and informally, and often are assumed to be experts about how to talk about sensitive topics, such as race, in diverse classrooms, and so colleagues often seek advice on these issues with them. And they may experience strange responses from students – of all races – who expect to call them by their first name or disregard their authority in other ways.

Also, students of color often expect and want faculty of color to mentor them and support them in their academic and personal journeys. Overall, these experiences take away from the time faculty of color have to devote to research and add an enormous amount of unofficial service, which is typically not adequately documented on annual reports or promotion or tenure dossiers since most of it is informal (Behari-Leak, 2017; Jones & Osborne-Lampkin, 2013).

Evaluation of Teaching

While research productivity continues to be the primary criterion for tenure decisions in public affairs programs (see The Volcker Alliance, 2017), effective teaching matters. However, there are challenges to adequately and fairly assessing teaching performance. Student course feedback is insufficient (see Boring, Ottoboni, & Stark, 2016; Hornstein, 2017) and prone to bias against women and teachers of color (Anderson & Smith, 2005; Punyanunt-Carter & Carter, 2015).

Critics have long noted that student feedback forms should not be used to constitute summative judgments on college teaching effectiveness, yet they are still routinely used to inform annual performance reviews and promotion and tenure decisions. Student course data are typically not representative (due to less-than-perfect response rates), have questionable measurement reliability, and do not provide a valid measurement of teaching effectiveness, yet we still treat them as if they do meet such standards (Hornstein, 2017).

Direct observation of teaching has been touted as a better tool to use to assess teaching, but peer visits also have their problems. Who should make the visits? More senior faculty members are typically expected to visit, but they also vote on promotion and tenure issues, and this presents a power differential not lost on the junior faculty members who are visited. Also, the peer visitors may not be comfortable offering critical feedback since they know the report goes into the official files. Thus, they may be incentivized to not go "on the record" with information that may be used against the junior faculty members.

Rewards for Community-Engaged Scholarship

There have always been slightly different expectations and rewards for applied research and service in public affairs programs from those in other disciplines. Given that public affairs programs typically have public service-oriented missions, their faculty members tend to be involved in practice-focused research and service. However, recent research verifies that publishing traditional scholarly research still presents the most important criterion for tenure and promotion decisions (The Volcker Alliance, 2017).

The need for more "community-engaged scholarship" has attracted attention, and the Volcker Alliance recently undertook research to ascertain what is needed to promote more of such practice-focused work. They found that incentives matter, and when practice-focused research and service does not count as heavily in promotion and tenure decisions, there are reduced incentives. In addition, most public affairs programs have faculty members from multiple disciplines. It may already be challenging to secure agreement on promotion and tenure decisions from faculty members with very differing disciplinary backgrounds, and especially when their disciplines do not value such practice-oriented work. The incentives for such work vary across schools, and there is not always consensus among faculty nor across public affairs programs about the appropriate rewards for what may be called service, or may be called community-based research.

Isolation

University faculty are increasingly more geographically distributed due to the growth of online programs and new work arrangements. But how can mentors and other senior faculty members effectively develop more junior faculty members from a distance? Previous research has shown that faculty prefer mentoring, personalized instruction, learning with peers, and informal help, but how can we do this effectively when faculty are not co-located (Herman, 2012, 2013)? Team-based professional development for university faculty members has also been shown to be especially effective, but the logistics to accomplish this with distributed faculty merit attention (Gast, Schildkamp, & van der Veen, 2017).

A Theory of Change for Effective Faculty Development

Given the challenges in the environment in which public affairs programs function, there are commonalities in requirements for effective faculty development. What should effective faculty development look like in practice? Figure 8.1 depicts a theory of change that graphically displays the basic processes that faculty development entails, as well as factors that affect the success of faculty development efforts. Theory-of-change models generally represent the causal relationships between planned efforts, expected outcomes, and context to explain how the program or policies are expected to work.

The ultimate goal of faculty development is for faculty members to thrive and be productive and enjoy successful careers. Relatedly, faculty retention in their department is a tangible and goal for academic leaders. The model in Figure 8.1 reiterates the key environmental factors covered above, and then displays the inputs, or resources needed, the activities required, and expected outcomes in both the short and longer term for effective faculty development.

Perhaps most importantly, our model also identifies the many contextual factors that may hinder successful faculty development at the organizational and individual level that are typically outside of the control of university administrators and departmental leaders.

Reading the theory of change model from left to right, the inputs include resources and guidance from both the university and department level. At the university level, we highlight the need for the formal faculty code to specify the need for and resources for faculty development, and that the upper-level university administrators both support faculty generally, and demonstrate a commitment to faculty development and prioritize providing the support that is needed. Similarly, at the departmental level, leadership commitment and support is the critical element. Also, given the importance of mentoring, having both the leadership and other faculty value mentoring (and community-building more generally) is key. Such support is critical to ensure that needed processes and activities are undertaken, which we discuss next.

Processes and Activities Needed for Effective Faculty Development

While there are likely many ways in which successful faculty development may play out in different contexts, there are five fundamental processes that are

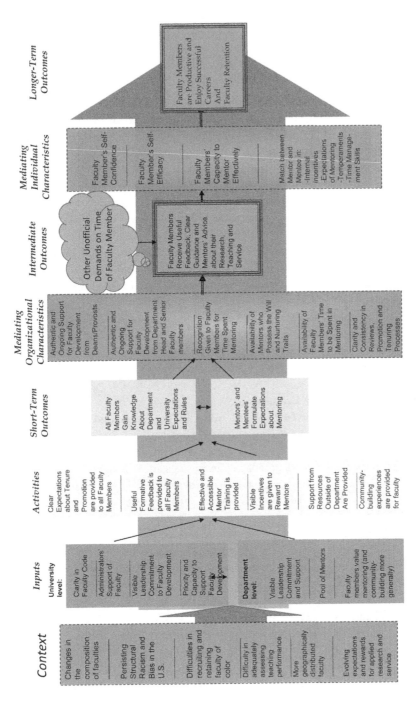

FIGURE 8.1 Theory of Change Model for Faculty Development

essential to support effective faculty development: Clear and consistent communication of expectations; provision of formative feedback; effective mentoring; provision of tailored support; and community building.

Clear and Consistent Communications

Clarity in expectations and communications about expectations is critical in any program or policy implementation effort, and it is in faculty development, as well. Department or program leaders need to be clear and consistent in their communications, but their organizational context may present challenges to accomplish this.

Ideally, within one's university, there are formal and consistent university guidelines and expectations for faculty development, as well as criteria for promotion and tenure, and there is consistency in such guidance across the various levels of the university. For example, there should be consistency across bylaws at college and departmental levels on processes, timelines, criteria, and such things as what constitutes "excellence" for promotion and tenure decisions. And then importantly, these rules and expectations should be clearly and consistently communicated to all faculty by not only the administrators and department chairs, but also by tenure and promotion committees and senior faculty members.

In reality, there may be a lack of clarity, and or inconsistencies across levels of the university. It is imperative that department or program leaders investigate and seek clarity to communicate expectations and criteria to all faculty members, for junior faculty may hear different things from different sources.

Tips for Department Leaders

- Learn about de facto as well as de jure regulations and expectations at the university level, school level, and department level for promotion for all faculty, as well as for tenure decisions. For example, it is helpful to become knowledgeable about how promotion and tenure committees and administrators above the department level weigh and value different materials, such as student feedback data, peer visits, external letters, and community-engaged scholarship.
- Monitor and ensure chairs of promotion and tenure committees and mentors are current on expectations, rules, and procedural requirements regarding faculty development. Expectations change at all levels of a university, from the president's or provost's office on down, and all senior faculty who may play a role in the promotion and tenure decisions need to be kept current.
- Ensure all regulations and expectations regarding promotion, as well as tenure, are communicated clearly and consistently to both tenure-track and non-tenure-track faculty members, including more senior faculty members so that there are not inconsistent messages given to more junior faculty members.

Provision of Formative Feedback

Within the evaluation profession, there is a clear difference drawn between formative and summative evaluation. *Formative* evaluation involves using evaluation methods to improve the way a program is delivered, while *summative* evaluation measures program outcomes and impacts during ongoing operations or after a program is completed to draw judgments on performance. Applying the notion of formative evaluation to faculty development highlights the need for department or program leaders in providing feedback to help faculty improve their teaching, research, or other aspects of their performance.

Faculty receive feedback from students and their academic leaders regularly. Students provide feedback on formal surveys at the end of each class, and the data provided can be used to help faculty members clarify their assignments and lectures, and make other adjustments in their teaching when appropriate. Annual reports present opportunities for departmental leaders to advise faculty on their performance in teaching as well as research and service.

Problems arise when feedback provided as a formative evaluation is used to inform judgments on faculty performance. As noted above, student course data are typically not representative, have questionable measurement reliability, and are not valid measures of teaching effectiveness (Hornstein, 2017). Accordingly, student feedback data should be used in a formative fashion to help faculty members improve. And if annual reports are used primarily to make judgments on faculty members, and they become part of formal documentation employed in promotion and/or tenure decisions, they do not provide an appropriate mode for providing formative feedback from departmental leaders.

Thus, mechanisms for providing formative feedback to help faculty members improve their performance need to be intentionally and consistently employed. Tools to provide formative feedback should be separated from any judgmental processes, such as decisions made on financial/merit salary increases, to ensure that the feedback can be candid and offered in what the receivers perceive as a safe space. And administrators and departmental leaders need to work to ensure there is consistency and clarity in feedback given to faculty members about their teaching performance from various sources such as promotion and tenure committees, deans' offices, formal mentors, and senior faculty.

Peer observations and peer team teaching efforts provide great opportunities to provide feedback to faculty members about their teaching – when undertaken in a formative mode, to encourage learning, rather than make judgments. Careful thought and design of the format and purpose of peer observations is needed, but, there are many models out there for adapting to specific contexts (Drew & Klopper, 2014).

Tips for Department Leaders

- Establish and formalize peer observations with clear criteria and expectations for the formative feedback that is provided to the faculty member who is observed.
- Communicate both the purpose and intended use of peer observations so that all faculty – senior and junior, tenured and contract, full-time and part-time – understand the value that they can reap from these visits.
- Clarify to all faculty when and how student course feedback data are used in any way that is not simply to help them improve.
- Make opportunities available for faculty (at all stages of their career) to team-teach courses, both with colleagues within their home department and with faculty in related departments and disciplines, to enable peer-to-peer learning.
- Alert all faculty members to the university-level resources to support their professional development, and then support faculty members who want to participate in cohort types of training and/or coaching from university centers offering such support services.

Mentoring

Within any organization, but especially within educational institutions, mentoring or reciprocal learning relationships characterized by trust, respect, and commitment provide valuable support for not only the mentored faculty members as they develop their careers but for other members of the university community, including the mentors and students. Mentors who are well received by their mentees are likely to present positive role models for them in giving useful feedback, and so the mentees are more likely to become good mentors when they become more senior, and also to be more skilled in giving valuable feedback to their students, as well. A sign of the increasing recognition of the importance of mentoring within higher education is the Mentoring Conference held annually since 2008. The conference, sponsored by the University of New Mexico Mentoring Institute, brings together faculty, researchers, and professionals in higher education to further understanding of effective mentoring (see Mentoring Institute, 2019).

Many of the studies on faculty mentoring have explored the benefits of faculty mentoring, and have found that mentoring facilitates the recruitment, retention, and advancement of faculty through many developmental processes. Mentoring is useful to socialize faculty members into an academic unit culture and can increase collegiality and build relationships and networks among protégés and mentors. And mentoring has been found to promote the professional growth and career development for protégés and mentors, as well as increase productivity and organizational stability (see Fountain & Newcomer, 2016; Mazerolle, Nottingham, & Coleman, 2018; Meschitti & Smith, 2017).

In recent research on mentoring in public affairs programs, the two institutional factors that appeared to be by far the most critical for effective mentoring were the academic unit head's support for mentoring, and faculty leadership commitment (Fountain & Newcomer, 2016). And the most frequently cited obstacle was the time commitment, as effective mentoring takes time (Fountain & Newcomer, 2016). In addition, there is also research that faculty should have mentors for each aspect of their work life (Higgins, 2000). Sustaining effective mentoring systems requires intentional and consistent attention.

Tips for Department Leaders

- Work collaboratively with faculty within your unit to clearly articulate the purpose and goals for a mentoring program.
- Align your mentoring program's goals with your program's mission and goals, and work to gain the support of all faculty and leadership upwards for the program.
- Discuss and develop intentional strategies for matching mentor-mentee pairs based on professional compatibility.
- Provide orientations for both mentors and mentees on the dynamics of mentoring, and provide written materials regarding the mentoring program's goals, desired outcomes, and expectations for activities on shared file space.
- Evaluate mentoring programs via annual surveys of both mentors and mentees to enable continuous improvement.
- Provide ongoing moral support for mentors and visibly reward them for their mentoring.

Provision of Tailored Support

There are typically many resources outside of departments but within universities that should be made available and safe for all faculty members to use. For example, university teaching centers and libraries typically offer relevant support that junior faculty members, in particular, should be encouraged to access. In addition, human resources offices that provide advice regarding maternity leave and health issues should be made available and easy to access. Additional sources of support on dealing with student issues, e.g., mental health issues, sexual harassment, and assault, should also be made easily accessible to all faculty.

Faculty leaders should also make it easy for faculty members to access support from relevant resources outside of the university when needed. For example, there are mentoring programs that reach across universities, such as the National Center for Faculty Development and Diversity (2019), and many consultants available to assist with diversity, inclusion, and equity efforts that can be brought into departments.

Tips for Department Leaders

- Develop useful and comprehensive faculty handbooks that are available from your university on shared file space for all faculty members that provide the email addresses and phone numbers of all pertinent support services for them, including but not limited to: Mental health support; human resource issues, such as family leave and maternity leave documentation requirements; grading expectations; offices that help with alleged cases of plagiarism; university-level teaching centers and programming; and helpful campus personnel to address sexual harassment and sexual assault complaints.
- Consult routinely with all faculty about development needs they have.
- Ensure all faculty members are aware of resources available for them to pay for development opportunities for them from outside of the university, such as honoraria for mentors from other schools, and professional coaches.

Community-Building

Establishing and sustaining communities of faculty where faculty members feel included and supported, and feel comfortable asking for feedback and support, requires planning and ongoing effort. Public affairs programs typically include faculty from many disciplines who bring diverse experiences with them into academe. Community-building entails hands-on efforts from both official leaders and other senior faculty and may involve such things as intentionally constructing opportunities for all faculty members (including part-time members) to socialize outside of the office regularly, and supporting co-authored research.

In addition, team-based professional development activities for university faculty have been growing in quantity and quality (see Gast, Schildkamp, & van der Veen, 2017). Given the many challenges present in the higher-education landscape discussed above, there are many topics for which team-based development interventions would be especially appropriate, and could advance community-building, such as: Building interdisciplinary connections and communities of practice; meeting the learning needs of an increasingly diverse student body; and moderating class discussions about important but sensitive topics such as racism.

Tips for Department Leaders

- Ensure all faculty members share a common title and affiliation on their business cards and related public media.
- Provide real incentives for faculty to co-author research and team-teach – especially matching more senior with more junior faculty members.
- Transparently and enthusiastically support joint research projects through the provision of support for things such as data collection/ purchase and software.

- Collaborate with faculty to build opportunities for team-based development activities for the entire faculty in areas that they suggest and/or on issues that may be emerging, e.g., rising (or declining) numbers of international students or first-generation students in the student body.

Local Challenges that May Impede Effective Faculty Development

In our theory of change, we list a variety of mediating factors that may hinder successful faculty development at the organizational and individual level to caution university administrators and departmental leaders to be alert, and be proactive when they face these obstacles. For example, at the organizational level, they may not be able to ensure they receive ongoing support for faculty development from deans and provosts, so they should be proactive to impede negative consequences of neglect from up top.

There are a set of potential pitfalls that face leaders as they try to shepherd effective mentoring processes. Departmental leaders may not be able to recruit mentors who possess both the will and the nurturing traits needed to serve as good mentors in their department, but they can look outside of their department or school. And they can and should monitor mentoring processes routinely, such as assessing the match between mentors and mentees in terms of incentives, expectations, temperaments, and time management.

Departmental leaders need to monitor communications and rumor mills consistently. They bear responsibility for ensuring there is clarity and consistency in communications about criteria used in reviews, promotion, and tenure processes, as well as the actual application of said criteria.

In terms of individual faculty members' responsibility for their development, and their self-efficacy and time management skills, there may not be much that department leaders can do. However, leaders should monitor faculty members regarding unofficial demands on the time of the faculty members that are not documented or rewarded, such as excessive advising for students of color, or family demands. It is likely more often the case that junior faculty members will be reluctant to ask for help, or to even realize they should do so until it is too late. It is up to good leaders to be watchful and supportive.

Conclusion

We have painted the challenging landscape in which our faculty members are trying to succeed. The kind and number of roles and responsibilities that our faculty members are expected to fulfill will no doubt continue to expand. And the nature of the student body and their needs will continue to change, as will the technological opportunities and challenges faculty face. For university faculty members, change continues to be the only constant. Faculty development needs and solutions need to keep up.

We have discussed faculty development processes and activities that can help advance faculty development and offered some practical tips for faculty leaders. We conclude now with some parting thoughts on navigating faculty development, first from a senior faculty leader's perspective and then from a junior faculty member's perspective.

Leaders shape culture and expectations. So understand your strengths and limitations that affect your leadership and managerial style. There are many resources available that help one to become more self-aware, as well as socially aware, and one especially accessible one is *Emotional Intelligence 2.0* by Bradberry and Greaves (2009). Relatedly, coping with conflict can be challenging too many, and *Difficult Conversations* by Stone, Patton, and Heen (2000) is especially helpful on this front.

Ensure all junior faculty members receive ongoing support, mentoring, reassurance, access to external resources, and tailored assistance. Given the increasingly high stakes to secure tenure, tenure-track faculty are likely to be especially nervous and deserve consistent attention to address concerns they have – about all aspect of the tenure process, as well as expectations of their service, their attendance at department or school events, etc.

Protect junior faculty from committing too much time to service to students, to the department, the university or profession until they earn tenure for tenure-track colleagues, or until they have built up their teaching repertoire and research agenda for non-tenure-track faculty colleagues.

And remember to give attention to developing more senior faculty and part-time faculty as well as pre-tenure faculty members! All of our colleagues require and deserve support as they develop throughout their careers. Maturing faculty members' needs change, thus the support they need will change as well. And part-time faculty members also require and deserve tailored support, and they are too easy to forget when out of sight.

Our practical advice on navigating faculty development from a junior faculty member's perspective includes the following recommendations. Although it may seem difficult to manage up, this is likely what you are going to do as a junior faculty member. First, we recommend establishing a daily writing practice. We recommend resources at the National Center for Faculty Development and Diversity (2019). This organization supports daily writing (Monday to Friday) and having a life. By making sure your writing is done first, you will have time for other matters.

Second, we hope you will establish a practice to work on your health. This can include exercise, meditation, or therapy – and prioritize these practices. It becomes easy to put your health second when you are in a new environment and often a new city, but focusing on health may clear your mind for the next big idea. Third, we recommend getting to know all of the faculty members in your department. One junior faculty we knew went up to her university in July and asked everyone in the department to coffee. This was a way for faculty to get to know her without the burden of a long awkward conversation. Although you will continue getting to know your colleagues, these first conversations can provide insight into how the university, college, and department function. Once these conversations occur, a trusted senior mentor will arise. This faculty member will help give you insight into your department's politics or explain what exactly happened in a recent faculty meeting.

Finally, continue to do your networking at your professional conferences. Reach out to senior colleagues and discuss their papers. A senior colleague shared with us that they tell junior faculty to reach out to senior colleagues via e-mail when they publish a paper in which they have heavily cited them. A quick e-mail with your paper attached sent in advance of a conference is an easy way to ask for a coffee to talk about research.

References

Anderson, K. & Smith, G. (2005). Students' preconceptions of professors: Benefits and barriers according to ethnicity and gender. *Hispanic Journal of Behavioral Sciences, 27*(2), 184–201.

Banaji, M. R. & Greenwald, A. G. (2013). *Blindspot: Hidden biases of good people.* New York: Delacorte Press.

Behari-Leak, K. (2017). New academics, new higher education contexts: A critical perspective on professional development. *Teaching in Higher Education, 22*(5), 485–500.

Boring, A., Ottoboni, K., & Stark, P. B. (2016). Student evaluations of teaching (mostly) do not measure teaching effectiveness. *ScienceOpen Research.* Retrieved January 2, 2020, from www.scienceopen.com/document?id=25ff22be-8a1b-4c97-9d88-084c8d98187a.

Bradberry, T. & Greaves, J. (2009). *Emotional intelligence 2.0.* San Diego, CA: TalentSmart.

Brown, K. S., Kijakazi, K., Runes, C., & Turner, M. A. (2019). *Confronting structural racism in research and policy analysis: Charting a course for policy research institutions.* Washington, DC: The Urban Institute.

Drew, S. & Klopper, C. (2014). Evaluating faculty pedagogic practices to inform strategic academic professional development: A case of cases. *Higher Education: The International Journal of Higher Education and Educational Planning, 67*(3), 349–367.

Fountain, J. & Newcomer, K. (2016). Developing and sustaining effective faculty mentoring programs. *Journal of Public Affairs Education, 22*(4), 483–506.

Gasman, M., Samayoa, A. C., & Ginsberg, A. (2017). Minority serving institutions: Incubators for teachers of color. *The Teacher Educator, 52*(2), 84–98.

Gast, I., Schildkamp, K., & van der Veen, J. (2017). Team-based professional development interventions in higher education: A Systematic Review. *Review of Educational Research, 87*(4), 736–767.

Herman, J. (2012). Faculty development programs: The frequency and variety of professional development programs available to online instructors. *Journal of Asynchronous Learning Networks, 16*(5), 87–106.

Herman, J. (2013). Faculty incentives for online course design, delivery, and professional development. *Innovative Higher Education, 38*(5), 397–410.

Higgins, M. C. (2000). The more, the merrier? Multiple developmental relationships and work satisfaction. *Journal of Management Development, 19*(4), 277–296.

Hornstein, H. (2017). Student evaluations of teaching are an inadequate assessment tool for evaluating faculty performance. *Cogent Education, 4*(1), 1–8.

Jones, T. & Osborne-Lampkin, L. (2013). Black female faculty success and early career professional development. *The Negro Educational Review, 64*(1–4), 59–75.

Lawrence, K., Sutton, S., Kubisch, A., Susi, G., & Fulbright-Anderson, K. (2004). *Structural racism and community building*. Washington, DC: The Aspen Institute.

Mazerolle, S., Nottingham, S., & Coleman, K. (2018). Faculty mentorship in higher education: The value of institutional and professional mentors. *Athletic Training Education Journal, 13*(3), 259–267.

Mentoring Institute (2019). 12th Annual mentoring conference: Towards the science of mentoring. *University of New Mexico.* Retrieved June 3, 2019 from http://mentor.unm.edu/conference.

Meschitti, V. & Smith, H. (2017). Does mentoring make a difference for women academics? Evidence from the literature and a guide for future research. *Journal of Research in Gender Studies, 7*(1), 166–199.

National Center for Faculty Development and Diversity (2019). *Faculty diversity.* Retrieved June 3, 2019 from www.facultydiversity.org.

Punyanunt-Carter, N. & Carter, S. (2015). Students' gender bias in teaching evaluations. *Higher Learning Research Communications, 5*(3), 28–37.

Sorcinelli, M. D., Austin, A. E., Eddy, P. L., & Beach, A. L. (2006). *Creating the future of faculty development: Learning from the past, understanding the present.* San Francisco, CA: Jossey-Bass.

Stone, D., Patton, B., & Heen, S. (2000). *Difficult conversations: How to discuss what matters most.* New York: Penguin Books.

The Volcker Alliance (2017). *Tenure and promotion at schools of public affairs* (Working Paper). Washington, DC: The Volcker Alliance.

9

CURRICULUM AND INSTRUCTIONAL DESIGN

Doug Goodman

This chapter focuses on the principles of developing a curriculum for public administration/affairs (including public administration, public policy, and public affairs) programs.[1] The chapter includes a brief discussion on the Network of Schools of Public Policy, Affairs, and Administration (NASPAA) accreditation standards and how to incorporate NASPAA's standards and competencies to individual program curriculum and design; a forthright discussion on how desired program outcomes are related to specific courses in individual programs; and a discussion on design of concentrations within a program and choices of program modality.

With the change in NASPAA's standards in 2009, the accreditation process migrated from an input-based to a competency-based accreditation process based on seven standards that include five universal competencies (Commission on Peer Review and Accreditation COPRA, 2014; Dunning, 2014). Rather than providing a list of courses, topics, and subject matter to be included in an MPA curriculum, NASPAA instead provided universal competencies to be used by programs to develop a curriculum that is designed for their mission for programs. Ten years later, more programs than ever are NASPAA-accredited or are seeking NASPAA accreditation across the globe. In 2019, NASPAA reported that 206 programs at 187 schools are now accredited (NASPAA, 2019a).

Not only do schools have to focus on NASPAA's accreditation standards, but some states like Texas are beginning to require universities to demonstrate that their degrees and programs provide students with marketable skills. The Texas Higher Education Coordinating Board's (THECB; 2015) strategic plan *60x30TX* requires that by 2030, 60 percent of Texans will have a college degree or certificate. In addition, the standards require all graduates from Texas public colleges and universities to have identified marketable skills, and universities will be transparent as to what those skills include. The THECB's strategic plan defines marketable skills as,

> those skills valued by employers that can be applied in a variety of work settings, including interpersonal, cognitive, and applied skills areas. These skills can be primary or complementary to a major and are acquired by students through education, including curricular, co-curricular, and extra-curricular activities.
>
> *(2015, p. 22)*

The strategic plan continues to say, "[w]here identified marketable skills exist within programs, institutions need to promote them; where identified skills don't exist, institutions need to incorporate them" (2015, p. 23). MPA/MPP programs are required to document, update, and communicate the marketable "skills students acquire in their [MPA] programs" (THECB, 2015, p. 22). NASPAA accreditation standards greatly help MPA programs meet additional requirements imposed on MPA/MPP programs by external boards.

NASPAA Accreditation

In 2009, NASPAA shifted from nine standards that were used for accreditation to seven standards (COPRA, 2014; Dunning, 2014). Accordingly, the new standards include the following.

- Standard 1. Managing the Program Strategically.
- Standard 2. Matching Governance to the Mission.
- Standard 3. Matching Operations with the Mission: Faculty Performance.
- Standard 4. Matching Operations with the Mission: Serving Students.
- Standard 5. Matching Operations with the Mission: Student Learning.
- Standard 6. Matching Resources with the Mission.
- Standard 7. Matching Communication with the Mission.

Curriculum and instructional design are covered by Standard 5's required "universal competencies." Programs must demonstrate that their students, upon completing the program, should be able to:

- lead and manage in public governance
- participate in and contribute to the policy process
- analyze, synthesize, think critically, solve problems, and make decisions
- articulate and apply a public service perspective
- communicate and interact productively with a diverse and changing workforce and citizenry

Additionally, programs that have mission specific competencies must also identify them and define those objectives (COPRA, 2014). Programs need to provide evidence through assessment of learning.

As part of the competency-based accreditation process NASPAA no longer directs the courses or subject matter to be covered in an MPA program. Accreditation now requires programs to demonstrate learning surrounding five universal competencies that should be mastered in each of the accredited programs. MPA programs are allowed latitude to determine what courses should be taught in their respective programs. Each core course should be linked to the program's mission and related to one or more of the universal competencies. The same is true with concentration or specializations. These courses should be tied to the program's mission. Although at this time NASPAA does not require programs to assess concentrations and specializations, programs are encouraged, however, to assess them internally.

The Importance of Mission

Before going into details about the universal competencies and program learning objectives, it is important to discuss program missions and how those relate to core courses. As mentioned above, Standard 1 required programs to be managed strategically. As part of their strategic planning process, programs develop and/or revise their mission statements and visions (see Chapter 5 on Strategic Planning). NASPAA indicates that each program is to have a mission statement "that guides performance expectations and their evaluation" (COPRA, 2014, p. 4). Standard 1 continues to say that a program mission for an accredited program or program seeking accreditation must include (COPRA, 2014, p. 4):

- its purpose and public service values, given the program's particular emphasis on public affairs, administration, and policy;
- the population of students, employers, and professionals the program intends to service; and
- the contribution it intends to produce to advance the knowledge, research, and practice of public affairs, administration, and policy.

Standard 1 also directs accredited programs or programs seeking accreditation to develop "observable program goals, objectives, and outcomes, including expectations for student learning, consistent with its mission" (COPRA, 2014, p. 4). NASPAA suggests that MPA/MPP programs range from 36 to 48 semester credit hours or equivalent. Further, a program must collect, analyze, and report data "about its performance and operations." The data are used for "continuous improvement" for the program and used to measure each of NASPAA's accreditation standards (COPRA, 2014, p. 4). Figure 9.1 illustrates the continuous improvement cycle for MPA programs that is used for

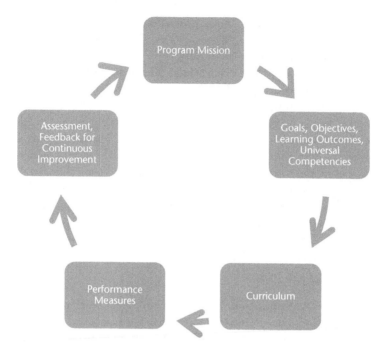

FIGURE 9.1 Strategic Program Curriculum Design

curriculum development. In other words, when designing or revising an MPA core curriculum it is *a priori*, as Figure 9.1 illustrates, that the program's mission, goals, objectives, and outcomes are utilized in developing program learning objectives. Each core course in the program should point back to at least one program learning objective. In turn, the program learning objective should be tied to at least one NASPAA universal competency. Assessment provides for continual feedback that is used to make periodic adjustments to the program mission. Rivenbark and Jacobson (2014) say that "mission drives competencies and competencies drive curriculum" (p. 191).

NASPAA's Standard 5 focuses on student learning and universal competencies for MPA and MPP programs. The five universal competencies should be related back to individual program's core learning objectives. Depending on the mission, programs may want to duplicate the universal competencies for their learning objectives, and in other cases, programs will devise their own learning objectives that tie into NASPAA's university competencies. Tables 9.1, 9.2, and 9.3 provide an example of a hypothetical university's curriculum mapping that matches its program's four learning objectives with NASPAA's universal competencies. For example, the rows in Table 9.1 report the four learning objectives for an MPA program. The columns represent each of NASPAA's five universal competencies. The check marks indicate the alignment of each learning objective with a specific universal competency.

TABLE 9.1 NASPAA Competencies/Learning Outcomes Crosswalk

MPA Learning Objectives	Competency 1: Lead and manage in public governance	Competency 2: Participate in and contribute to the policy process	Competency 3: Analyze, synthesize, think critically, solve problems, and make decisions	Competency 4: Articulate and apply a public service perspective	Competency 5: Communicate and interact productively with a diverse and changing workforce and citizenry
SLO #1: Students will demonstrate an understanding of the theoretical foundations of public management, policy making, and leadership in government and nonprofit settings	✓		✓	✓	
SLO #2: Students will demonstrate proficiency in organizational and decision analysis	✓	✓	✓		
SLO #3: Students will demonstrate sound preparation for careers in the public and nonprofit sectors	✓	✓	✓	✓	✓
SLO #4: Students will demonstrate a mastery of persuasive written and oral communication	✓				✓

TABLE 9.2 MPA Assessment Matrix

Core Courses	SLO 1: Students will demonstrate an understanding of the philosophical, theoretical, and legal foundations of public management, policy making, and leadership in government and nonprofit settings	SLO 2: Students will demonstrate a proficiency in organizational and decision analysis, research and evaluation practice, and quantitative and qualitative techniques	SLO 3: Students will demonstrate a sound preparation for careers in the public and nonprofit sector	SLO 4: Students will demonstrate a mastery of persuasive written and oral communication
Public Management	I, P		I, P	P
Public Policymaking and Institutions	I, P			P
Introduction to Quantitative Methods		I, P, M		P
Evaluating Program and Organizational Performance		P, M	P	I, P
Organizational Theory	M	M		
Government Financial Management and Budgeting		P	P	
Human Resource Management	I, P, M	I, P	I	I, P, M
Nonprofit Management	I, M		P	P, M
Capstone in Public Affairs		M	M	M
Internship			M	

Note
I = Introduce; P = Practice; M = Master

TABLE 9.3 MPA Assessment Matrix with NASPAA Universal Competencies

Core Courses	Competency 1: Lead and manage in public governance	Competency 2: Participate in and contribute to the policy process	Competency 3: Analyze, synthesize, think critically, solve problems, and make decisions	Competency 4: Articulate and apply a public service perspective	Competency 5: Communicate and interact productively with a diverse and changing workforce and citizenry
Public Management	I, P	I, P	I, P	I, P	
Public Policymaking and Institutions	P	I		P	P
Introduction to Quantitative Methods	P	I	I	P	P
Evaluating Program and Organizational Performance	I, P		P, M	P	P
Organizational Theory	I, P	I, P	I, P	I	
Government Financial Management and Budgeting	P	P	P	P	I, P
Human Resource Management	P, M	P, M	P, M	I, P, M	I, P, M
Nonprofit Management	I, P			I, P	P
Capstone in Public Affairs	M	M	M	M	M
Internship	M			M	
Timeframe for assessment	2021–2023	2022–2024	2023–2025	2019–2021	2020–2022

Note
I = Introduction; P = Practice; M = Master

Tables 9.2 and 9.3 report how each core course in the hypothetical MPA program is related to the program's student learning objectives and NASPAA's universal competencies, respectively. Each learning objective is introduced, practiced, and/or mastered in the MPA program's core courses. In each course students are introduced, practice, or demonstrate mastery of at least one learning objective. If a core course does not introduce, practice, or master a program learning objective, the course needs to be reevaluated, realigned, or perhaps removed from the core curriculum if the course is no longer integral to the mission. Table 9.3 goes a step further and provides a timeframe for assessment for each of NASPAA's universal competencies. Notice that each competency is not assessed every year. Nonetheless, each year at least three competencies are being assessed.

There are a lot of resources available to MPA programs, faculty, and directors to help them decide appropriate courses, measures, assessment tools, etc. NASPAA's accreditation website provides information about accreditation, its standards, and education and training modules to assist programs through the process (NASPAA, 2019b). In addition to this book, there are several websites and academic journals with numerous articles to assist with program design, course design, learning objectives, assessment, performance measures, rubrics, teaching, etc. These resources include specialty journals such as the *Educational Resources Information Center*, *Journal of Public Affairs Education*, and *Teaching Public Administration*; field and specialty journals such as *Public Integrity*, *Review of Public Personnel Administration*, *American Review of Public Administration*, and *Public Administration Review* also includes curriculum development articles from time to time. Other helpful resources for faculty include teaching conferences, NASPAA's Annual Conference, Rubric-maker.com, RubiStar, and the Atlas of Public Management. The Atlas website is especially comprehensive and helpful for MPA/MPP program administrators (more to follow).[2]

Curriculum Development and Course Design

There are many reasons curricula change over the years. Some changes are mandated by state legislatures, university administrators, or accrediting agencies. Other times changes are suggested by students, faculty, stakeholders, technology, or other relevant sources. University and program missions change, thereby necessitating curriculum changes.

As programs begin to develop or update their curriculum, they should map their courses, especially core courses, to the NASPAA's universal competencies (Clark, Eisen, Lennon, & Pal, 2015). Adapting Bloom's Taxonomy (Anderson, Krathwohl, & Bloom, 2001; Bloom, 1956; Shabatu, 2018) can help faculty ensure higher forms of learning in the curriculum (see Figure 9.2). Bloom's Taxonomy includes six cognitive domains or levels of learning that are associated with action verbs (Anderson et al., 2001; Shabatu, 2018). Similar to

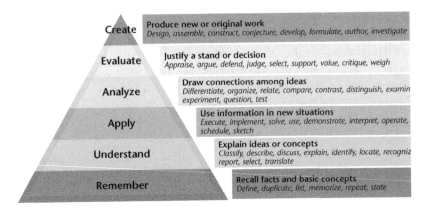

FIGURE 9.2   Bloom's Taxonomy of Learning

Source: Armstrong (2016).

Maslow's (1943) hierarchy of needs, the taxonomy is a hierarchy or continuum that moves from lower levels of learning such as remembering and understanding to higher levels of learning that include evaluating and creating new knowledge. Courses in an MPA/MPP curriculum follow the same ordering that progresses from introduction to practice to mastery (Dunning, 2014). The idea behind Bloom's Taxonomy is that:

> [b]efore you can *understand* a concept, you must *remember* it. To *apply* a concept you must first *understand* it. In order to *evaluate* a process, you must have *analyzed* it. To *create* an accurate conclusion, you must have completed a thorough *evaluation.*
>
> *(Shabatu, 2018)*

Bloom's Taxonomy is illustrated in Figure 9.2. The bottom row of the pyramid focuses on *remembering* where students are asked to recall concepts by defining, duplicating, listing, memorizing, and repeating or restating concepts. These are mainly accomplished through assignments, quizzes, and exams. Being able to remember helps build a foundation for further elevations in the taxonomy. The second level of blooms taxonomy is *understanding*, students should be able to explain ideas or concepts. Once a student can explain the concepts they can begin to *apply* those concepts. Case studies are great examples that allows students to apply materials they have learned through class and reading. The next level of Bloom's Taxonomy is the ability to *analyze*. At this level students are expected to draw connections between ideas or among ideas. Critical essays that ask students to critically assess an article or synthesize articles or case studies are good tools to better help students learn to analyze. The next step in Bloom's Taxonomy is to *evaluate*. This step involves students learning how to judge, critique, or defend their arguments. Evaluating provides students with the necessary skills needed for decision-making. Finally, as students begin to master subject matter or skills they are able to *create* new knowledge and original work. They take the skills that they have learned throughout their MPA/MPPA program or in the course and culminate with new knowledge.

When an MPA/MPP program is designing or changing its curriculum, it will want to include courses that introduce concepts, practice those concepts, and allow for their mastery. Sometimes the introduction, the practice, and the mastery are all included in one course. For other subjects, the introduction, practice, and mastery might be spread across multiple courses (see Tables 9.2 and 9.3).

Table 9.4 provides some rudimentary steps for curriculum changes. First, courses need to tie back to the program's mission and learning objectives. It is essential that courses and curricula are relevant and meet the needs for the students and stakeholders. Each course should be designed with assessment in mind. Appropriate assignment items need to be created that introduce, practice, and/or master skills and learning objectives. Assignments should have direct ways to measure student learning. Direct tools are exams, portfolios, final papers, oral presentations, and case analysis, to name a few. Indirect methods include surveys and reflection assignments (Shenoy, 2016).

MPA faculty will need to gather data about their curriculum, courses, and learning. There are many sources for data. Surveys can be used as a source of relevancy of the subject matter. Focus groups and advisory board meetings are excellent tools to gather data about the curriculum and topics for future coverage. Faculty should evaluate course syllabi each year to ensure all courses are up to date. It is also a good idea, especially for MPA directors, to view faculty course evaluations and address deficiencies and highlight innovation and excellence.

Finally, brainstorming is always a good exercise (Center for New Designs in Learning & Scholarship, 2019). Saint-Germain, Ostrowski, and Dede (2000) discuss the use of e-mail Delphi to ascertain the skills and knowledge employers want in MPA graduates. During these exercises, be sure to listen to junior faculty. They are much more current with the literature and the state of the field than many seasoned faculty members.

As part of the strategic planning process, programs will ensure the relevancy and currency of its curriculum and the individual courses. Stakeholders (Hornbein & King, 2012; Peters, 2009; Saint-Germain et al., 2000), including students (Larson, Wilson, & Chung, 2003), should be involved in the process to ensure relevancy and the needs are met by the program. Courses should be added and deleted as necessary based on the mission and needs of the stakeholders. Further, courses should be updated often to make sure materials and readings are still relevant and current.

TABLE 9.4 Steps for Curriculum Change and Planning

Mission
- Are the courses relevant to the mission?
- Has the mission changed? If so, has the curriculum changed to reflect the changes in the new mission statement?

Relevancy and Needs
- Are the courses and course content still relevant?
- Are the curriculum and courses up to date and constantly updated to reflect changes in the literature?
- What are the desired results?

The Role of Assessment
- Student learning
- Teaching methods and course content
- Appropriate tools for measuring learning are in place
- Create assignments that introduce, practice, and master concepts and learning objectives
- Use direct measures to assess learning
- Use rubrics

Gather and Analyze Data
- Surveys
  - New students, graduating students, alumni, stakeholders, employers
- Advisory boards
- Focus groups
- Course syllabi
- Course evaluations
- Current literature
- Current events
- Listen

Brainstorm
- Faculty meetings
- Advisory board meetings
- Student meetings
- Capstone seminars

Helpful Web Resources
- Center for New Designs in Learning and Scholarship (CNDLS): https://cndls.georgetown.edu/support/assessment/eightsteps/
- DQP Assignment Library: www.assignmentlibrary.org/
- The Atlas of Public Policy and Management: www.atlas101.ca/pm/about/

Sources: CNDLS (2019), NASPAA (2019c), and Shenoy (2016).

The following vignette provides an example of how a hypothetical MPA program made appropriate changes to its curriculum.

The faculty was meeting with its advisory board; the discussion turned to the currency of the curriculum. A city manager mentioned that she would like to see more emphasis placed on program management either as a stand-alone course or as components of other courses. The discussion began to focus on the need of graduates who are able to manage programs that might last multiple years involving many departments and outside contractors. Advisory board members agreed that graduates should be able to plan, oversee program implementation, prepare performance measures, evaluate those measures, and make program decisions based on the analyzed evidence.

Following the advisory board meeting, the faculty began a series of discussions on whether or not their program would benefit from a new course in program management or should incorporate project management into various courses. It was decided to contact alumni and more employers to gather additional data. Once data were gathered the faculty decided to move forward; they then mapped program management back to the appropriate universal competencies and student learning objectives. Course syllabi were adjusted and course learning objectives related to program management were formulated. The faculty then brainstormed on appropriate assignments, projects, and other tools that could be used to assess student program management learning.

After offering the course/module on program management, as part of the assessment process, the faculty then "closed the loop" and discussed how incorporating program management course/modules met the goals and objectives of the program's mission. Faculty then made necessary adjustments to help meet the program goals and objectives (see Chapter 10 on assessment, this volume).

Each MPA/MPP program needs to include evaluation standards and assessment practices that demonstrate student learning and that their program is fulfilling its missions. Programs need "consistent evaluation standards, or grading rubrics" (Rivenbark & Jacobson, 2014, p. 188).

Programs can also implement assessment mechanisms that require input from stakeholders and students (Getha-Taylor, Hummert, Nalbandian, & Silvia, 2013). Any assessment process needs to provide feedback to programs so programs can evolve (Aristigueta & Gomes, 2006; Durant, 2002). Collection of data is an important part of the assessment process and does not need to be difficult or burdensome. Chapter 10 provides more details on assessment and how to best gather and analyze assessment data.

The Atlas of Public Management website is an excellent resource where program heads, directors, and deans who are designing or refining MPA/MPA curricula should begin. The Atlas was funded by the Canada School of Public Service and the Social Sciences and Humanities Research Council. Although the websites were created and maintained by a Canadian university, the sites were designed with the 2009 NASPAA standards in mind (SPPG, 2019).

As part of the Atlas project, Clark and Pal (2014) and Clark, Eisen, and Pal (2014) synthesized NASPAA standards along with United Nations Department of Economic and Social Affairs/International Association of Schools and Institutes of Administration (UNDESA/IASIA) accreditation standards and arrived at four broad course domains for MPA and MPP programs. The domains include general preparation courses that include "Tools and Skills" and "Institutions and Context." Specific practice domains include management functions and policy sectors (see Tables 9.5 and 9.6). MPP programs will generally draw most of their course components from the analysis and skills, institutions and context, and policy sectors domains while MPA programs will draw heavily on tools and skills, institutions and context, and management functions domains. The Atlas also has ready-made curricula available for MPA and MPP programs. The Atlas links to sample syllabi, assessment tools, and rubrics (SPPG, 2019).

In Tables 9.5 and 9.6, the General Preparation and Specific Preparation domains show a number of learning concepts that are tied back to NASPAA's universal competencies. For example, when looking for subject matter appropriate to the first competency, "to lead and manage in public governance," one notes that concepts surrounding policy analysis and contemporary governance, implementation and policy, models and policymaking, and organizational behavior are all appropriate concepts that programs can cover in their courses that link back to the first universal competency. The tables include many entries for the other universal competencies. If one accesses the website, the list is more comprehensive. Links are available to access sample syllabi, assignments, test questions, assessment mechanisms, and other web resources needed to build and enhance MPA and MPP curricula. It is important for programs when designing curricula and courses to match knowledge, skills, and learning objectives from the course to program learning objectives and goals, which in turn are to be linked back to NASPAA's universal competencies and the program's mission (see Figure 9.1).

Suggested Topics Based on Missions

Many reading this chapter will be interested in what types of courses are found in MPA programs and how those courses align with the universal competencies. Ultimately, the courses offered by programs are program decisions. Courses need to be connected back to the needs of the community, university, college, and individual program missions. NASPAA provides a lot of leeway to programs in designing curricula and courses. Programs do, however, need to tie their curriculum back to the NASPAA universal competencies (Rivenbark & Jacobson, 2014).

Revising mission statements is part of the strategic planning process. NASPAA requires that MPA and MPP programs be managed strategically (COPRA, 2014) (see Chapter 5 of this volume for more details on strategic planning). As part of that process NASPAA requires programs to have a mission statement, performance expectations, and program evaluation. The strategic

TABLE 9.5 Atlas Framework for Portraying Curricular Content for General Preparation Courses*

Tools and Skills

Institutions and Context

Policy and Management Analysis

- Policy Analysis and Contemporary Governance (1)
- Implementation and Policy (1)
- Models and Policymaking (1)
- Program Evaluation (3)
- Policy Design and Instrument Choice (3)
- Rules versus Discretion (2)
- Recent Trends from Comparative Public Administration (1)
- The Meaning of Strategy in Public Management (3)
- Performance Information as a Management Tool (3)
- Organizational Performance and Management Reform (2)
- Organization Behavior (1)
- The Shift to Public Governance (2)
- The Role of Leadership in Strategy and Implementation (3)
- Managing Conflict (1)
- Working in Teams and Motivation (1)
- Implementing Through Markets (1)
- Implementing with Partners (2)

Economic Analysis

- Theory of the Firm (3)
- Consumer Theory (3)
- Externalities (2)
- Public Goods and Commons Problems (3)
- Market Failure and Optimal Intervention (3)
- Monopoly, Oligopoly, and Cournot Competition (3)
- Asymmetric Information and Signaling (3)
- Game Theory (3)
- Taxes and Lump-Sum Transfers (3)
- Trade (3)
- Welfare Economics and Welfare Policy (4)
- Supply and Demand (3)

Communication Skills

- Effective Rhetoric and Generating Emotional Impact (5)
- Writing Memos, E-Mails, and Internal Documents (5)
- Writing Op-Eds, Blogs, and Public Documents (5)

Democratic Institutions and Policy Process

- The Political Context of Policy Making (2)
- The Policy Cycle (2)
- Federalism (2)
- Political and Administrative Responsibilities (3)
- The International Context of Domestic Institutions
- Indigenous Rights and Institutions
- Executive Leadership in Government
- Westminster Parliamentary Systems (2)
- Courts and Judicial Review (4)
- Public and Para-Public Institutions (4)
- Bureaucracy and the Formation of Public Policy (2)
- Institutional Designs and Paths (4)
- New Public Management (4)

Ethics, Rights, and Accountability

- Ethics in Public Management (4)
- Implementation and Accountability (2)
- Means and Ends – The Problem of Dirty Hands (4)
- Liberty and its Limits: Speech, Harm, Paternalism, and Moralism (3)
- Lying, Deception, Privacy, and Transparency (4)
- Compromise and Disagreement (4)

Socioeconomic and Political Context

- Race, Gender, and Other Group Identities (1)
- Indigenous Peoples (5)
- The Immigrant Society (5)
- Income Inequality (2)
- Changing Family Structures: Gender, Work, Inequality, and Poverty (2)
- Education, Labor Markets, and Low-Skilled Workers (2)

- Multi-Level Governance (1)

Quantitative Methods
- Descriptive Statistics (3)
- Looking at Data (3)
- Probability Concepts (3)
- Sampling (3)
- Confidence Intervals and Hypothesis Testing (3)
- Simple Regression (3)
- Multivariate Analysis (3)
- Omitted Variable Bias (3)
- Randomized Trials (3)
- Research Design (3)
- Ethical Issues in Research (3)
- Panel Data Fix Effects and Instrumental Variables (3)

Analytic Methods
- Decision Analysis (3)
- Agency Theory (3)
- Cost-Benefit Analysis (3)
- Project Management (1)
- Risk Management (1)
- Impact of Bias Under Decision-Making and Insights from Behavioral Economics (3)

Leadership Skills
- Operational skills (5)
- Networking (5)
- Acting Like a Professional (5)
- Leadership in Public, Nonprofit, and Private Organizations (1)
- How Values Differ: Psychological Types and Moral Foundations (5)
- Setting Goals and Strategy (3)
- Identifying Resources for Leading Change (2)
- Mobilizing Potential Stakeholders (5)
- Negotiation (5)

- Public Opinion, Ideas, and Policy Frames (1)
- Political Parties and Elections (4)
- Representation and Accountability (3)
- Media, Framing, and Agenda Setting (1)
- Actors, Interests, and Lobbying (2)

Global Context
- The Global Context (2)
- National Interest (2)
- Federal, Unitary, and Hybrid States (2)

Source: Adapted from Clark et al. (2015).

Note
* NASPAA Universal Competency number in parentheses.

TABLE 9.6 Atlas Framework for Portraying Curricular Content for Specific Preparation Courses*

Management Functions	Policy Structures	
Public Financial Management • Financial Statements and Accounting Concepts (2) • Planning and Budgeting (2) • Costing and Forecasting (2) • Capital Budgeting (2) • Management Control: Risk-Based Approach (3) • Audit and Oversight in Managing Public Money (1) **Evaluations and Performance Management** • Evaluation Purposes, Types, and Questions (2) • Fundamental Identification Program: Causality, Counterfactual Responses, Heterogeneity, Selection (2) • Assessing the Confounding Effects of Unobserved Factors (2) • Sensitivity Analysis (3) • Data Collection Strategies (3) • Performance Measurement and Performance Management (3)	**Macroeconomic Policy** • Understanding a Nation's Fiscal Architecture: Building Appropriate Revenue and Expenditure Systems (3) • Government Deficits, Government Debt, and Fiscal Consolidation (4) • Fiscal Stabilization Policy (3) • Monetary Policy (3) **International Development** **Public Finance and Social Policy** **Health** **Education**	**Employment, Labor, and Immigration** **Cities, Urban and Regional Development** **Environment and Sustainability** • Defining Environmental Issues and Policy problems (4) • Environmental Risks and Hazards (4) • Regulatory Choices in Environmental Policy (4) **Agriculture** **Science, Technology, and Innovation** **Industry, Trade, and Investment** **Energy, Transport, and Infrastructure** **Defense, Security, and Foreign Relations** **Policing and Justice Administration** **Arts and Culture** **Financial Markets** **Other Policy Sectors**
Human Resource Management • Managing People: Performance, Recruitment, Renewal (1) • Evaluating Talent (3) • Workplace Issues and Labor Relations (5) • Civil Service Systems (4) • Employment Law and Legal Issues (1) **Information and Technology Management** • IT in the Public Sector: Costs and Challenges (1) • Online Service Delivery (1) • Open Government (1) **Regulatory Policy and Management** **Local Government Management** **Nonprofit Management and Advocacy**		

Source: Adapted from Clark et al. (2015).

Note
* NASPAA Universal Competency number in parentheses.

planning process is dynamic and evolves over the years. Generally, programs more formally revisit their mission statements during their self-study year. During this time programs should bring work with faculty, students, advisory boards, and stakeholders. They conduct SWOT analyses to get a better idea of their strengths, weakness, opportunities, and threats. Programs should also pay close attention to opportunities that surround them.

After conducting a SWOT analysis and gathering data from various sources, programs should revisit their mission to determine what changes and updates, if any, need to be made. Once changes are made, programs will need to ensure the curriculum meets the revised mission objectives.

Calls for competency-based curricula began years ago (Tompkins, Laslovich, & Greene, 1996). The literature is rife with articles and suggestions for courses and concepts that should be covered in contemporary MPA programs. Even with the move to competency-based curricula there is still a tendency for scholars to suggest that specific courses, and to a lesser extent concepts, be required in MPA/MPP programs rather than courses that incorporate universal competencies. Some scholars call for more leadership-oriented courses (Crosby & Bryson, 2005; Fairholm, 2006; Haupt, Kapucu, & Hu, 2017). Others suggest that programs need courses that emphasize important concepts such as diversity (Beaty & Davis, 2012; Bernotavicz, 1997; Hatch, 2018; Johnson & Rivera, 2007; Riley & Johansen, 2019; Rubaii, 2016; Ryan, 2012; White, 2004; Wyatt-Nichol & Antwi-Boasiako, 2008), social equity (Alvez & Timney, 2008; McCandless & Larson, 2018; Rosenbloom, 2005; Svara & Brunet, 2005), and cultural competencies (Lopez-Littleton & Blessett, 2015).

Many have expressed the need to better integrate public policy and analytic skills in the curriculum (Aristigueta & Raffel, 2001; Haupt et al., 2017; Tankha & Gasper, 2010). Some suggest that courses should include rule of law and constitutional issues (Newbold, 2011), religion/spirituality (Leland & Denhardt, 2005), comparative and global contexts (Haruna & Kannae, 2013; Purón-Cid, 2019; Rauhaus & Sakiev, 2018; Yu, Rubin, & Wu, 2012), sustainability practices (Rangarajan & Joshi, 2019), and ethics (Edlins & Dolamore, 2018; Jurkiewicz & Nichols, 2002; Molina & McKeown, 2012; Svara & Baizhanov, 2019).

There are suggestions that programs should cover nonprofit, nongovernmental organizations, and social entrepreneurship topics (Appe & Barragán, 2013; Denison & Kim, 2018; Gelles, 2016; Saidel & Smith, 2015; Vaughan & Arsneault, 2015; Wiley & Berry, 2015). Other scholars see the need for more instruction in areas such as emergency management (Haupt & Knox, 2018; Reddy, 2000), information technology, management, and security (Christian & Davis, 2016; Ganapati & Reddick, 2016; Mauldin, 2016; Mergel, 2016; Ni & Chen, 2016; Purón-Cid, 2017).

There have been calls for experiential learning that include internship experiences (Reinagel & Gerlach, 2015), service learning (Bushouse & Morrison, 2001; Dicke, Dowden, & Torres, 2004; Reinke, 2003; Witesman, 2012), and problem-based learning (Goodman, 2008). Adding to that, capstone courses and experiences have become popular and have been adopted by many programs (Fenger & Homburg, 2011; Roberts & Pavlak, 2002).

The important thing when designing curricula is not to get lost in the "courses" but rather to focus on the subject matter that points back to the universal competencies and the program's mission in a systematic fashion. For example, an MPP program that focus on public policy evaluation and analysis might not include a specific course on human resource or information management, whereas an MPA program that focuses on local government management may include courses in human resource management, information management, program management, and local government management. As mentioned above, The Atlas provides a long list of courses and subjects that point back to each of NASPAA's competencies.

As MPA directors and faculty fine-tune their programs they may come across readings or a survey of local government mangers that finds an emphasis on continuing to build leadership and management skills for MPA students (Haupt et al., 2017). They use that evidence to make the appropriate changes to their programs.

Another option for programs when designing courses and curricula is to think about marketable skills as discussed above. What marketable skills can a student or graduate include on their resume from the program or a particular course? Many sources are available to programs and instructors to supplement classroom learning. Third parties such as LinkedIn Learning, FEMA's Emergency Management Institute, TRAIN, and the Society for Human Resource Management have readily available sources to supplement classroom learning.

Many university libraries partner with LinkedIn Learning to provide learning courses for students, staff, and faculty at no extra costs (LinkedIn, 2019). Those short courses provide marketable skills that can be included on resumes for job applications. Thousands of courses are available to enhance business or managerial skills, creativity skills, and technology skills. Once a learning module is completed it is attached to the student's LinkedIn profile as a marketable skill. By taking advantage of these training modules faculty can assign students to complete training modules as part of classroom assignments. For example, faculty who teach human resource management can assign students to complete several relevant training modules as an assignment. There are courses available in Compensation and Benefits, HR Administration, HR Software, HR Strategy, Hiring and Interviewing, and Learning and Development. Statistics and methods courses can assign short courses in SQL, Big Data, Analytics, SPSS, STATA, SAS, etc. Somebody teaching an emergency management course can assign students to complete FEMA certification courses. Completion of these courses provides evidence of learning for assessment purposes.

Conclusion

In conclusion, in 2009 NASPAA moved from an input-based accreditation system to a competency-based accreditation system. Programs were required to tie their mission-based curricula back to five universal competencies. More important, programs have to demonstrate student learning and a mastery of skills obtained by the time students graduate from an MPA program. This chapter has discussed Bloom's Taxonomy in the importance a designing curricula and courses that move along the continuum to better enhance student learning. Also provided in this chapter are resources that programs can access to help with designing their curriculum. Especially helpful is the Atlas Public Management website. Faculty can use the website to find course ideas, subject matter, cases studies, assignments, and learning objectives that point back to NASPAA's universal competencies.

Notes

1. The term "public affairs" is used to include public administration, public affairs, and public policy programs since all three types of programs are accredited by NASPAA. "MPA" is used generically to include all three types of programs.
2. The Atlas of Public Management can be accessed online by going to www.atlas101. ca/pm/about/.

References

Alvez, J. D. S. & Timney, M. (2008). Human rights theory as a means for incorporating social equity into the public administration curriculum. *Journal of Public Affairs Education, 14*(1), 51–66.

Anderson, L. W., Krathwohl, D. R., & Bloom, B. S. (2001). *A taxonomy for learning, teaching, and assessing: A revision of Bloom's Taxonomy of educational objectives.* New York: Longman.

Appe, S. & Barragán, D. (2013). Strategies outside the formal classroom: Nonprofit management education in transparency and accountability. *Journal of Public Affairs Education, 19*(4), 591–614.

Aristigueta, M. & Gomes, K. M. (2006). Assessing performance in NASPAA graduate programs. *Journal of Public Affairs Education, 12*(1), 1–18.

Aristigueta, M. P. & Raffel, J. A. (2001). Teaching techniques of analysis in the MPA curriculum: Research methods, management Science, and "the third path." *Journal of Public Affairs Education, 7*(3), 161–169.

Armstrong, P. (2016). *Bloom's Taxonomy.* Nashville, TN: Vanderbilt University Center for Teaching.

Beaty, L. & Davis, T. J. (2012). Gender disparity in professional city management: Making the case for enhancing leadership curriculum. *Journal of Public Affairs Education, 18*(4), 617–632.

Bernotavicz, F. (1997). A diversity curriculum: Integrating attitudes, issues, and applications. *Journal of Public Administration Education, 3*(3), 345–360.

Bloom, B. S. (1956). *Taxonomy of educational objectives.* New York: D. McKay Co., Inc.

Bushouse, B. & Morrison, S. (2001). Applying service learning in the Master of Public Affairs programs. *Journal of Public Affairs Education*, 7(1), 9–17.

Center for New Designs in Learning & Scholarship (2019). Eight steps to curricular change. *Georgetown University*. Retrieved August 6, 2019 from https://cndls.georgetown.edu/support/assessment/eightsteps/.

Christian, P. C. & Davis, T. J. (2016). Revisiting the information technology skills gap in Master of Public Administration programs. *Journal of Public Affairs Education*, 22(2), 161–174.

Clark, I. D. & Pal, L. A. (2014, April). *The new world standards in public management pedagogy: Comparing universal accreditation competencies with the actual content of MPP and MPA programs*. Paper presented at the annual meeting of the International Research Society for Public Management, Ottawa, Canada.

Clark, I. D., Eisen, B., & Pal, L. A. (2014, March). *What are the core curricular components of master's-level public management education and how is learning within them assessed?* Paper presented at the annual meeting of the Canadian Association for Programs in Public Administration Research Conference, Kingston, Canada.

Clark, I. D., Eisen, D., Lennon, M. C., & Pal, L. A. (2015, May). *Mapping the topics and learning outcomes of a core curriculum for MPP and MPA programs*. Paper presented at the annual meeting of the Canadian Association for Programs in Public Administration Research Conference, Toronto, Canada.

Commission on Peer Review and Accreditation (2014). *NASPAA standards*. Washington, DC: Network of Schools of Public Policy, Affairs and Administration.

Crosby, B. C. & Bryson, J. M. (2005). Challenges of introducing leadership into the public affairs curriculum: The case of the Humphrey Institute. *Journal of Public Affairs Education*, 11(3), 193–205.

Denison, D. V. & Kim, S. (2018). Linking practice and classroom: Nonprofit financial management curricula in MPA and MPP programs. *Journal of Public Affairs Education*. https://doi.org/10.1080/15236803.2018.1443690.

Dicke, L., Dowden, S., & Torres, J. (2004). Successful service learning: A matter of ideology. *Journal of Public Affairs Education*, 10(3), 199–208.

Dunning, P. T. (2014). Developing a competency-based assessment approach for student learning. *Journal of Public Affairs Education*, 32(1), 55–67.

Durant, R. F. (2002). Toward becoming a learning organization: Outcomes assessment, NASPAA accreditation, and mission-based capstone courses. *Journal of Public Affairs Education*, 8(3), 193–208.

Edlins, M. & Dolamore, S. (2018). Ready to serve the public? The role of empathy in public service education programs. *Journal of Public Affairs Education*, 24(3), 300–320.

Fairholm, M. R. (2006). Leadership theory and practice in the MPA curriculum: Reasons and methods. *Journal of Public Affairs Education*, 12(3), 335–346.

Fenger, M. & Homburg, V. (2011). The studio approach in public administration teaching: Bringing coherence and practice into the curriculum. *Journal of Public Affairs Education*, 17(3), 385–405.

Ganapati, S. & Reddick, C. G. (2016). An Ostrich burying its head in the sand? The 2009 NASPAA standards and scope of information technology and E-Government curricula. *Journal of Public Affairs Education*, 22(2), 267–286.

Gelles, E. (2016). Perhaps easier said than done: Is there a downside to integrating nonprofit substance into the MPA core curriculum? *Journal of Public Affairs Education*, 22(3), 415–434.

Getha-Taylor, H., Hummert, R., Nalbandian, J., & Silvia, C. (2013). Competency model design and assessment: Findings and future directions. *Journal of Public Affairs Education*, *19*(1), 141–171.

Goodman, D. (2008). Problem-based learning in the MPA curriculum. *Journal of Public Affairs Education*, *14*(2), 253–270.

Haruna, P. F. & Kannae, L. A. (2013). Connecting good governance principles to the public affairs curriculum: The case of Ghana Institute of Management and Public Administration. *Journal of Public Affairs Education*, *19*(3), 493–514.

Haupt, B. & Knox, C. (2018). Measuring cultural competence in emergency management and homeland security higher education programs. *Journal of Public Affairs Education*, *24*(4), 538–556.

Haupt, B., Kapucu, N., & Hu, Q. (2017). Core competencies in Master of Public Administration programs: Perspectives from local government managers. *Journal of Public Affairs Education*, *23*(1), 611–624.

Hatch, M. E. (2018). Quiet voices: Misalignment of the three Cs in public administration curriculum. *Journal of Public Affairs Education*, *24*(2), 152–172.

Hornbein, R. & King, C. S. (2012). Should we be teaching public participation? Student responses and MPA program practices. *Journal of Public Affairs Education*, *18*(4), 717–737.

Johnson, R. G. & Rivera, M. A. (2007). Refocusing graduate public affairs education: A need for diversity competencies in human resource management. *Journal of Public Affairs Education*, *13*(1), 15–27.

Jurkiewicz, C. L. & Nichols, K. L. (2002). Ethics education in the MPA curriculum: What difference does it make? *Journal of Public Affairs Education*, *8*(2), 103–114.

Larson, R. S., Wilson, M. I., & Chung, D. (2003). Curricular content for nonprofit management programs: The student perspective. *Journal of Public Affairs Education*, *9*(3), 169–180.

Leland, P. J. & Denhardt, K. G. (2005). Incorporating spirituality into the MPA curriculum: Framing the discussion. *Journal of Public Affairs Education*, *11*(2), 121–131.

LinkedIn (2019). LinkedIn Learning. Retrieved from April 19, 2019 on www.linkedin.com/learning.

Lopez-Littleton, V. & Blessett, B. (2015). A framework for integrating cultural competency into the curriculum of public administration programs. *Journal of Public Affairs Education*, *21*(4), 557–574.

Maslow, A. (1943). A theory of human motivation. *Psychological Review*, *50*(4), 370–396.

Mauldin, M. D. (2016). No MPA left behind: A review of information technology in the Master of Public Administration curriculum. *Journal of Public Affairs Education*, *22*(2), 187–192.

McCandless, S. & Larson, S. J. (2018). Prioritizing social equity in MPA curricula: A cross-program analysis and a case study. *Journal of Public Affairs Education*, *24*(3), 361–379.

Mergel, I. (2016). Big data in public affairs education. *Journal of Public Affairs Education*, *22*(2), 231–248.

Molina, A. D. & McKeown, C. L. (2012). The heart of the profession: Understanding public service values. *Journal of Public Affairs Education*, *18*(2), 375–396.

Network of Schools of Public Policy, Affairs, and Administration (2019a). *2019–2020 roster of accredited programs*. Retrieved October 1, 2019 from www.naspaa.org/sites/default/files/docs/2019-10/Annual%20Roster%20of%20Accredited%20Programs%2010.01.2019.pdf.

Network of Schools of Public Policy, Affairs, and Administration (2019b). *Accreditation.* Retrieved April 4, 2019 from www.naspaa.org/accreditation.

Network of Schools of Public Policy, Affairs, and Administration (2019c). *Standards and guidance.* Retrieved August 8, 2019 from www.naspaa.org/accreditation/standards-and-guidance.

Newbold, S. (2011). No time like the present: Making rule of law and constitutional competence the theoretical and practical foundation for public administration graduate education curriculum. *Journal of Public Affairs Education, 17*(4), 465–481.

Ni, A. Y. & Chen, Y. C. (2016). A conceptual model of information technology competence for public managers: Designing relevant MPA curricula for effective public service. *Journal of Public Affairs Education, 22*(2), 193–212.

Peters, R. A. (2009). Using focus groups and stakeholder surveys to revise the MPA curriculum. *Journal of Public Affairs Education, 15*(1), 1–16.

Purón-Cid, G. (2017). Information technology strategy and management curricula in public administration education in Latin America. *Journal of Public Affairs Education, 23*(3), 903–924.

Purón-Cid, G. (2019). A comparative analysis of public affairs master's programs in the United States and the Latin American region. *Journal of Public Affairs Education, 25*(4), 495–523.

Rangarajan, N. & Joshi, S. (2019). Sustainability education in public administration and policy: A multi-method study of NASPAA accredited programs. *Journal of Public Affairs Education, 25*(3), 343–363.

Rauhaus, B. M. & Sakiev, A. (2018). A comparative analysis of public administration education in the United States and post-Soviet Central Asia. *Journal of Public Affairs Education, 24*(1), 27–42.

Reddy, S. D. (2000). Introducing an emergency management curriculum into public affairs. *Journal of Public Affairs Education, 6*(3), 183–192.

Reinagel, T. P. & Gerlach, J. D. (2015). Internships as academic exercise: an assessment of MPA curriculum models. *Journal of Public Affairs Education, 21*(1), 71–82.

Reinke, S. J. (2003). Making a difference: Does service-learning promote civil engagement in MPA students? *Journal of Public Affairs Education, 9*(2): 129–138.

Riley, L. & Johansen, M. (2019). Creating valuable indigenous learning environments. *Journal of Public Affairs Education, 25*(3), 387–411.

Rivenbark, W. C. & Jacobson, W. S. (2014). Three principles of competency-based learning: Mission, mission, mission. *Journal of Public Affairs Education, 20*(2), 181–192.

Roberts, G. E. & Pavlak, T. (2002). The design and implementation of an integrated values-and competency-based MPA core curriculum. *Journal of Public Affairs Education, 8*(2), 115–129.

Rosenbloom, D. (2005). Taking social equity seriously in MPA education. *Journal of Public Affairs Education, 11*(3), 247–252.

Rubaii, N. (2016). Bringing the 21st-century governance paradigm to public affairs education: Reimagining how we teach what we teach. *Journal of Public Affairs Education, 22*(4), 467–482.

Ryan, S. E. (2012). Assessing diversity in public affairs curricula: A multi-methodological model for student-led programmatic self-study. *Journal of Public Affairs Education, 18*(4), 757–774.

Saidel, J. R. & Smith, S. R. (2015). Nonprofit management education in schools with public affairs curricula: an analysis of the trend toward curriculum integration. *Journal of Public Affairs Education, 21*(3), 337–348.

Saint-Germain, M. A., Ostrowski, J. W., & Dede, M. J. (2000). Oracles in the ether: Using and e-mail Delphi to revise and MPA curriculum. *Journal of Public Affairs Education, 6*(3), 161–172.

School of Public Policy and Governance (2019). *The Atlas of Public Management: Concepts, topics, and courses taught in leading MPP and MPA programs.* Retrieved August 6, 2019 from www.atlas101.ca/pm/.

Shabatu, J. (2018). Using Bloom's Taxonomy to write effective learning objectives. University of Arkansas. Retrieved March 19, 2018 from https://tips.uark.edu/using-blooms-taxonomy/.

Shenoy, G. (2016). Assessing student learning outcomes. *University of Texas at Dallas.* Retrieved August 6, 2019 from https://dox.utdallas.edu/presentation1018.

Svara, J. H. & Baizhanov, S. (2019). Public service values in NASPAA programs: Identification, integration, and activation. *Journal of Public Affairs Education, 25*(1), 73–92.

Svara, J. H. & Brunet, J. R. (2005). Social equity is a pillar of public administration. *Journal of Public Affairs Education, 11*(3), 253–258.

Tankha, S. & Gasper, D. (2010). Trees and water: Mainstreaming environment in the graduate policy analysis curriculum. *Journal of Public Affairs Education, 16*(4), 621–644.

Texas Higher Education Coordinating Board (2015). *Texas higher education strategic plan: 2015–2030.* Retrieved March 28, 2019 from www.thecb.state.tx.us/reports/PDF/9306.PDF?CFID=57485581&CFTOKEN=60423954.

Tompkins, J., Laslovich, M. J., & Greene, J. D. (1996). Developing a competency-based MPA curriculum. *Journal of Public Administration Education, 2*(2), 117–130.

Vaughan, S. K. & Arsneault, S. (2015). A core issue: The inseparable relationship between nonprofits and public policy. *Journal of Public Affairs Education, 21*(3), 349–366.

White, S. (2004). Multicultural MPA curriculum: Are we preparing culturally competent public administrators? *Journal of Public Affairs Education, 10*(2), 111–123.

Wiley, K. K. & Berry, F. S. (2015). Teaching social entrepreneurship in public affairs programs: A review of social entrepreneurship courses in the top 30 US public administration and affairs programs. *Journal of Public Affairs Education, 21*(3), 381–400.

Witesman, E. M. (2012). Faculty research-driven vs. community-driven experiential learning in the quantitative public administration curriculum. *Journal of Public Affairs Education, 18*(4), 775–796.

Wyatt-Nichol, H. & Antwi-Boasiako, K. B. (2008). Diversity across the curriculum: Perceptions and practices. *Journal of Public Affairs Education, 14*(1), 79–90.

Yu, W., Rubin, M., & Wu, W. (2012). An Executive MPA program for China: Lessons from the field. *Journal of Public Affairs Education, 18*(3), 545–564.

10

FUNDAMENTALS OF PROGRAM ASSESSMENT

Kathleen Hale

Assessment is now a well-established dimension of academic program development across the nation (Deardorff & Folger, 2005; Fox & Keeter, 1996; Mitchell & Manzo, 2018; Young, 2012). Graduate programs in public administration, public affairs, and public policy are no exception. In particular, programs accredited by the Network of Schools of Public Policy, Affairs, and Administration (NASPAA) – or which seek to become accredited – assess the ability of their programs to establish mastery of specific knowledge, skills and abilities germane to public service in general and, in some cases, with respect to specific specializations (Meek, 2018).

At its core, assessment is a systematic approach to understanding whether our students are learning what we want them to learn, and whether our programs are designed to support that learning. Assessment is the process of gathering systematic evidence to inform decisions about programs and student learning. Suskie (2018, p. 11) describes assessment as "cousin to traditional empirical research," which suggests that the process should be rather more inherently familiar to educators than mysterious. Although we don't use assessment to test hypotheses, we conduct it as a method of improving our programs and our execution of curricula.

At the outset, it is important to note that assessments of NASPAA programs will vary in design and approach, as all programs are uniquely constructed around program-specific missions. Although assessment documents and reports may look different, they are all designed to answer the same questions: Is the program accomplishing what it intends to accomplish? Are improvements or changes needed? How can those be accomplished?

This chapter begins with a brief summary of the evolution of assessment in higher education. The chapter next organizes the assessment process into four major stages of development including outcomes, curriculum, methodology, and results. These assessment stages are used to frame assessment in universal terms and as a specific adaptation to the NASPAA protocol. This dual focus recognizes that many programs must consider how to address the particulars of their institution's assessment culture as well as NASPAA's requirements (Bishu, Guy, & Heckler, 2019; Riley & Johansen, 2019). This dual focus also reflects the normative view that the success of assessment plans depends on an institutional culture of assessment in which the plan is embedded in institutional content; otherwise, the effort expended may occur only in response to external mandates and may therefore fail to achieve sustainable legitimacy (Deardorff & Folger, 2005; National Institute for Learning Outcomes Assessment, 2016; Suskie, 2018).

Chapter sections illustrate how these stages can be used to develop an assessment plan for any NASPAA-accredited program.[1] A few examples are also provided to illustrate how assessment can be applied to a specialized graduate certificate in public service that is a part of an MPA program. Examples contain templates that can be used to develop an assessment program that will serve multiple audiences and constituencies. Throughout, the terminology that is used is directed at the program level; it is important to note that assessment can be (and is) conducted at any organizational level. The principles that follow apply equally to assessment conducted at different subunit levels including the course level and the experiential level. The terminology about each stage may vary; however, the conceptual path follows these stages.[2]

Putting Assessment in Context

Assessment in higher education is not new. In fact, the seeds of today's articulated approach to assessment are rooted in observations of the imperiled status of American higher education as early as the 1980s. *A Nation at Risk*, issued by President Ronald Reagan's National Commission on Excellence in Education in 1983, argued that American higher education lagged behind the world in the face of rapidly changing technology and new conceptualizations of literacy including competence in the workplace (National Commission on Excellence in Education, 1983). Fast-forward 25 years. The Department of Education reported that, although improvements had been made, significant challenges persisted in demonstrating the accountability of higher education. The Department of Education issued a call for evaluating the ways in which higher education was accomplishing the mission of educating students to meet new demands for global and technological literacy, and to improve the standing of American programs on the world stage (Department of Education, 2006). Public and private constituencies responded, identifying the divergent distribution of various skills and forms of literacy across the American landscape in the face of a growing and more diverse population, and gaps between skills and literacy and the needs of the private sector in a changing world economy (e.g., Baer, Cook, & Baldi, 2006; Business Roundtable, 2005; Committee on Science, Engineering, and Public Policy, 2007; Kirsch, Braun, Kendaro, & Sum, 2007; UNESCO Institute for Statistics, 2009). The evolution of the assessment landscape in American higher education was mapped (e.g., Dwyer, Millett, & Payne, 2006; Ewell, 2006; Millett, Stickler, Dwyer, & Payne, 2007; Millett, Payne, Dwyer, Stickler, & Alexiou, 2008), and literature now identifies processes for assessment plan development (e.g., National Institute for Learning Culture Assessment, 2016; Suskie, 2018).

Before beginning with the specifics, it is important to note that assessment is not an end in and of itself. Rather, it is a method of reflection that supports continuous program improvement. Assessment is tied always to the program mission, curriculum, and course offerings. Within the NASPAA context, graduate programs in public administration, public affairs, and public policy exercise substantial determining influence over these program elements, which are essentially the heart of the program. Typically, program assessment also occurs within the broader context of a department or school. This environment incudes a range of stakeholders outside the program who may have an interest in the results of assessment although they will not be directly involved in the faculty effort to develop the assessment plan or to implement its steps. Perhaps more fundamental, all programs face resource constraints that limit the number of faculty that can be hired, and their rank as tenured, tenure-earning or neither, the number of courses that can be offered, and the frequency of course rotations. More broadly, graduate programs in public administration, public affairs, or public policy may be expected to fill a particular niche within the larger department. Programs housed within a larger unit (e.g., a department of political science) may need to stretch to find common ground on a mission that reaches across the department and satisfies multiple stakeholders.

Assessment is also different to grading, although grades may be part of an assessment plan. In summarizing the reports of academic professional associations, Suskie (2018) notes that grades provide information on student performance on particular assignments and in particular courses but do not provide evidence of particular knowledge or skills. Grades also reflect student performance in areas not directly tied to learning outcomes (e.g., attendance, timeliness, and participation when communication is not a specific course goal). This information may not reflect student ability in cross-cutting areas such as critical thinking or writing. Course grades also do not reflect the range of learning experiences that higher education provides to students including co-curricular experiences with community and organizations, and through internships and service projects. Assessment provides a vehicle for synthesizing course content across a program, and also for synthesizing faculty grading approaches and interpretations of student performance across courses.

The discussion in this chapter begins with the assumption that a graduate program has identified and specified its mission. Although there are no universal, commonly used measures to determine effectiveness of American higher education defined in terms of student learning (Dwyer et al., 2006), it is possible to assess graduate program effectiveness through articulated student learning outcomes linked to the mission of the graduate program. The NASPAA accreditation approach is grounded in this program mission. Typically, a program mission is relatively stable for a period of time. That said, assessment is a method of continuous improvement and should be used to identify areas of strength in the curriculum, and areas that need to be shored up in relation to the mission or jettisoned. At the most basic level, assessment can also identify soft spots in the program mission; aspirational elements may be foreclosed by current and future resources or may require a reconfiguration of the curriculum.

Student Learning Outcomes

Student learning outcomes (SLOs) are the foundation of any assessment. SLOs reflect the specific knowledge, skills, and abilities that students should gain from a program, course, or experience. In order to develop SLOs, program faculty must be clear about what students should be able to do when they graduate. SLOs should be both specific and comprehensive, and should be communicated widely to the program's stakeholders.

Specific SLOs are phrased through precise learning verbs and about precise knowledge, skills, and attitudes. SLOs reflect the thing that students should learn, the level of knowledge that is expected, observable behavior at the desired level of learning, and context that identifies how, when, and where the SLOs are observed. A typical "formula" for an SLO is: [A]t the conclusion of [*this program, course, experience*], students should be able to [*learning verb + explicit, observable term(s)*].

Bloom's original Taxonomy (1956) and its subsequent revision (Anderson & Krathwohl, 2001) establish a useful starting point for considering program knowledge, skills and abilities and the process of crafting these as SLOs. Bloom's Taxonomy is a hierarchy of levels of thinking across learning domains that include cognitive (knowledge), affective (attitudes), and sensory/psychomotor (skills) dimensions. The levels of learning are scaffolded and include remembering, understanding, applying, analyzing, evaluating, and creating.[3] This chapter focuses on the cognitive dimension as the most common.

Remembering is the ability to recall information and is considered to be the basic building block in any discipline or subject. It is essential to be able to recall basic terminology and definitions that include institutions, actors, and behaviors. *Understanding* takes remembering a step further. Understanding means the ability to discuss terms and concepts, distinguish them from one another, and place them in historical perspective. *Applying* means using the information in a real-world situation to accomplish a task. It involves translating a theory into an administrative or policy setting. *Analyzing* builds on application by investigating and identifying components of a concept, identifying patterns, and comparing or connecting these. *Evaluating* is the ability to make informed choices about a collection of information. Evaluation includes interpreting information, recognizing subjectivity, and grappling with the presence or absence of various values. *Creating* is the ability to synthesize knowledge across areas, draw conclusions, and compose new ideas or plans.

This taxonomy of levels of learning is conceptualized around verbs that indicate observable behavior (Anderson & Krathwohl, 2001). Specific terminology fosters a precise form of thinking about learning, making it easier for educators to create clear objectives for lesson planning and student evaluation. It also makes it simpler for students to understand what is expected of them. The modern taxonomy further refines our understanding of knowledge by separating the cognitive domain into four categories: Factual, conceptual, procedural, and metacognitive. Factual knowledge is characterized by terminology and discrete facts. Conceptual is characterized by categories, principles, theories, and models; the relationships are examined across a system or structure. Procedural means how to do something, and involves knowledge of specific methodologies, processes, and techniques. The meta-cognitive category reflects the capacity of students to self-assess their own knowledge, skills, and abilities. This chapter does not point out specific illustrations of each of these four conceptual categories; however, taken as a whole, the illustrations cover each of the four categories.

Table 10.1 presents the levels of thinking, some of the common observable behaviors designated by actionable verbs used for developing SLOs, and activities and questions that can guide student assignments toward the desired outcomes. The list of verbs, activities, and questions is illustrative but not exhaustive; there are myriad resources that can expand on these illustrations. The activities and questions are prompts that can be used to create assignments applicable to any course delivery format, including traditional face-to-face courses, activity-based flipped classrooms, online platforms, and blended learning designs.

SLOs are based on these observable behaviors, activities, and questions. This is where the curriculum comes to life. In this step, faculty express what they want students to learn, and how they expect students to go about doing that. The SLOs have a reciprocal relationship to faculty effort and activities; in designing activities, faculty essentially commit to delivering these. At this stage, the activities are not necessarily tied to any course(s), although it is likely that faculty will suggest activities to accomplish particular objectives by drawing upon the methods that they use in their courses. Keeping the discussion at the program level at this stage allows multiple ideas to surface, and can give faculty permission to explore new approaches that could move the program beyond what it is doing currently.

TABLE 10.1 Levels of Thinking and Examples of Observable Behaviors and Associated Activities and Questions

Level of Thinking	Definition	Observable Behaviors	Questions and Activities
A Remembering	Recalling ideas and concepts	Define, identify, label, list, name, outline, recall, recognize	Simple question-and-answer sessions; multiple-choice tests; list creation; fact charts; find the meaning of …; is X true or false?; who/what/where/when/why?
B Understanding	Explaining ideas and concepts; paraphrasing knowledge and generating analogies	Describe, discuss, explain, generalize, paraphrase, summarize, translate	Chart of similarities and differences; illustration of a main point; summary report of an event; provide an example of what you mean; write in your own words; why is [fact] important?
C Applying	Using information in new situations; Extending knowledge outside classroom	Apply, demonstrate, determine, examine, predict, solve, use	Case studies; think-pair-share about next steps; panel discussion about views; what do you think will be the end result? what additional information is needed?
D Analyzing	Establishing connections between concepts; critical thinking	Break down, compare, connect, differentiate, deconstruct, investigate	Diagrams; network maps; organizational relationship charts; report that connects multiple concepts to practice; what are the results of relationships or connections? what problems can occur? How can this line of thought be extended?
E Evaluating	Making educated judgments about material; justifying a decision	Appraise, assess, conclude, critique, decide, evaluate, explain, measure, support, summarize	Prepare a case that presents your view; prepare a survey of a group of interest; draw conclusions about a set of facts and opinions; critique a process; prepare recommendations; how effective was …?; are there other possible solutions or better ones?; classify the most important rules/practices
F Creating	Creating new and original work; building something that demonstrates knowledge	Compose, develop, design, formulate, generate, integrate, plan, synthesize	Prepare flow charts, booklets, and recommendations; write a report to provide advice about changes needed; develop an analogy to a new area of study or practices; write or revise a manual; what next steps are recommended?; what questions still need to be addressed?; how can our current understanding be expanded

Note
Levels of thinking and definitions from Bloom (1956) and Anderson & Krathwohl (2001).

Organizing SLOs and the NASPAA Universal Competencies

Recent research argues that although the SLO approach may provide tools to direct the student mindset, assessment learning objectives may also be perceived by faculty to be nothing more than an administrative requirement (Mitchell & Manzo, 2018). The peer-reviewed framework established by NASPAA addresses a key faculty concern, which is that they want to be active participants in assessment and particularly in determining SLOs. Specifically, faculty want to have the ability to create learning objectives rather than respond to a compliance regime of mandated goals.

Under the NASPAA framework, faculty are fully active participants; each program creates its SLOs in furtherance of its unique mission. NASPAA assessment focuses on the attainment of the five universal competencies, which are: (1) To lead and manage in public governance; (2) to participate and contribute to the policy process; (3) to analyze, synthesize, think creatively, solve problems, and make decisions; (4) to articulate and apply public service perspectives; and (5) to communicate and interact productively with a diverse and changing workforce and citizenry. The university competencies reflect the state of the field in public service education as the product of collective and continuous peer review by program faculty and program leaders first in the United States and now around the world (Jennings, 2019). For assessment plans in graduate programs of public administration, public affairs, or public policy, these five universal competencies provide a useful framework for organizing SLOs for programs and for specializations. The NASPAA competencies also provide evidence to support the comprehensive nature of the SLOs, which is noted above as an essential component of assessment plans.

Tables 10.2 through 10.6 illustrate the alignment of SLOs and activities at each level of thinking across the five universal competencies for a generic MPA program. Programs seeking to demonstrate assessment performance under the NASPAA accreditation protocol will recognize the general approach.

This "levels of learning" approach is a comprehensive scaffold that reflects everything from terminology to creation of products useful in the field, and for each of the universal competencies. This highly articulated framework functions as a template for developing SLOs that can meet both university and NASPAA requirements. It also functions as an analytic framework for identifying points within the curriculum where additional attention is required. As a result, for graduate programs, the scaffold can be streamlined in a couple of ways. First, SLOs could emphasize the highest levels of learning such as evaluation and creation. Embedded in these are the assumptions that students have synthesized the lower-order skills of memory, understanding, application, and analysis. During feedback sessions, faculty can determine whether deficits exist in the more basic skills, knowledge, and abilities and enhance curricula accordingly. The SLOs linked to evaluating and creating are highlighted in Tables 10.2 through 10.6; the products and activities used to demonstrate attainment of these SLOs are typical major project assignments in core courses in graduate programs in public service.

Another approach is to specify SLOs and fit them to the universal competencies after the fact. Table 10.7 illustrates this more generalized approach to SLO articulation with examples of specific activities that could be used to fulfill the SLO.

TABLE 10.2 MPA Program SLOs and NASPAA Competency 1: To Lead and Manage in Public Governance

Level of Thinking	Examples of SLO-Based Activities and Products
A Remembering	Generate lists to identify major theories, major principles, and concepts in public service broadly.
B Understanding	Compare and contrast various approaches to the study of public administration, leadership, or management.
C Applying	Reflect on aspects of leadership, management, and public service institutional structure observed in an internship or other public service setting.
D Analyzing	Diagram the formal and informal leadership and management roles and relationships from data gathered in an assignment to interview public servants about a particular issue.
E Evaluating	Critique a management proposal to address the use of social media by office staff.
F Creating	Design an employee selection, evaluation, and/or appraisal system.

TABLE 10.3 MPA Program SLOs and NASPAA Competency 2: To Participate in and Contribute to the Public Policy Process

Level of Thinking	Examples of SLO-Based Activities and Products
A Remembering	Outline the stages of the public policy process and the relevant public, nonprofit, and private-sector actors in each.
B Understanding	Defend the role of citizen participation in public policy the American democratic system.
C Applying	Demonstrate the ways in which local community advocacy could influence a public policy issue.
D Analyzing	Create a planning document that articulates and contrasts the roles of nonprofit groups, public agency representatives, and private-sector organizations in the design and implementation of a public policy initiative.
E Evaluating	Assess the efficiency of a new public program using original data from designers and implementers.
F Creating	Compose legislative planning document for a policy proposal from design through legislative adoption.

Each SLO can be linked to one or more of the universal competencies. Graduate programs in public service build curricula around the universal competencies as broad guiding principles, so these connections can be made easily. Each program makes unique decisions about how to link SLOs to the universal competencies based on program mission. In one program, for example, the SLO "apply basic management principles to case studies of typical public organization problems" could be intended to demonstrate skill in leading and managing in public service (Competency 1). In another program, this same SLO might be

TABLE 10.4 MPA Program SLOs and NASPAA Competency 3: To Analyze, Synthesize, Think Creatively, Solve Problems, and Make Decisions

Level of Thinking	Examples of SLO-Based Activities and Products
A Remembering	Identify different models of decision making and their stages.
B Understanding	Describe the unique role of qualitative methods in the study of public service issues.
C Applying	Construct an array of alternative variables to measure particular concepts.
D Analyzing	Differentiate between types of research methods used to study a community issue.
E Evaluating	Appraise the strengths and weaknesses of a mixed methods research design that combines original and secondary data.
F Creating	Collect original data through a survey and interviews of public-sector stakeholders and write a report of the findings.

TABLE 10.5 MPA Program SLOs and NASPAA Competency 4: Articulate and Apply Public Service Perspectives

Level of Thinking	Examples of SLO-Based Activities and Products
A Remembering	Reproduce the array of actors and institutions in public service.
B Understanding	Describe the roles of public agencies and nonprofit organizations in public service issues.
C Applying	Construct an array of potential roles for public agencies and nonprofit organizations in case study fashion.
D Analyzing	Differentiate between public and nonprofit resource development approaches used to address a community issue.
E Evaluating	Appraise the strengths and weaknesses of an array of budget proposals.
F Creating	Collect original data through a survey and interviews of public-sector stakeholders, and prepare a budget proposal.

TABLE 10.6 MPA Program SLOs and NASPAA Competency 5: To Communicate and Interact Productively with a Diverse and Changing Workforce and Citizenry

Level of Thinking	Examples of SLO-Based Activities and Products
A Remembering	Name the major federal laws that preserve civil rights in public-sector life and public-sector employment.
B Understanding	Summarize the evolution of the concept of cultural competence.
C Applying	Apply hiring criteria to a pool of hypothetical applicants.
D Analyzing	Deconstruct an informal community network to compare stakeholder motivations and likely paths of action on a particular issue.
E Evaluating	Critique a professional code of ethics for a field of public service.
F Creating	Develop a plan to create a new community collaboration to address a local issue.

used to demonstrate the ability to analyze, synthesize, and think creatively about a public service issue.

The concept of assessment and the development SLOs can also be utilized for specialized curriculum within the overall graduate program in public service. The most closely specified specializations are typically aligned with graduate certificates, and graduate certificates are often also included in college and university assessment regimes that apply to all degree-granting programs. Financial management, emergency management, and project or city/county management are but a few of the many examples.

Table 10.8 presents student learning products and activities expressed for a specialization – here, the emerging field of election administration.[4] These products and activities reflect current or prospective faculty assignments or sub-assignments. The information in Table 10.8 is not aligned with the five universal competencies, although it certainly could be. That alignment will differ across programs and depends on the ways in which faculty view a particular exercise – for example, whether the focus of an exercise is directed at honing a public service perspective or on initiating basic skills in data analysis.

As the rest of this chapter illustrates, the foundation of each assessment process rests on acquiring and demonstrating knowledge, skills, and abilities at the program level and for substantive categories that the program feels are appropriate beyond the program as a whole – i.e., additional frameworks for any concentrations, specializations, or graduate certificates. And although the subject matter varies, the process remains essentially the same.

Of course, the outcomes portion of an assessment plan requires more than simply developing SLOs and activities. The outcomes must be both

TABLE 10.7 Generic SLOs with Activity and Product Examples

Level of Thinking	Generic SLO	Examples of SLO-Based Activities and Products
A Remembering	Students exhibit the ability to articulate the basic structures of public administration.	Recall the bureaucratic structure of the US government and the corresponding bureaucratic structure in at least one state.
B Understanding	Students understand the primary activities involved in governing and policy development.	Articulate the stages in the policy cycle and the importance of key stakeholders in each stage.
C Applying	Students are capable of applying pre-existing principles of public administration and management to common cases and scenarios.	Apply basic management principles to case studies of typical public organization problems.
D Analyzing	Students develop the skills to analyze existing data to solve public problems.	Use secondary data to present evidence of a policy problems with descriptive and bivariate statistical analysis.
E Evaluating	Students develop the ability to make reasoned decisions about policy options and administrative choices.	Identify strengths and weaknesses of competing policy solutions and articulate which is potentially better and why.
F Creating	Students demonstrate basic abilities to create new products or processes related to public administration.	Develop a statement of public service philosophy.

comprehensive and public. Comprehensive means that the outcomes reflect the state of the field. To establish that outcomes are comprehensive, programs can look to disciplinary standards. Disciplinary standards should be reflected in the consensus of the program faculty and based on their qualifications in the field. External referents could include reports that synthesize learning objectives for the field or program goals. Not least, comprehensive SLOs in graduate programs of public administration, public affairs, and public policy reflect the field of practice itself. The views of those who do the work that students are being educated to undertake are invaluable. There are a variety of ways to gather this information including surveys and focus groups. A community advisory board is already likely in place for a NASPAA-accredited (or accreditation seeking) program, and its input on SLOs should be documented and considered in faculty deliberations.

An assessment plan should also be public. Publicity here means that SLOs should be communicated to current students through student orientations and advising as well as through course syllabi (which is discussed with curriculum maps). It also means that program faculty should be aware of the plan, which should be the case if they are involved in its development. Advisory boards should also be included in communications about SLOs and can also be involved in co-creating SLOs and in providing feedback generally. Websites can also easily provide this information to prospective students. An assessment plan should include documentation of both the comprehensive nature of the SLOs and the methods of dissemination to relevant audiences.

Curriculum Maps

So far, the assessment process has been proceeding at the program level. Through curriculum mapping, the process becomes more specific. It also becomes more iterative. Curriculum maps illustrate three related information sets. The first set of information displays alignment between courses and SLOs. The second set of information displays the scaffolding of the SLOs across the curriculum that supports mastery and the progression of student learning of the SLOs from introduction to reinforcement to emphasis. The third set of information indicates the assignments that reflect the SLOs.

It is technically possible to combine all of this information on one map; however, in practice this can become unwieldy. As a result, two types of maps are typical. The first curriculum map aligns SLOs with the available learning opportunities. Available learning opportunities include courses, internships, practicums, and other student experiences including opportunities for research and civic engagement – the composition of this array depends on the program. The second map demonstrates the extent to which each SLO is developed within the learning opportunity; e.g., introduced, reinforced, and emphasized (following the framework advanced by Good [2016]). To assist in interpretation, a code is typical: 1 = introduced; 2 = reinforced; and 3 = emphasized.

TABLE 10.8 Examples of Products and Activities for a Specialization in Election Administration

Level of Thinking	Products and Activities
A Remembering	• Identify the array of methods by which election officials are selected. • Identify the array of state/local and local office structures. • Generate a glossary of election administration as an interactive intergovernmental system. • Identify methods of voter registration and electoral participation around the world. • Name the federal laws that preserve civil rights in voter registration and election administration.
B Understanding	• Explain the implications for public understanding of selecting election officials through elections. • Describe methods of election reform over time. • Examine the development of measurement of election administration. • Describe different methods of voter convenience in American elections and in other countries. • Explain why some groups merit particular treatment in the election administration process.
C Applying	• Apply an election office social media policy to election–day activities. • Discuss implications of recent US Supreme Court decisions on election operations in specific states. • Express measures that could be used to capture performance in a key area of election administration. • Create a panel to discuss stakeholder perspectives about a method of election designed to improve voter convenience. • Determine how Section 2 of the Voting Rights Act of 1965 applies to a decision of a local election office.

D Analyzing
- Diagram reporting and influence relationships across the election administration system on a specific administrative problem.
- Map the state, local, and national election offices, advocacy groups, and vendors involved in a major policy issue in election administration (e.g., voter identification methods).
- Investigate contemporary vendor products and methods designed to address a particular election administration issue.
- Construct a network map of information sources that could be accessed to better understand an election administration issue.
- Map a community network of advocacy groups and government offices that support accessibility for voters with disabilities.

E Evaluating
- Write a job description for a new position in a local election office.
- Reflect on lessons learned and best practices in cyber-security policy in election administration.
- Appraise the strengths and weaknesses of various methods of auditing elections.
- Prepare an evaluation of community outreach efforts to provide language assistance to voters.
- Synthesize research about the voting experience and poll-worker race and ethnicity.

F Creating
- Prepare a budget proposal to address staffing needs and other resources needed for a transition to a new policy requirement.
- Develop a plan to implement a specific election reform in a state.
- Design staff training for an election issue in an election office.
- Create a flow chart of a plan to increase voter satisfaction with the voting experience.
- Develop a plan to provide technology support for a local election office.

A third type of map can present the major assignments that are used in each course; this is not intended to constrain academic freedom but rather to provide information about the techniques and methods that are being used to deliver the program.

Some assessment plans include all learning opportunities, and some focus only on those that are required. Focusing only on required opportunities will yield information about the SLOs that can be accomplished with a "core" set of courses, and this is valuable information in and of itself. Most graduate programs in public service incorporate a balance of required and elective courses and other learning opportunities for students, and most "require" a certain number of elective hours. The more comprehensive approach is to focus on all learning opportunities.

The curriculum maps are prepared by using course syllabi. In the ideal case, SLOs and activities that have been developed earlier in the process are already included in course syllabi. It is likely, however, that new SLOs have been identified or the wording has been revised. It is also highly likely that the array of activities has been amplified through faculty discussion about the SLOs. It is best to plan for an iterative review of both, as this process can involve considerable dialogue and revision of SLO wording and activities.

Course syllabi are also key in communicating assessment plan details to students. Course syllabi should identify all the SLOs and NASPAA competencies that are addressed, and the assignments in each course that will be used to assess student learning. In this way, students know how course expectations relate to overall program goals.

Table 10.9 presents an illustration of a course-level curriculum map for a typical MPA program. This map includes seven required courses. In this and the subsequent curriculum maps, course names are used rather than course call numbers so that the content arrangements are clearer. The primary value of this map is to demonstrate that each SLO and each competency is linked to at least one course, and that all the NASPAA competencies are addressed. The visual display makes concentrations or gaps readily apparent; i.e., whether and how SLOs and competencies are distributed across the curriculum and whether SLOs or competencies have fallen through the cracks. Both circumstances should prompt reflection. If every course addresses a particular SLO, perhaps that content can be eliminated from some courses in order to make room for other content, or perhaps courses are not sufficiently varied. If an SLO is omitted, perhaps that SLO is not necessary, or needs to be added to one or more courses.

Faculty reflection on what the curriculum should accomplish, and whether it is designed to do that, is a very important aspect of developing an assessment plan. Faculty should resist the temptation to indicate that each class addresses each of the universal competencies, and at every level of learning. All of the courses in a public service curriculum should relate to each other, and so themes of public service values, management skills, public policy activities, equitable practices, and decision skills should be expected to appear in every course and learning experience. This second level of curriculum mapping is designed to direct attention (and faculty discussion) toward the depth of treatment that the material in the course provides with respect to the SLOs and also the NASPAA competencies. Table 10.10 illustrates for each course the degree of emphasis on SLOs that pertain to each of the universal competencies. Darker shading

TABLE 10.9 Course-Level Curriculum Map for an MPA Program

Course	NASPAA Universal Competency				
	Lead and Manage	Participate in Public Policy	Analyze and Synthesize	Public Service Perspective	Diversity in Public Life
Seminar in Public Service	*			*	*
Public Policy Analysis		*	*	*	
Public and Nonprofit Resource Management	*	*	*		*
Leadership and Ethics	*			*	*
Public-Sector Personnel Management	*				*
Research Methods		*	*		
Internship	*	*	*	*	*

Note
* indicates that the competency is addressed in the course.

TABLE 10.10 Curriculum Map for Levels of Exposure to Competencies in an MPA Program

Course	NASPAA Universal Competency				
	Lead and Manage	Participate in Public Policy	Analyze and Synthesize	Public Service Perspective	Diversity in Public Life
Seminar in Public Service	I			I, E	I
Public Policy Analysis		I, E	R	R	
Public and Nonprofit Resource Management	R	R	R		R
Leadership and Ethics	E			E	R
Public-Sector Personnel Management	E				E
Research Methods		R	I, E		
Internship	E	R	R	R	E

Note
I = introduced; R = reinforced; E = emphasized

illustrates greater emphasis or degree of exposure. The ideal result is a relatively even distribution of SLOs and competencies across the curriculum, and emphasis on each competency in at least one course.

Methodology

As demand for assessment information has increased, so has the conversation about the types of information that constitute "evidence" in an assessment protocol. Broadly, methods used in assessment can be guided by the field of practice – here, public service. The diversity of public service as a field of practice and the inherent diversity of values that it embodies call for multiple methods, multiple stakeholder inputs, and recognition of the complexity of the public service environment. Applied research methods are embedded in the study of public organizations (government agencies and nonprofit organizations) through the use of theories of change, contextual elaboration, and uncovering unintended consequences and surprise occurrences (e.g., Brown & Hale, 2014; Gerring, 2007). A deep body of research argues that a wide range of goals and methodologies are appropriate for assessing public service administration and third-party governance activities including case studies, comparative methods, and the explicit use of triangulation (Khagram & Thomas, 2010; Riccucci, 2010). Similarly, the scholarship of public service, broadly defined, continues to generate new paradigms for organizing and explaining the field. Among these are "new public service" (e.g., Denhardt & Denhardt, 2000); "public value" (e.g., Moore, 1995; O'Flynn, 2007); the "new governance" paradigm (e.g., Bingham, Nabatchi, & O'Leary, 2005); and "network governance" (e.g, Salamon, 2002); and specific focus on nonprofit organizations (e.g., Brown & Cornforth, 2013).[5]

Within this broader framework of multiple and mixed methods of inquiry, assessment plans typically require a plan for data collection and two types of evidence. The assessment plan provides information that describe the measures, how data are collected, the source(s) of the data, how data are rated, how data are analyzed, by whom, and how frequently. Direct and indirect measures are required by many institutional assessment programs. Following Young (2012), direct measures collect evidence of student course work or test performances where faculty look at actual student work (e.g., portfolios, simulations, capstones, internally developed exams, external review of nationally recognized exams) (see also Kapucu & Koliba, 2017). Indirect measures collect evidence from other sources within the program or institution and outside it, including student and alumni interviews or surveys, non-course work from students, national surveys, and other data from alumni and other stakeholders. For direct measures, a rubric is typically used to evaluate the data (Sandberg & Kecskes, 2017). Indirect measures are evaluated according to the measure.

Table 10.11 illustrates the data collection framework for an MPA program, the timing of review, and the standards of review. The data collection approach

TABLE 10.11 Summary of Data Collected for MPA Program

Assessment Vehicle	E-Portfolio	Public-Service Presentation	Community Stakeholders	MPA Program Alumni
Type of measure	Direct	Direct	Indirect	Indirect
Use of rubric	Yes	Yes	No	No
Collection method	Websites developed by each student	Written material and observation of presentation	Survey and meeting discussion	Survey
Data source	Material provided by students	Material provided and presentation given by students	MPA Advisory board*	MPA Program alumni*
Rating method	Faculty applications of rubric – minimum four faculty	Faculty application of rubric – minimum four faculty	Faculty discussion of themes and observations; directed at use of results	Faculty discussion of themes and observations; directed at use of results
Method of analysis	Scores averaged per and across students; open-ended responses. Analyzed for emerging themes and trends	Scores averaged per and across students; open-ended responses analyzed for emerging themes and trends	Scores averaged; open-ended responses analyzed for emerging themes and trends	Scores averaged; open-ended responses analyzed for emerging themes and trends
Frequency of review	twice/year, fall and spring semesters	twice/year, fall and spring semesters	Annually	Annually

Note
* Consider a separate advisory board for specializations, or identify particular advisors to provide additional stakeholder perspectives on the content and context of the specialization in practice.

is based on two direct measures and two indirect measures. The measures reflect the signature efforts of students in each program. Here, MPA students prepare an e-portfolio with examples of their work. The e-portfolio is presented as a website that includes artifacts for each of the universal competencies, as well as student self-reflection about how their work demonstrates their ability relative to the competency. Students are required to demonstrate an array of artifacts that reflect a higher level of learning (analysis, evaluation, or creation) in each competency. In preparing the e-portfolio, faculty serve as advisors for groups of students to ensure that appropriate materials are selected. Data are also drawn from the MPA advisory board and program alumni.

Feedback and Capacity Considerations

The combination of SLOs with NASPAA universal competencies can create an administrative bottleneck in even the smallest programs. A single direct measure generates five data points per student (one per competency) without taking into consideration other direct measures or any indirect measures from stakeholders. Faculty interest in creating highly articulated SLO frameworks with meaningful activities is to be encouraged – this sort of foundation is the heart of a program.

Granularity must be balanced, however, against the capacity of faculty to review the data, compile results, and reflect in a meaningful way. If levels of learning are utilized, one management strategy is to create a schedule of review for SLOs based on levels of learning so that all SLOs are reviewed over a period of time (e.g., three years). By beginning with the SLOs that reflect higher-order learning, information can be generated about what is happening (or not happening) at lower levels of the learning scaffold. As an illustration, a SLO review cycle could proceed as follows: Year 1 = creating and evaluating; Year 2 = application and analysis; and Year 3 = remembering and understanding. There are no hard-and-fast rules, and programs may find other approaches to be useful such as focusing SLOs on the highest levels of learning (evaluating and creating).

The results category of an assessment plan includes reporting of results of chosen measures, interpreting those, communicating to appropriate stakeholders, and processing feedback through reflection and a plan for next steps. Assessment results should be communicated broadly. A good place to start is the range of communication strategies identified for SLOs. All program faculty, students, and community advisory board members should be made aware of the results. As with SLOs, communication with some stakeholder groups can be accomplished through website postings, or as an item on a meeting agenda. Faculty involvement will be more extensive.

The feedback loop in an assessment plan should be purposeful and reflective. Whether and how results are used is a critical part of the assessment process.

This part of the assessment process should be facilitated by establishing a dedicated time for faculty to discuss results and next steps. Common changes that could occur as a result of faculty reflection run the gamut from changes within courses to changes across the program. Examples of changes that could occur following faculty discussion include scaffolding assignments or courses, or adding pre-requisites through course sequencing. Courses could be removed. Capstone courses or internships could be added to provide opportunities for experiential learning. Courses could be added to address content gaps within the existing curriculum to reflect new developments in the field.

Results could also reveal that the assessment plan does not capture the essence of the program; this result suggests the need to review both methods and measures to better reflect student learning.

The feedback loop is essential in assessment – it is in fact largely the point. The faculty conversations are necessary. Faculty should schedule opportunities for purposeful dialogue and reflection to identify needs for change, and develop plans for implementing these changes. This can seem overwhelming; however, in practice, engaged faculty actually do this sort of thing regularly. Many times, changes evolve informally; the assessment plan approach provides structure and predictable opportunities for input and discussion.

Conclusion

Assessment can appear daunting – and it is entirely true that assessment takes time and effort, and the engaged effort of all program faculty. This chapter provides a road map for establishing assessment as a systematic tool for continuous program improvement. The illustrations in this chapter can be easily adapted to specific program missions and student populations. For programs accredited by NASPAA, the universal competency framework provides a ready template to use in organizing SLOs and can also be used in assessment regimes developed for other institutional purposes.

The goal of the assessment plan is to improve the likelihood of student learning of knowledge, skills, and abilities advanced by a program. Yet, Banta, Jones, and Black (2009) found that it is rare that an assessment program demonstrates improved student learning (6 percent of the nation's top 150 assessment programs) (see also Banta & Blaich, 2011). To be successful as an instrument of continuous improvement (and not an added burden), assessment has to be incorporated into faculty workloads that are already full of scholarship responsibilities. This then requires that the leadership, political will, and resources exist to support the faculty time and effort required to conduct assessment as a value proposition, and to support faculty time and effort (and perhaps other administrative efforts) needed to implement recommended changes.

Notes

1. Throughout, "assessment plan" refers to the overall plan and planning process; in the norm, a "report" about assessment would include most if not all of the elements discussed in the chapter.
2. The labels for these stages synthesize common terminology (e.g., Suskie, 2018) and reflect the assessment approach implemented at Auburn University (Good, 2016), which guides the assessment approach for its NASPAA-accredited MPA program and graduate certificates in nonprofit organizations and community governance, and in election administration.
3. In the original version of the taxonomy (Bloom, 1956), the levels of learning were knowledge, comprehension, application, analysis, evaluation, and synthesis.
4. Election administration is a newly recognized subfield of public administration, and as such provides a case of first impression for developing SLOs and for other aspects of the assessment process. The SLOs and activities displayed here represent those developed by the Auburn University faculty for its Graduate Certificate in Election Administration.
5. The scholarship in each of these areas is extensive; references are illustrative and intended as a point of departure for additional reading.

References

Anderson, L. & Krathwohl, D. (2001). *A taxonomy for learning teaching, and assessment: A revision of Bloom's taxonomy of educational objectives.* New York: Longman.

Baer, J. D., Cook, A. L., & Baldi, S. (2006). *The literacy of America's college students.* Washington, DC: American Institutes for Research.

Banta, T. W. & Blaich, C. (2011). Closing the assessment loop. *Change: The Magazine of Higher Learning, 43*(1), 22–27.

Banta, T. W., Jones, E. A., & Black, K. E. (2009). *Designing effective assessment: Principles and profiles of good practice.* San Francisco, CA: Jossey-Bass.

Bingham, L. B., Nabatchi, T., & O'Leary, R. (2005). The new governance: Practices and processes for stakeholder and citizen participation in the work of government. *Public Administration Review, 65*(5), 547–558.

Bishu, S. G., Guy, M. E., & Heckler, N. (2019). Seeing gender and its consequences. *Journal of Public Affairs Education, 25*(2), 145–162.

Bloom, B. S. (1956). *Taxonomy of educational objectives.* New York: D. McKay Co., Inc.

Brown, M. & Hale, K. (2014). *Applied research methods in public and nonprofit organizations.* San Francisco, CA: Wiley.

Brown, W. A. & Cornforth, C. (2013). *Nonprofit governance: Innovative perspectives and approaches.* New York: Routledge.

Business Roundtable (2005). *Tapping America's potential: The education for innovative initiative.* Washington, DC: Business Roundtable.

Committee on Science, Engineering, and Public Policy (2007). *Rising above the gathering storm: Energizing and employing America for a brighter economic future.* Washington, DC: National Academies Press.

Deardorff, M. D. & Folger, P. J. (2005). Assessment that matters: Integrating the "chore" of department-based assessment with real improvements in political science education. *Journal of Political Science Education, 1*(3), 277–287.

Denhardt, R. B. & Denhardt, J. V. (2000). The new public service: Serving rather than steering. *Public Administration Review, 60*(6), 549–559.

Department of Education (2006). *A test of leadership: Charting the future of U.S. higher education*. Washington, DC: Department of Education.

Dwyer, C. A., Millett, C. M., & Payne, D. G. (2006). *A culture of evidence: Postsecondary assessment and learning outcomes*. Princeton, NJ: Educational Testing Services.

Ewell, P. (2006). *Making the grade: How boards can ensure academic quality*. Washington, DC: Association of Governing Boards of Colleges and Universities.

Fox, J. C. & Keeter, S. (1996). Improving teaching and its evaluation: A survey of political science departments. *PS: Political Science and Politics, 29*(2), 174–180.

Gerring, J. (2007). *Case study research: Principles and practices*. Cambridge: Cambridge University Press.

Good, M. (2016). *Quality of assessment rubric*. Auburn, AL: Auburn University Office of the Provost.

Jennings, E. T. (2019). Competencies and outcomes in public affairs education. *Journal of Public Affairs Education, 25*(1), 12–17.

Kapucu, N. & Koliba, C. (2017). Using competency-based portfolios as a pedagogical tool and assessment strategy in MPA programs. *Journal of Public Affairs Education, 23*(4), 993–1016.

Khagram, S. & Thomas, C. W. (2010). Toward a platinum standard for evidence-based assessment by 2020. *Public Administration Review, 70*(1), s100–s106.

Kirsch, I., Braun, H., Kendaro, Y., & Sum, A. (2007). *America's perfect storm: Three forces changing our nation's future*. Princeton, NJ: Educational Testing Services.

Meek, J. W. (2018). Making a difference: Good governance in disrupted states. *Journal of Public Affairs Education, 24*(2), 135–151.

Millett, C. M., Stickler, L. M., Dwyer, C. A., & Payne, D. G. (2007). *A culture of evidence II: Critical features of assessments for postsecondary student learning*. Princeton, NJ: Educational Testing Services.

Millett, C. M., Payne, D. G., Dwyer, C. A., Stickler, L. M., & Alexiou, J. J. (2008). *A culture of evidence III: An evidence-centered approach to accountability for student learning outcomes*. Princeton, NJ: Educational Testing Services.

Mitchell, K. M. W. & Manzo, W. R. (2018). The purpose and perception of learning objectives. *Journal of Political Science Education, 14*(4), 456–472.

Moore, M. (1995). *Creating public value: Strategic management in governance*. Cambridge, MA: Harvard University Press.

National Commission on Excellence in Education (1983). *A nation at risk: The imperative for educational reform*. Washington, DC: National Commission on Excellence in Education.

National Institute for Learning Outcomes Assessment (2016). *Higher education quality: Why documenting learning matters*. Urbana, IL: National Institute for Learning Outcomes Assessment.

O'Flynn, J. (2007). From new public management to public value: Paradigmatic change and managerial implications. *Australian Journal of Public Administration, 66*(3): 353–366.

Riccucci, N. M. (2010). *Public administration: Traditions of inquiry and philosophies of knowledge*. Washington, DC: Georgetown University Press.

Riley, L. & Johansen, M. (2019). Creating valuable indigenous learning environments. *Journal of Public Affairs Education, 25*(3), 387–411.

Salamon, L. (ed.) (2002). *The tools of government: A guide to the new governance*. New York: Oxford University Press.

Sandberg, B. & Kecskes, K. (2017). Rubric as a foundation for assessing student competencies: One public administration program's creative exercise. *Journal of Public Affairs Education, 23*(1), 637–652.

Suskie, L. A. (2018). *Assessing student learning: A common sense guide.* San Francisco, CA: Wiley.

UNESCO Institute for Statistics (2009). *Literacy skills for the world of tomorrow: Further results from PISA 2000.* Paris: Organisation for Economic Co-operation and Development.

Young, C. C. (2012). Program evaluation methods and assessment: Integrating methods, processes, and culture. In Deardorff, M. D., Hamann, K., & Ishiyama, J. (eds), *Assessment in political science* (pp. 117–137). Washington, DC: American Political Science Association.

11

IMPROVING STUDENT OUTCOMES

D. Ryan Miller

Student outcomes are defined as "the educational, societal, and life effects that result from students being educated" (Great Schools Partnership, 2013), which include such examples as academic achievement, degree completion, employment, and enhanced salary. Helping students achieve these outcomes is the *raison d'être* of academic programs. The central role of student outcomes in education can be seen in their importance in the standards established by accrediting institutions (see, for example, Standards 1, 5, and 7 developed by the Network of Schools of Public Policy, Affairs, and Administration [NASPAA]). The quality of student outcomes is also important due to the relationship between outcome quality and program survival, with quality and reputation being among the top reasons graduate students choose to pursue an education at a particular school (Aslanian, Clinefelter, & Magda, 2019; Mercado, 2018). Accordingly, the directors of Master of Public Affairs (MPA) programs need to focus their attention on ensuring positive student outcomes to ensure program quality and survival. This chapter examines the student outcomes of MPA programs, and specific actions that MPA programs can take to improve the outcomes of their students.

As the definition given above suggests, there are several categories of student outcomes. To better cover the topic, this chapter focused on educational outcomes with emphasis given to student learning (i.e., achievement). Educational outcomes, particularly student learning, warrant special attention because they are the basis for students achieving societal and life outcomes. Each aspect of an MPA program has the potential to affect student outcomes. Whether the effects are positive or negative depends on how the aspect impacts each student's ability to meet learning outcomes. The remainder of this chapter is dedicated to examining how choices related to admissions requirements, curriculum and andragogy, and learning outcomes affect student achievement.

To illustrate the effect of these choices on student outcomes, the following analogy is utilized throughout the chapter. The student experience in an MPA program is like a journey where the destination is the attainment of educational outcomes. A student's ability to reach the destination depends on the distance to be traversed, the speed at which the student travels, and the time allotted to make the journey. In this analogy, the distance to be traversed is the learning gains a student must make in order to successfully attain the educational outcomes (i.e., the difference between a student's initial level of achievement and the level of achievement required by the outcomes). Speed is the learning rate of the student, or how quickly the student makes learning gains. The time allotted for the journey is the amount of time in which a student is expected to make the requisite learning gains (e.g., the length of a course or the expected time to degree completion). Using this analogy, the chapter explores the factors program directors and faculty should consider when designing or modifying admissions requirements, curriculum and andragogy, or learning outcomes. For each of these areas, specific recommendations for improving student learning outcomes are presented.

Admissions Requirements

The first aspect of an MPA program that impacts student success is the choice of admissions requirements. Program leadership and faculty should rely on their mission statement when drafting and/or revising admission requirements. Admissions requirements establish the minimal level of knowledge required to enter an MPA program. Together with the learning outcomes, the admissions requirements set the maximum learning gains students are expected to achieve in order to graduate from the program. In other words, the requirements indicate the minimum level of knowledge a student can possess at the beginning of the degree program and still be able to succeed in the program (i.e., achieve the learning outcomes). When the admissions requirements are set too low, some students may be unable to successfully complete the degree requirements. If a program finds its drop-out rate to be too high, raising the admissions requirements (e.g., increasing the minimum GPA, requiring writing samples, or requiring standardized tests) can help improve student achievement, persistence, and graduation rates by reducing the extent of the learning gains required for success.

In addition to setting maximum learning gain expectations, admissions requirements also affect learning rates. Students who possess prerequisite competencies are able to make greater learning gains than students who do not possess the prerequisites (Dochy, de Ridjt, & Dyck, 2002). Programs can improve educational outcomes by establishing admissions standards that clearly indicate any prerequisite competencies necessary to be successful in the program. Once standards are established, programs must share them with prospective students so that prospective students are aware of what they need to know (or learn) in order to be successful in the program. Programs then improve student outcomes by either not admitting students lacking the prerequisites or by providing opportunities and resources for admitted students to obtain the missing competencies.

The following example illustrates the importance of establishing prerequisites and how an MPA program might provide students opportunities to obtain prerequisites. Consider an MPA program that teaches inferential statistics as part of its core curriculum. In order to be successful in inferential statistics, students need a solid foundation in descriptive statistics. If the MPA program does not include descriptive statistics in its curriculum, then prospective students need to be made aware that they are expected to enter the program with a solid foundation in descriptive statistics. As part of its admissions requirements, the program could require prospective students to demonstrate knowledge of descriptive statistics (e.g., through transcripts showing prior coursework in statistics, work experience in a position that regularly utilized descriptive statistics, or scores on a test that assesses statistical knowledge). Alternatively, the program could admit students without a background in descriptive statistics and require those students to complete additional learning through a descriptive statistics workshop provided by program faculty, an undergraduate course offered by the institution, or a course offered at a local community college.

Admissions requirements are the important first step to improving student outcomes. The requirements established by an MPA program, in conjunction with the program's learning outcomes, set the maximum learning gains students are expected to make to pass courses, to persist through the curriculum, and to graduate with their MPA. In addition, admissions requirements affect the speed at which students will make learning gains by requiring students to possess prerequisite competencies. Students who possess prerequisites are better prepared to learn the program's curriculum, allowing them to make quicker learning gains. The next section examines how decisions about the program curriculum and methods of instruction affect student educational outcomes.

Curriculum and Andragogy

The academic component of an MPA program consists of a curriculum and a set of teaching methods (andragogy). Together the curriculum and the andragogy are the means by which students attain educational outcomes. The curriculum defines the courses and the sequencing of curricular content (both within and across courses). Andragogy defines the methods of teaching used throughout the program (e.g., flipped-classroom, case study method, etc.). Continuing with the analogy that a student's experience is a journey, the curriculum and the andragogy affect the speed (i.e., learning rates) students travel on their way to their destination (i.e., academic achievement, graduation, etc.). This section begins by presenting how program-level decisions related to curriculum and scheduling affect student outcomes. The section concludes with a discussion of how course-level decisions related to curriculum and andragogy affect student outcomes.

Program-Level Decisions

At the program level, decisions related to course sequencing and course scheduling influence student outcomes. The following subsections explain the relationships between course sequencing, scheduling, and student educational outcomes. Examples of actions MPA programs can take to improve student outcomes are provided.

Sequencing

Course sequencing refers to the prescribed order in which courses in the MPA program curriculum should be completed. Courses should be sequenced in such a way that the curriculum builds upon itself. For example, a research methods course should precede a program evaluation course when the content of the methods course will be used by students in the evaluation course. Likewise, any co-requisite courses (those courses designed to be taken concurrently) should be sequenced so that students may take them at the same time.

Proper course sequencing ensures students are exposed to curricular content in an order that enhances their ability to learn the material quickly. To use the journey analogy, sequencing is equivalent to mapping out the quickest path to a destination when multiple stops (i.e., courses) must be made along the way. Similar to establishing prerequisites for program admission, sequencing courses in the curriculum prepares students for each course by exposing them to any course-level prerequisite competencies that are also part of the program's curriculum.

Another consideration when sequencing courses is the time requirements of courses intended to be taken concurrently. When possible, avoid sequencing together multiple courses that place substantial demands on student time. In the journey analogy, this is comparable to trying to visit two attractions that require substantial time on the same day (e.g., Disney World and Universal Studios). Trying to visit both attractions on the same day will result in only partial, and likely unfulfilling, visits to both places. The same is true for high-demand courses. Taking multiple high-demand courses at the same time can leave students achieving only some of the learning objectives and earning lower grades than they would have had the sequencing been different. The proper balance of courses will depend on the backgrounds and demographics of the students (e.g., full-time versus part-time, pre-service versus in-service), the content of individual courses, and the course requirements established by individual faculty. Work with students and faculty to gain an understanding of which courses work well together and which do not. Then, apply that understanding to sequencing courses.

Course sequences can be either mandatory or voluntary for students. To enforce required sequencing, establish prerequisite courses. These courses should be listed as prerequisites in the course catalog and in the institution's enrollment management system. Establishing prerequisites in the enrollment management system will prevent students from enrolling in courses for which they have not yet completed the prerequisites. A word of caution: Too many prerequisites can make it difficult for students to progress through the program. Select prerequisites carefully and, prior to implementation, always map out how students will progress through the program once the prerequisites are in place (see discussion below on course maps). Students should usually have multiple paths by which they can complete the program. If this is not the case, then prerequisites may need to be removed. As an alternative to (or in combination with) prerequisites, use the course schedule to limit student course options per semester. By limiting course options, programs can enforce the course sequence without incurring the restrictions inherent to the use of prerequisites.

In the case of both mandatory and voluntary sequencing, students and their advisors should be made aware of the prescribed sequence, and any changes made to the sequence, on an annual basis. Course maps are a convenient way to convey the prescribed course sequence to students and academic advisors. These maps visualize the courses students should take each term throughout the program. It is also beneficial to create multiple maps, with each map providing an alternative path to completion requiring different amounts of time (e.g., completing in two years, three years, or four years). Multiple maps are especially useful in programs with a mix of full-time and part-time students as part-time students will take longer to complete the program than full-time students. Tables 11.1 and 11.2 provide examples of course maps designed for students to complete a fictitious MPA program in two years or three years, respectively. Two final notes about course maps: For MPA programs with multiple concentrations (or specializations), maps should be created for each combination of concentration (or specialization) and time to completion; MPA programs with multiple dates for students to start the program should have sets of course maps for each start date.

MPA programs can improve student outcomes by sequencing courses so that prerequisite and co-requisite courses are taken by students in the proper order. When students enter a course prepared, they do not need to spend time learning prerequisite knowledge or skills while simultaneously learning the course content. Once sequencing is complete, the path(s) through the program must be conveyed to students and their advisors. It is often helpful to convey this information in a visual format such as a program map. In addition to sequencing the curriculum, the program must schedule courses so that students can follow the prescribed sequence without interrupting their progression through the program.

TABLE 11.1 Course Map for Completion in Two Years

Year 1					
Fall		*Spring*		*Summer*	
Course	*Credits*	*Course*	*Credits*	*Course*	*Credits*
PAD 5001	3	PAD 5003	3	Concentration Course	3
PAD 5002	3	PAD 5004	3	Concentration Course	3
Concentration Course	3	Concentration Course	3		
Total Credits	9	*Total Credits*	9	*Total Credits*	6

Year 2			
Fall		*Spring*	
Course	*Credits*	*Course*	*Credits*
PAD 5005	3	PAD 5007	3
PAD 5006	3	Concentration Course	3
Concentration Course	3	PAD 5008 MPA Capstone	3
Total Credits	9	*Total Credits*	9

Scheduling

Once the course sequence is established, it must be operationalized by scheduling courses in the appropriate terms and at the appropriate times. Course maps (see the examples in Tables 11.1 and 11.2) only indicate in which terms courses should be scheduled. When scheduling courses, additional consideration must be given to the following factors: Course section modality, number of program starts, day and time of course sections, faculty coverage, and student academic progress requirements. While a detailed discussion of scheduling is beyond the scope of this chapter, it is important to mention how scheduling relates to student outcomes.

Poor scheduling impedes students' progress toward graduation. Progress is impeded when courses are not offered in the semesters listed in the course maps, course meeting times conflict, or sections are not offered in the necessary modality (e.g., online sections are not available for students who can only take courses online). Scheduling can also affect the ability of students to fund their education by preventing them from meeting academic progress requirements imposed by funding sources. For example, to receive federal financial aid,

TABLE 11.2 Course Map for Completion in Three Years

Year 1

Fall		*Spring*		*Summer*	
Course	*Credits*	*Course*	*Credits*	*Course*	*Credits*
PAD 5001	3	PAD 5003	3	Concentration Course	3
PAD 5002	3	PAD 5004	3	Concentration Course	3
Total Credits	6	*Total Credits*	6	*Total Credits*	6

Year 2

Fall		*Spring*		*Summer*	
Course	*Credits*	*Course*	*Credits*	*Course*	*Credits*
PAD 5005	3	PAD 5007	3	Concentration Course	3
PAD 5006	3	Concentration Course	3	Concentration Course	3
Total Credits	6	*Total Credits*	6	*Total Credits*	6

Year 3

Fall

Course	*Credits*
Concentration Course	3
PAD 5008 MPA Capstone	3
Total Credits	6

students must take a prescribed number of credit hours each semester. If the schedule does not allow students to take enough credit hours to meet requirements, then funding can be denied. Likewise, students receiving tuition reimbursement from their employers may be required to complete a specified number of credit hours each semester. Help students avoid funding issues by ensuring the program's sequencing, scheduling, and course maps meet students' needs.

A final note regarding scheduling. When making a change to the program schedule, keep in mind the potential impacts of any changes on current students. For example, offering a course one semester later than it has historically been offered can interrupt student progress through the program, delay graduation, or negatively affect student access to financial aid. Always have a contingency plan for how to assist any students negatively affected by schedule changes (e.g., offer an additional section of the course at its historical time for one year, provide for independent studies, or substitute other courses).

The Course Level

At the course level, decisions affecting student outcomes are made primarily by the faculty designing, teaching, or overseeing a course. These decisions can affect the time a student has available to engage in learning, the time a student spends engaged in learning, and the rate at which a student learns. The following subsections explain the relationships between these effects and faculty decisions related to content sequencing, non-learning activities, and andragogy. This section concludes with a discussion of student motivation, its relationship to student outcomes, and how instructional decisions influence it. Examples of actions MPA faculty can take to improve student outcomes are provided.

Content Sequencing

Within a single course, sequencing refers to the order in which concepts are presented to students. As with the overall program curriculum, concepts presented in individual courses should be sequenced so that curriculum builds upon itself. For example, in a research methods course the fundamentals of measurement would be taught before methods of experimentation.

The proper sequencing of concepts ensures students are exposed to curricular content in an order that enhances their ability to learn the material quickly. Like program-level sequencing, course-level sequencing is equivalent to mapping out the quickest path to a destination when multiple stops (i.e., concepts) must be made along the way. Failure to sequence concepts in an organized way slows the learning process (Dochy et al., 2002) and can frustrate students. Frustration can reduce students' motivation to learn, which leads to less time spent engaged in learning and, ultimately, poor learning outcomes (Kahu, Stephens, Leach, & Zepke, 2015).

Reduce Time Spent on Non-Learning Tasks

A key inhibitor of student achievement is the allocation of time to non-learning activities. Students have a limited amount of time to learn course concepts. The more time they spend actively engaged in learning, the more they can achieve (Carroll, 1963). In terms of the travel analogy, when a traveler must reach a destination by a certain time (e.g., a student must pass a class by the end of the semester), sitting in traffic (e.g., waiting for instruction) or getting lost (e.g., receiving incorrect instruction) can prevent arrival by the specified time.

Instructors and course designers can take a number of actions to reduce the time students spend on unproductive or non-learning activities. Begin by ensuring that the course assessments align with the course outcomes (i.e., assessment validity) and that the curriculum aligns with the course assessments (i.e., teach only what is tested and test only what is taught). Misalignment at either of these stages results in students spending time on activities that are unrelated to the learning goals of the course.

Faculty should ensure that curricular inputs (e.g., lectures, readings, assignments, etc.) are accurate. Factual errors require students to spend additional time relearning material. Furthermore, correcting errors is more difficult and time-intensive than initially learning the content correctly. In addition to correcting errors in curricular inputs, instructors should also provide students the errata sheets for any textbooks or other materials used in the course.

When designing and updating courses, always develop high-quality materials. The design of a course should minimize the time a student spends on processes that do not increase learning. For example, provide a course structure that is easily navigable. Ease of navigation reduces the time students waste searching for instructional materials and assignments. For online, hybrid, and web-enhanced courses, standardizing elements of course websites across the program and providing navigational videos in individual courses can improve the course navigability.

Faculty should provide frequent, meaningful, and timely feedback. Good feedback identifies student errors and recommends corrections. This process saves students time and encourages them to correct errors by lowering the barriers to finding the correct solutions.

Last, set and communicate clear goals, objectives, and expectations for each class session, activity, learning module, etc. By setting and communicating goals, objectives, and expectations, students know what material to focus on to achieve the learning objectives (Dean, Hubbell, Pitler, & Stone, 2012). As a result, students reduce the time spent on learning content unrelated to the learning objectives of the course and have more time to learn relevant course content.

Andragogy

Andragogy is the "the art or science of teaching adults" (Andragogy, 2019). Andragogy connotes the methods and practices instructors use in teaching. An instructor's choice of teaching methods and practices affects the rate at which students learn (Carroll, 1963). To illustrate, consider a student who sets out independently to learn how to conduct a program analysis. This student could find a variety of resources to learn the material without formal instruction. One of the benefits of formal instruction, however, is that it would enable this student to learn how to correctly conduct a program analysis in less time than would be required by independent learning. In the travel analogy, this is akin to having a knowledgeable navigator give turn-by-turn directions on how to best reach a destination while also avoiding obstructions such as traffic or road work. The quicker a student learns, the more the student can learn in a semester and, as a result, the better the educational outcomes.

Enhancing learning rates requires instructors to manage the process by which students take in information, process that information, and store the processed information in long-term memory. When we learn, we take in new information from the environment, which is then stored and processed in working memory before being transferred into long-term memory (Mayer, 2008). When processing new information, working memory is limited in its capacity to store new information (Miller, 1956), the duration for which it can store the information (Peterson & Peterson, 1959), and its capacity for processing information (Cowan, 2001). Given the limitations of working memory, instructors can enhance the rate at which new information is accurately processed and transferred to long-term memory by managing the demands placed on students' working memory.

The demands placed on working memory by a learning task (i.e., cognitive load) result from either the intrinsic nature of the learning task (intrinsic cognitive load) or the means by which the information is presented (extraneous cognitive load) (Kirschner, Sweller, Kirschner, & Zambrano, 2018; Sweller, 2011). Intrinsic cognitive load can be altered by changing what is to be learned or changing the expertise of the student (i.e., the knowledge the student already has stored in long-term memory) (Sweller, 2011). Extraneous cognitive load can be reduced or eliminated by choosing more efficient instructional procedures (Sweller, 2011). The goal is to minimize extraneous cognitive load and maximize intrinsic cognitive load, without overloading the learner's working memory capacity, so as to enhance student learning rates.

There are a variety of ways instructors can manage intrinsic cognitive load. When the intrinsic cognitive load of a task is low, instructors should increase the variability in the learning activity. Variability in this context refers to the variation in the learning tasks. For example, when teaching descriptive statistics, rather than having students practice repetitively calculating the means of lists of numbers, word problems that vary the context of the problem to be solved could be used to increase variability. More variability increases cognitive load, improves the utilization of working memory capacity, and results in greater learning gains for the amount of time spent learning (Sweller, 2011).

When the intrinsic cognitive load of a task is high, exceeding the capacity of students' working memory, the elements of the learning task should be isolated. By breaking the learning task into independent elements requiring less cognitive load, students can more quickly master the learning task. Once the isolated elements have been learned, they can be recombined into a single learning task (Sweller, 2011). For example, when teaching hypothesis testing and interpretation, the process for conducting a t-test would be taught separately from the process for interpreting the test results. Once students mastered both skills independently, problems requiring them to both conduct t-tests and interpret the results would be introduced.

Another strategy for managing intrinsic cognitive load is to gradually increase task complexity as students develop expertise (Leppink & van den Heuvel, 2015). For example, in a budgeting course, students would begin with problems that involve only fixed costs. Once proficiency was achieved, variable cost problems would be introduced.

A final way to manage intrinsic cognitive load is to gradually increase the fidelity of learning tasks (i.e., the degree to which the learning tasks replicate real-world scenarios). Gradually increasing fidelity increases the complexity of the task and the cognitive load while building on a foundation of prior knowledge developed through less complex tasks (Leppink & van den Heuvel, 2015). By building on prior knowledge, the increase in cognitive load does not overwhelm the student. For example, when teaching financial statement analysis, an instructor may begin with purely numerical examples (i.e., examples that do not use word problems). An instructor can add fidelity by introducing word problems that utilize simplified financial statements for a fictitious organization. The instructor can then further increase fidelity by introducing problems that utilize the actual financial statements of a real organization.

In addition to managing intrinsic cognitive load, there are also a variety of ways instructors can manage extraneous cognitive load. When possible, instructors should introduce new problems without specific goals. When a new problem is introduced with a specific goal to achieve, cognitive load is increased as students must identify the specific means that will achieve the goal. Cognitive load can be reduced by making the goal open-ended, such as by asking students to identify as many solutions as they can (Leppink & van den Heuvel, 2015; Sweller, 2011). For example, when teaching information and technology management, an instructor may ask students to identify as many explanations as they can for the failure of information system implementation rather than asking students to identify the most likely explanation for a given scenario.

To reduce extraneous cognitive load, instructors can provide students with worked examples that demonstrate the detailed steps to solving a problem. Worked examples reduce extraneous cognitive load by assisting students in developing mental models of how to solve problems (Sweller, 2011). For example, when teaching program evaluation, an instructor might provide an example demonstrating the work to be completed at each stage of the process. As students gain proficiency in a task, instructors can begin to introduce partially completed problems (where learners fill in the missing details) as an intermediary step between worked examples and unassisted problem-solving (Leppink & van den Heuvel, 2015). Following the example above, an instructor would provide a program evaluation exercise with some parts completed and other parts left for the student to complete.

To reduce cognitive load, physically integrate information sources so that students' attention is not split across space (e.g., searching for information between text and figures) or time (e.g., remembering instructions from the beginning of a lecture to solve homework problems at a later time). When attention is split, cognitive load is increased due to the need to search for related information (Sweller, 2011). For example, when teaching human resource management, an instructor would provide instructions for writing a part of a job description when the student is attempting to write that section, rather than providing instructions for how to write all parts of a job description and then having students attempt to write a complete description. As an alternative to physically integrating information sources, information from multiple sources may be combined by presenting one source visually and a second source aurally (e.g., narrating a video). Working memory can process visual and aural information simultaneously. Presenting information sources simultaneously using different modalities can therefore reduce cognitive load (Leppink & van den Heuvel, 2015; Sweller, 2011). For example, when explaining systems theory, an instructor may provide students a graphic depicting the systems theory model to which they can refer during the lecture.

Instructors should avoid presenting redundant information. Presenting the same information in multiple formats (e.g., visually and aurally, visually and visually, or aurally and aurally) increases cognitive load without benefit. Cognitive load is increased because learners have to process the same information twice and they will attempt to relate the redundant information (Leppink & van den Heuvel, 2015; Sweller, 2011). An example of redundant information is presenting a fully intelligible graphic with accompanying text that describes the details of the graphic.

It is imperative to understand that these recommendations do not produce the desired effect (i.e., reduced cognitive load) in all circumstances. The effectiveness of each recommendation is dependent on the characteristics of the learning task and the students' cognitive architectures (Sweller, 2011; for a more extensive explanation of cognitive load theory and the circumstances under which these recommendations manage cognitive load, see Sweller, 2011).

In addition to managing cognitive load, instructors can increase student learning rates by affecting the transfer of information from working memory to long-term memory. Transfer is aided by practice and repetition (Kandel, 2006). To promote the transfer of knowledge to long-term memory, repetition and practice should be built into the course and program (i.e., concepts are introduced in one course and reinforced in another).

Motivation

One additional way instructors can influence student learning outcomes is by increasing student motivation and preventing demotivation. Motivated students are expected to allocate more time to learning and spend more of that time engaged in learning activities. The more time students spend engaged in learning, the better their outcomes will be (Carroll, 1963). The following are examples of actions instructors and course designers can take to influence student motivation.

To increase motivation, instructors and course designers can utilize principles of universal design (UX) when constructing online course sites. When course materials are not accessible, students are excluded from participating. Incorporating UX principles into course site design (e.g., machine-readable captions, alternative text, closed captioning) creates an inclusive environment motivating students to persist and engage with course materials.

Motivation is enhanced by quality educational resources (e.g., videos, handouts, podcasts, lectures, textbooks, research articles, assignments, etc.). High-quality resources are engaging and update-to-date, accurate and reliable, well-designed and attractive, culturally diverse and free of bias, accessible to all students, and related directly to the learning objectives (Association of American Publishers, 2019; Quality Matters, 2018).[1] In contrast, poor-quality educational resources are a source of frustration to students and can negatively affect motivation and attention. Examples of quality resources include video and audio resources with high resolution and good sound quality, well-written reading assignments, and concept visualizations that are understandable without explanation.

Instructors should ensure all hyperlinks, whether in documents or course websites, are active and link to the correct content. Inactive or incorrect links frustrate students and require additional time to locate the intended content. Instructors should also ensure all written materials are free of spelling and grammatical errors. Errors of spelling and grammar inhibit understanding, suggest a lack of professionalism on the part of the instructor, and frustrate the reader.

Last, instructors and course designers may consider incorporating principles of gamification in course design. Kapp (2012) defines gamification as "using game-based mechanics, aesthetics and game thinking to engage people, motivate action, promote learning, and solve problems" (p. 10). It is important to note that gamification is not the same as using a game as a learning tool. Rather, it is the use of game design elements to engage and motivate (Buckley & Doyle, 2016; Kapp, 2012). The elements of gamification include the use of goals; rules; conflict, competition, or cooperation; time; reward structures; feedback; levels; storytelling; curves of interest; aesthetics; and replay or do-over (Kapp, 2012). An example of using gamification elements is the use of case studies where the student is asked to assume the role of one of the actors in the case (for a detailed explanation of gamification, see Kapp, 2012).

Student Outcomes

The above explanations of how decisions affect student achievement of outcomes and the recommendations for how to improve achievement have taken the outcomes to be achieved as a given. In reality, NASPAA permits each MPA program great flexibility in defining the outcomes for its students. While NASPAA requires that outcomes cover the program's required, elective, and professional competencies, each program gets to define its competencies relative to the five domains prescribed by NASPAA (see the current NASPAA accreditation standards for more information about competencies and domains). Once the competencies are defined, programs have substantial latitude in developing learning outcomes as long as the outcomes are consistent with the competencies and the program's mission. This chapter concludes with a discussion on developing program and course-level student outcomes relative to a program's established mission and competencies. The development of student outcomes warrants special attention because of the relationship between outcomes and admissions requirements, curricular design, and andragogic choices.

When programs and instructors develop student learning outcomes, they define what is to be learned as well as to what degree of complexity and to what level of proficiency it is to be learned. The first component of a learning outcome, the learning objective, is defined across two dimensions: Breadth of learning and depth of learning. Breadth is the number of concepts to be learned. For example, will students be required to learn only one model of public policy or will they be required to learn several? Depth of learning refers to the complexity of the concept to be learned, often stated as a level on the revised Bloom's Taxonomy (Anderson et al., 2001). For example, will students be required to remember the models of public policy or to apply the models to explain the adoption of a particular policy? The revised Bloom's Taxonomy specifies six levels of cognitive complexity: Remember, understand, apply, analyze, evaluate, and create. Knowledge and skills required by higher levels of the taxonomy build on knowledge and skills attained at the lower levels. The remember, understand, and apply levels describe lower-order thinking skills, while the analyze, evaluate, and create levels describe higher-order thinking skills.

For each level, a list of verbs describes the types of actions students should be able to successfully demonstrate at that level. For example, at the remember level, student actions include identifying people, places, or things and recalling information. These verbs are used when writing learning objectives to indicate what students should be able to achieve after a learning activity, a course, or an MPA program. While objectives at each level of the taxonomy are likely to be included in individual learning activities, at the course level and program level objectives should be related to higher-order thinking skills (i.e., analyze, evaluate, and create). An example of a course-level learning objective for an introductory public administration course is "Analyze the role of public administration and public administrators in the U.S. governance structure." A full discussion of how to write learning objectives using Bloom's Taxonomy is beyond the scope of this chapter but interested readers can find extensive resources related to the revised Bloom's Taxonomy online.

In addition to defining the learning objectives, instructors and programs define the level of performance, or proficiency, students must demonstrate on learning objectives in order to pass classes (e.g., minimum level of performance to earn a passing grade) or graduate from the program (e.g., minimum GPA requirements). A student's aggregate level of proficiency on a set of concepts at the prescribed depths of learning is a measure of the student's overall level of achievement. The choice of learning objectives and proficiency standards define the outcomes students are expected to attain (i.e., the level of achievement that students must attain to pass a course or graduate from a program).

When establishing learning outcomes at the course or program level, the goal is to set students up for success. This is not to imply that learning outcomes should be easy or lack rigor. Rather, it is to say that given the students admitted to an MPA program, and the time allotted to them for completing a course or the program, the learning outcomes should be achievable by students within the time available. When choosing achievement standards, think in terms of the achievement gains the outcomes will require of students rather than the achievement level they represent. If the gains require more time than the students can reasonably allocate to learning, then the students will not be successful, resulting in poor grades, low motivation to learn, and lower persistence and graduation rates. For example, consider a course where the objective is for students to conduct an independent statistics-heavy policy evaluation within eight weeks. If students enter the class without any knowledge of descriptive and inferential statistics, then their likelihood of successfully meeting the learning objective is low. In such a scenario, either the curriculum needs to be sequenced so that students enter the course with the prerequisite knowledge, the admissions requirements need to be changed to reflect the prerequisite knowledge and skills students need in order to be successful in the program, or the course objectives need to be modified.

The guiding principle when establishing learning outcomes at the course or program level is to define objectives and set proficiency standards so that it is possible for the students admitted to the program to attain or surpass the outcomes within the time available. While there is no *a priori* way to know the optimal outcomes a program's students can achieve, the steps outlined below are a guide for thinking about how to define program- and course-level outcomes. In addition to these steps, MPA programs can examine student and faculty experiences in the classroom, student demographics, program and course failure rates, course withdrawals, and dropout rates to assess how well students are meeting current outcomes and what actions are needed to improve achievement of the outcomes (e.g., improved instruction, access to support services, changes in admissions standards, or modifications to learning outcome definitions).

When defining learning outcomes, begin by establishing a reasonable expectation for the amount of time students should allocate to learning. What constitutes a reasonable expectation will depend on the characteristics of the MPA program (e.g., length and progression rate) and the students (e.g., funding source, enrollment status, family status, and employment status). A program's length (i.e., number of courses in the program) and desired progression rate (i.e., time to completion) affect the overall amount of time available for allocation to learning. When choosing a program's length and progression rate, remember that for students, the rate of progression is impacted by their funding source. Employer reimbursement programs may have deadlines for students to finish the degree and the federal student loan program requires students to take a pre-scribed number of credit hours each semester to be eligible for financial aid.

Make sure learning outcome definitions align with the students' reality. Student characteristics, including enrollment status (full-time versus part-time), family status, and employment status, impact the amount of time students can allocate to learning. Students with families, especially families with children or aging parents, have additional demands for their time. Employment also places additional demands on time. Based on the program's length and progression rate, and the characteristics of its students, estimate a reasonable expectation for the amount of time students should allocate to learning to be successful in the program.

After establishing an expectation for the time students should allocate to learning, determine a reasonable expectation for learning gains based on the time allocation expectation and a guestimate of students' learning rates. The experience of the MPA program faculty can provide a reasonable guestimate of how quickly the students in a program learn. The goal here is to set reasonable expectations for students, not to measure the exact learning rates. Learning gains should be chosen so that the time students need to achieve the gains is consist-ent with the allocated time expectation, otherwise students may be unable or unmotivated to allocate enough time to achieve the gains.

When setting learning objectives and proficiency standards for the program or individual courses, set expectations for learning gains that are attainable by students within the time available. In doing so, MPA programs create paths to success for their students. The concepts in this section (e.g., time allocations, learning rate, etc.) do not represent exact measurable quantities. Rather, the concepts indicate ideas that need to be considered when establishing learning outcomes. Exactitude is not necessary for the concepts to be useful. Over time, the program can experiment with different standards and expectations as a means of improving student performance.

Conclusion

This chapter discusses how program choices and instructional practices affect student outcomes, particularly student learning outcomes. Three areas where program choices can affect student learning outcomes are the choice of admissions standards, the curriculum and andragogy, and the definition of student outcomes. The chapter also provides recommendations of actions that programs and instructors can take to improve student outcomes.

MPA program directors interested in improving the learning outcomes of their students should dedicate themselves to developing a clear understanding of how adult students learn and how the actions of programs and instructors inhibit or enhance student learning. While this chapter introduces many of the key concepts related to these topics, research in psychology, education, and neuroscience is continuously developing better understandings of the teaching and learning processes. Keeping abreast of developments in these fields will help MPA directors to develop strategies for continuously improving student outcomes.

Note

1. Open educational resources are a source of high-quality, often free, teaching materials and are widely available online. Quality Matters (2018) provides a list of websites hosting high-quality open educational resources.

References

Anderson, L. W., Krathwohl, D. R., Airasian, P. W., Cruikshank, K. A., Mayer, R. E., Pintrich, P. R., Raths, J., & Wittrock, M. C. (eds) (2001). *A taxonomy for learning, teaching, and assessing: A revision of Bloom's Taxonomy of educational objectives.* New York: Longman.

Andragogy (2019). In *Merriam Webster Online.* Retrieved June 21, 2019, from www. merriam-webster.com/dictionary/andragogy.

Aslanian, C. B., Clinefelter, D. L., & Magda, A. J. (2019). *Online college students 2019: Comprehensive data on demands and preferences.* Louisville, KY: Wiley.

Association of American Publishers (2019). *Quality content for learning resources.* Retrieved June 23, 2019 from https://publishers.org/our-markets/prek-12-learning/quality-content-learning-resources.

Buckley, P. & Doyle, E. (2016). Gamification and student motivation. *Interactive Learning Environments, 24*(6), 1162–1175.

Carroll, J. (1963). A model of school learning. *Teachers College Record, 64*(8), 723–733.

Cowan, N. (2001). The magical number 4 in short-term memory: A reconsideration of mental storage capacity. *Behavioral and Brain Sciences, 24*(1), 87–114.

Dean, C. B., Hubbell, E. R., Pitler, H., & Stone, B. J. (2012). *Classroom instruction that works: Research-based strategies for increasing student achievement.* Alexandria, VA: Association for Supervision and Curriculum Development.

Dochy, F., de Ridjt, C., & Dyck, W. (2002). Cognitive prerequisites and learning: How far have we progressed since Bloom? Implications for educational practice and teaching. *Active Learning in Higher Education, 3*(3), 265–284.

Great Schools Partnership (2013). *Student outcomes.* Retrieved June 23, 2019 from www. edglossary.org/student-outcomes/.

Kahu, E., Stephens, C., Leach, L., & Zepke, N. (2015). Linking academic emotions and student engagement: mature-aged distance students' transition to university. *Journal of Further and Higher Education, 39*(4), 481–497.

Kandel, E. R. (2006). *In search of memory: The emergence of a new science of mind*. New York: W. W. Norton and Company.

Kapp, K. M. (2012). *The gamification of learning and instruction: Game-based methods and strategies for training and education*. San Francisco, CA: John Wiley and Sons.

Kirschner, P. A., Sweller, J., Kirschner, F., & Zambrano, J. R. (2018). From cognitive load theory to collaborative cognitive load theory. *International Journal of Computer-Supported Collaborative Learning, 13*(2), 213–233.

Leppink, J. & van den Heuvel, A. (2015). The evolution of cognitive load theory and its application to medical education. *Perspectives on Medical Education, 4*(3), 119–127.

Mayer, R. E. (2008). Applying the science of learning: Evidence-based principles for the design of multimedia instruction. *American Psychologist, 63*(8), 760–769.

Mercado, D. (2018). The top reason why graduate students choose their school: Hint, it's not cost. *CNBC*. Retrieved June 23, 2019 from www.cnbc.com/2018/01/16/top-reason-why-graduate-students-choose-a-school-hint-its-not-cost.html.

Miller, G. A. (1956). The magical number seven, plus or minus two: Some limits on our capacity for processing information. *Psychological Review, 63*(2), 81–97.

Peterson, L. & Peterson, M. J. (1959). Short-term retention of individual verbal items. *Journal of Experimental Psychology, 58*(3), 193–198.

Quality Matters (2018). *Open educational resources*. Retrieved June 23, 2019 from www.qualitymatters.org/qa-resources/resource-center/articles-resources/open-ed-resources.

Sweller, J. (2011). Cognitive load theory. In Mestre, J. P. & Ross, B. H. (eds), *The psychology of learning and motivation: Vol. 55* (pp. 37–76). San Diego, CA: Elsevier Academic Press.

12

RECRUITING AND RETAINING A DIVERSE STUDENT BODY

William Hatcher and Martha Humphries Ginn

The goal of the chapter is to examine issues of recruitment and retention for public affairs programs in order to provide advice for the directors of Master of Public Administration (MPA) degrees and similar programs in public affairs. Recruiting and retaining diverse student bodies contributes to the goals of fairness and effectiveness in public administration. For instance, when managed properly, diversity in an organization appears to contribute positively to the overall effectiveness of the organization (Choi & Rainey, 2010; Groeneveld & Verbeek, 2012; Pitts, 2009). Gender and minority representativeness also increases inclusivity in organizations and decreases negative workplace occurrences, such as discrimination and bullying (Andrews & Ashworth, 2015). Furthermore, research shows that women in leadership positions are more likely to be democratic (Fox & Schuhmann, 1999; Weikart, Chen, Williams, & Hromic, 2007) and transformational (Eagly, Johannesen-Schmidt, & Van Engen, 2003) compared to men in leadership positions. Thus, MPA programs need to help the public service achieve the benefits of having diverse and inclusive organizations by educating a diverse student body.

Additionally, MPA programs need to maintain sustainable enrollment levels to be viable academic units in their home universities and to serve the needs of the local governments and nonprofits in local communities. MPA directors list recruitment as one of their most important tasks. For instance, 90 percent of surveyed MPA directors of small programs identified recruitment as a part of their responsibilities (Hatcher, Meares, & Gordon, 2017). However, MPA program directors encounter various pressures in the areas of recruitment and retention. Program directors are given little to no money for recruitment, and many MPA programs have difficulties standing out in their home universities (Hatcher, Meares, & Gordon, 2017). Furthermore, professional programs are often viewed as revenue generators for their universities, which only intensifies recruitment pressure (Brainard, 2017).

Given that MPA program graduates presumably staff the bureaucracy, directors also feel additional pressures to ensure that their student bodies reflect the demographics of the population at large. By effectively training a diverse student body within MPA programs, these programs help to facilitate active representation where underrepresented groups and their policy preferences are taken into account in the policy making process (Meier & Stewart, 1992; Selden & Selden, 2001). However, while the number of women and minorities recruited into MPA programs is increasing, we still do not have demographic parity with the population in the programs or the workforce and, additionally, most public agencies in the United States do not have demographic parity with the populations that they serve (Beaty & Davis, 2012; Guy, 1993; Hsieh & Winslow, 2006; Kim & Lewis, 1994; Lee & Cayer, 1987; Naff, 2001; Primo, 2013; Riccucci, 2009; Rivera & Ward, 2008; Sabharwal & Geva-May, 2013; Selden & Selden, 2001). Sabharwal and Geva-May (2013) found "that a majority (63%) of public affairs and related programs have less than 34% of their student body from underrepresented populations" (p. 672). Moreover, furthermore, recent research of the US federal government provides evidence that the contracting out of public services decreases the representative of women and minorities in positions of public management (Brown & Kellough, forthcoming).

The public sector is currently experiencing a wave of retirements from the baby-boomer generation, which provides a window of opportunity for MPA programs to increase demographic representation within the bureaucracy. By paying attention to the educational pipeline, these programs can provide a diverse, knowledge-based workforce who can jumpstart their careers within the general service ranks by having an MPA (Sabharwal & Geva-May, 2013). There is a consensus within the discipline that graduate programs in public affairs need to increase enrollment and attract a pool of qualified minority candidates to meet the need for workplace diversity in the public sector (Kohler & Cropf, 2007; Rice, 2004; Sabharwal & Geva-May, 2013; Selden & Selden, 2001; Soni, 2000; White, 2004). However, Sabharwal and Geva-May (2013) point out that these programs struggle to recruit and retain students from underrepresented minorities. This dilemma is only exacerbated by the reality that African American male recruitment numbers in undergraduate programs are decreasing while other ethnic groups' enrollment numbers are on the rise (Brooks, Jones, & Burt, 2013). Therefore, while the pool of applicants for MPA programs may be growing for some underrepresented populations, it is shrinking for African American males.

While facing the need to help build inclusive public workplaces, MPA directors often receive little to no training to assist them with drafting and implementing recruitment and retention plans for their programs (Hatcher, Meares, & Gordon, 2017). When surveyed, only 25 percent of MPA directors in small programs (ones with fewer than 100 students) reported receiving adequate training for their administrative responsibilities. Many of these directors point to the need for more resources and adequate training to help them implement successful recruitment strategies.

This chapter provides the faculty and leaders of MPA programs with strategies to recruit and retain diverse student bodies. To do this, we review the literature to help identify strategies to recruit and retain students from underrepresented populations. Next, we discuss commonly used recruitment strategies and suggest improved efforts for programs. We follow this section by discussing commonly used retention strategies and suggest improved efforts. Last, we present a case study to illustrate how these recruitment and retention strategies can work in practice.

The Research on Recruitment and Retention in Academic Programs

To assist in recruitment and retention, we reviewed the literature on these topics in general academic programs and public affairs programs. Foremost, the literature on recruitment stresses the importance of "student-centered" strategies (Elliott & Healy, 2001). In particular, the perceived satisfaction of students with the educational experience will motivate the decision to select an institution and specific academic programs. Elsharnouby (2015) found that the reputation of universities and the perceived competency of faculty members are two stronger predictors of student satisfaction with their educational experience. Research shows that student satisfaction is a variable that affects both recruitment and retention. Students who are satisfied with their experiences are more likely to succeed in the university setting, and they are more likely to take additional courses in the area of learning that positively affected their satisfaction (Sinclaire, 2014). Accordingly, from a recruitment and retention standpoint, universities, based on Elsharnouby's finding, should focus on cultivating their reputations among potential students and developing their faculty.

Recruitment and retention for public affairs programs are more target-marketing exercises than mass-marketing (Lewison & Hawes, 2007). In the next few paragraphs, we discuss some of the main target areas that affect recruitment and retention in public affairs programs.

One critical factor identified to help recruit and retain students from underrepresented populations is having a diverse faculty (Breihan, 2007; Brooks, Jones, & Burt 2013; Rogers & Molina, 2006; Sabharwal & Geva-May, 2013). In order to have a diverse faculty, we need to have a diverse professoriate, and unfortunately that is not the current state of affairs. Farmbry (2007) outlines strategies to expand diversity in public affairs doctoral programs including educating underrepresented populations about the benefits of and opportunities involved with a doctoral degree, developing a pool of academic mentors, minimizing barriers in the recruitment process, and developing support networks to help students finish their degree programs. Diversifying the professoriate is a prerequisite to recruiting and retaining a diverse faculty, and diversifying student bodies in master's-level programs is also beneficial to this goal. Schools with higher minority populations are able to attract more diverse faculty (Sabharwal & Geva-May, 2013). Further, many of the strategies identified by Farmbry (2007) to recruit students to doctoral programs apply to the MPA as well.

A primary way to recruit all students is through mass media. Websites are a common method of recruitment, but in order to be effective in recruiting from underrepresented populations, the photos displayed on the pages should reflect student diversity in terms of race, gender, and age (Breihan, 2007). Websites also need to be up-to-date with, at a minimum, monthly updates. NASPAA suggests updating your site weekly on a set day, perhaps having something like a Tuesday Update, so that consumers will check your website more often for new information (NASPAA, 2015a). Local newspapers and local broadcast media are other great avenues for recruiting, particularly in outlets that provide programming directed to minority populations. Beyond advertising, inviting these outlets to cover events where you celebrate the success of minority students will provide content that will resonate with your target populations (Breihan, 2007). Breihan (2007) also has a suggestion for programs that lack the financial resources for advertising. Programs in need of funds to promote themselves in mass media should include requests for media budgets in all grant applications.

Another way to advance recruitment efforts with underrepresented populations is to cultivate relationships with leaders within those communities (Breihan, 2007). This can be done in several ways, including recruiting members to serve on your boards and showing them the value they add to the board and participating in their organizations and events if possible so that you can meet your potential students at these endeavors. If you actively support the minority-led organizations in your community, recruitment through networking should naturally follow. Keeping an updated alumni directory is also beneficial (NASPAA, 2015a). If some of your alumni are leaders in the targeted communities, they can mentor new and potential students to help grow a more diverse program.

A common theme in the recruitment literature is the need to develop individual and personalized relationships with potential future students. With all the advances we have seen with technology and virtual interconnectivity, personalized letters, and campus visits remain the predominant method of effective recruitment (Lee & Cayer, 1987; Sabharwal & Geva-May, 2013). These avenues allow program directors to explain why a program will be uniquely valuable to an interested student. Another important component in this type of recruiting is to build a reputation of being responsive to students. This can be done by making simple changes in accessibility by offering services after work hours and consulting current and potential students about future course schedules to address major conflicts or barriers to enrollment (Breihan, 2007).

Recruiting effectively should also involve serious reflection and critique of your admissions process by asking if there are unnecessary barriers to students applying. Program directors should be asking if the admissions process itself is straightforward and accessible. Application deadlines should be evaluated to determine if they are too early and are therefore precluding a substantial number of late appliers from enrolling. Turn-around time on applications decisions should be examined to see if matters can be expedited. Required application materials need to be explored to determine if the admissions criteria are good predictors of success (Breihan, 2007). A common admission requirement is a minimum score on the Graduate Record Exam (GRE). The quantitative portion of GRE puts midcareer applicants at a disadvantage unless they were in situations to maintain mathematical knowledge from undergraduate degree programs (Clark, 1984; Hartlle, Joan, & Clark, 1983).

Many schools have successfully implemented GRE waivers for certain populations. Some accelerated BA to MPA programs waive the GRE provided the undergraduate has a high enough GPA, and students are attracted to these programs as a result (Kohler & Cropf, 2007). There has long been a debate over whether GRE scores have predictive validity with experienced midcareer adult students. Menifield et al. (2007) found that GRE waivers did not adversely affect the quality of the program studied and that the waiver increased applications for working African Americans and women who traditionally experienced test bias. Similarly, Gibson, Leavitt, Lombard, & Morris (2007) found that the students who received waivers were typically older in-service professionals with greater work experience and that they performed better (measured by GPA) than those without a waiver.

Ultimately, predicting student success in a graduate program is not an exact science, but multiple studies suggest that the GRE is not a very good predictor. Leavitt, Lombard, and Morris (2011) find that the best predictor of MPA student success (measured by final GPA) is undergraduate GPA. Thompson and Kroback (1983) find that student performance in first courses has double the predictive power of success of all admissions criteria, while Oldfield and Hutchinson (1996) find that performance in a methods course in the first semester has more predictive validity than a GRE score. Given that the GRE requirement may discourage some in underrepresented populations from applying and given that the test's predictive power is marginal at best, schools may want to consider waiving this requirement, either for select populations or altogether. Programs may find that greater predictors of success are personal essays or having applicants read and evaluate a professional article similar to ones they will encounter in the program (Breihan, 2007).

Expanding targeted populations can help with recruitment. Adult learners are an undertapped market for the majority of MPA programs (Loutzenhiser &

Orman, 2005). For example, cultivating a collaborative effort between a professional studies program offering a BA to adult learners and a department of public policy with an MPA to offer an accelerated degree to those students could increase enrollment, particularly in underrepresented populations (Kohler & Cropf, 2007). Accelerated programs are advantageous in general because you can recruit directly from your undergraduate population and, as mentioned previously, waiving the GRE requirement is a strong incentive for students to apply.

A challenge in public policy and public administration is the lack of a common undergraduate preparation (Light, 1999). While students coming from various fields can expand recruitment opportunities, and the wide array of educational backgrounds can lead to more experiences, interests, skill sets, and expectations about careers, there is a downside to this variety. The variability in undergraduate education, as well as the gap that may occur between completion of that degree and enrollment in a graduate program, can result in the students lacking training in foundational subjects like American government, political science, mathematics, statistics, and economics (Wechsler & Baker, 2004). The lack of foundational knowledge may discourage applicants from applying or may result in students who enroll deciding to withdraw from the program due to feelings of intellectual inadequacy.

Strategies to overcome deficits in prior educational backgrounds include recommending prerequisite courses, remedial coverage of foundational material in the core coursework, or systematic, intensive instruction outside the regular academic year. Gathering data from NASPAA-affiliated program websites, Wechsler and Baker (2004) found that a majority of programs have recommended prerequisites, with the most common being statistics and mathematics. They found most were just recommended because it is impossible to determine if the student has the baseline that programs are seeking, particularly if time has elapsed. The authors identified "camping" as a promising approach to help students from nontraditional backgrounds get prepared for graduate coursework. Camping is offering intensive instruction outside the regular academic year. For instance, the LBJ School at the University of Texas at Austin offers a four-week day camp in the summer to prepare students for graduate work, and the Truman School at the University of Missouri at Columbia offers a two-week camp during fall semesters. According to Wechsler and Baker (2004) these programs have the following advantages: They help to level the playing field in terms of educational backgrounds; they help students learn important concepts with context about how they apply to the field of public affairs; they help students overcome the fear of failing statistics in the program; and they provide connections with other students and faculty. The problems with these intensive programs include the cost, particularly in faculty labor, and the fact that they are not accessible to students who work full-time.

The creation of these camping programs does highlight the needs of new students, particularly those whose educational backgrounds may be lacking, as well as reinforcing the reality that recruitment and retention are on the same continuum. Program directors must continue recruiting students while they are in the program to ensure progression to graduation (Breihan, 2007). Although schools are making an effort to recruit and retain students from under-represented populations, there is still more to be done in terms of minority engagement and persistence (Harper, 2009; Peltier, Laden, & Matranga, 2000). Practices that help underrepresented students graduate include mentoring by a diverse faculty, facilitating social integration, addressing foundational skills, pro-viding paid internships, and providing other forms of financial assistance (Brooks, Jones, & Burt, 2013; Sabharwal & Geva-May, 2013). Breihan (2007) provides additional concrete steps to take to help with retaining a diverse student body including providing the appropriate sequencing of coursework taking into account the nature of the material and introducing more the applied, interesting, and relevant coursework early. Other suggestions include adjusting teaching styles to meet preferences of students, creating assignments that apply to what students care about with well-defined expectations, and providing prompt feedback. Breihan (2007) also emphasizes the need for direct and per-sonal communication between the students and faculty, as well as the import-ance of recognizing and sharing student success.

Recruitment Strategies in Public Affairs Programs

In this section, we present an overview of recruitment strategies used by many MPA programs. According to marketing advice given by the Network of Schools of Public Policy, Policy, and Administration (NASPAA), MPA directors need to focus on alumni, online resources, employers, media, and students (NASPAA, 2015a). Tables 12.1 and 12.2 present an overview of recruitment strategies and the actions that many MPA programs put in place to recruit students.

For most MPA programs, their websites are their front doors, where most potential students first go to find information. NASPAA also requires MPA programs to post data on their websites reporting their completion rates and alumni job placement statistics. Having a fully functional website that is accessible is a standard requirement for MPA programs to recruit new stu-dents. Many potential students today first turn to social media to learn about academic programs. These potential students want to see programs that offer experiential learning opportunities, networking opportunities, and employ-ment placement data. Additionally, current students and alumni can use social media sites to network with members and supporters of the public affairs pro-grams. Directors of public affairs programs can also use social media sites to push out information about potential employment and academic offerings. Thus, MPA programs need to be active on social media sites, such as Face-book, Twitter, and Instagram.

TABLE 12.1 Possible Recruitment Strategies by Media Type

Online and Social Media	Traditional Media
Maintain a functional website with information on the program and its coursework, job placement, curriculum offerings, community projects, faculty research, and other areas	Encourage faculty to offer their expertise to the media
	Promote the program's community work to local media
Utilize resources like LinkedIn to identify possible students	Consider writing a local column for your community's newspaper on public service
Be active on social media sites, such as Facebook and Twitter	Secure free media when possible
	Consider purchasing advertisements on local radio and television
Provide testimonials of students and alumni through online and social media	Create student pamphlets and promotional materials that emphasis how the program can advance the careers of potential students
Provide information about the program faculty	
Use the sites as forums to advertise potential employment for students, alumni, and potential students	Consider hiring marketing professionals to secure traditional media
Consider purchasing social media ads on a limited basis	

Highly ranked MPA programs have access to resources to conduct significant marketing to local, regional, and national media outlets. Small and regional MPA programs are more limited. The leaders of these programs need to be creative with their efforts to obtain media attention. By being involved in community outreach and applied research, MPA programs can garner free media from local media stories. As long as the attention is positive, media stories will help market the local MPA program and assist MPA directors and faculty with recruitment.

Current students are often the best recruiters for MPA programs. Students have a vested interest in seeing their programs succeed, and they can help spread positive sentiment through multiple networks, compared to the more limited outreach networks of just faculty and staff. To involve students with recruitment efforts, programs should encourage active student associations that help plan professional events such as a speaker series, social events such as graduation celebrations, and volunteer outreach such as encouraging involvement in local nonprofits.

MPA programs rely on their alumni to help with recruitment efforts. Programs that integrate their alumni in marketing efforts can leverage the professional networks of their alumni to provide a positive message to potential students. To accomplish this, programs need to have updated alumni directories

TABLE 12.2 Possible Recruitment Strategies by Actor

Program Students	Alumni Marketing	Community Employers
Ask the program's student association to help promote the program	Leverage alumni networks	Build pipelines with local employers for their employees to earn MPA degrees
Ask students to help program faculty and staff at recruitment-related events	Update alumni directories	Offer an effective job shadowing and internship program and advertise the benefits of the program to potential students
Provide student testimonials of the program	MPA newsletters	
	Create and maintain an alumni association	Build active community advisory boards comprised of local employers to help recruit for the program
	Provide information on alumni job trends	
		Build curriculum offerings that help students secure jobs and serve the public organizations in the community and advertise the benefits of these partnerships
		Schedule information meetings where MPA directors visits local employers to talk about the benefits of their programs

and regular contact with alumni. The creation of alumni associations can be a tool to help leverage alumni for recruitment purposes. Programs can provide alumni updates on their websites, alumni newsletters, and information on the job trends of alumni.

MPA programs can work with community employers to build pipelines for their employees to earn degrees. Programs in public affairs offer internship programs, jobsite shadowing, and even fellowships, with tuition waivers, to build partnerships with community employers. For example, the University of North Carolina at Charlotte's MPA program offers a public service fellowship that places students in local public agencies and nonprofits to work while they are completing their degrees (University of North Carolina at Charlotte, 2017). Additionally, MPA programs should have local community advisory boards that assist in such governance areas as curriculum revisions, internship placement, and program evaluation. MPA directors can use their advisory boards to help recruit students from the board members' agencies and professional networks.

Strategic Recruitment for Public Affairs Programs

NASPAA's advice for marketing MPA programs is a place to start with recruitment strategies, but the broad suggestions do not provide significant help to faculty and leadership who lack backgrounds and experience in recruitment. The problem for public affairs programs is how broad these actions suggested by NASPAA are, and these strategies work for some programs and fail for others. Additionally, the limited research on recruitment and retention, reviewed in this chapter, points to a few common strategies that may work for MPA programs; however, these strategies do not always produce the intended results. Sabharwal and Geva-May (2013) found that public affairs schools "with a lower percentage of students from underrepresented groups use scholarships, tuition waivers, and teaching assistantships to recruit students from these populations" (p. 657). Accordingly, MPA programs need to be strategic in how they develop recruitment plans. To develop a strategic recruitment plan, MPA programs need to do the following.

First, MPA faculty and staff need to collect information from students, alumni, university leaders, and community employers to learn where their programs are succeeding and areas where their programs can be improved. The data can be collected through surveys, focus groups, one-on-one interviewing, and other methods that give program leaders a good understanding of the program's strengths and areas of improvement. Additionally, the stakeholder data needs to include information about the program's students and potential students.

Second, MPA programs need to use stakeholder data to develop their recruitment materials and strategies. Programs often develop recruitment materials and content without reliable data on their potential audience. By using stakeholder data, programs can develop marketing materials and strategies that appeal to potential students. The data may include information on potential students in the program's region. Stakeholder data can include information from opinion surveys of local employers. For example, at Augusta University, we collect information on what local employers want in MPA graduates, and we use this information to help us craft our curriculum but also our marketing efforts to potential students. Data on the educational attainment of a program's potential students is information that should be used in creating marketing strategies, especially social media strategies that can target potential students with specific degrees, career interests, likes, dislikes, etc.

Third, MPA programs need to develop strategies that are unique to their communities and potential students, but there are certain recruitment efforts that work across MPA programs. The following are a few of those efforts. MPA programs need to have a strong presence in their communities. It is a cliché, but it is still true for academic programming. Word of mouth is the best marketing. By being active in their communities through internship programs, applied research partnerships, and employment pipelines, MPA programs can build a strong reputation that will help with the recruitment of students. Next, MPA programs with a strong reputation among other academics normally are successful in their recruitment efforts. For instance, the ranking developed by the US News and World Report are influential with potential students. In public affairs, the graduate rankings are determined by peer surveys sent to program leaders. Accordingly, a program's reputation among others in the field is an area that affects recruitment for most MPA programs. Most importantly, programs recruit students by offering a valuable product. This can include having a cutting-edge curriculum, effective instructors, strong partnerships with practitioners, innovative fellowships, beneficial active learning opportunities, strong internship programs, and strong career placement.

When it comes to recruiting students from underrepresented groups, two studies provide evidence for strategies that may work across MPA programs. In a survey of the nation's public administration programs, Lee and Cayer (1987) found that personal appeals, financial aid, and mentoring services were key strategies to recruit students from underrepresented groups. In a more recent survey of public administration programs, Sabharwal and Geva-May (2013) found similar recruitment strategies being used. The authors' findings stress the need for MPA programs to link recruitment and retention efforts. For instance, the authors found that public administration programs with more faculty from underrepresented groups are more likely to have students from those populations, which demonstrates the important of including retention plans alongside recruitment strategies.

Retention Strategies for Public Affairs Programs

As with their recruitment plans, MPA programs need to be strategic in their retention efforts. On its accreditation website, NASPAA provides peer examples of diversity plans and retention strategies for public affairs programs (NASPAA, 2015b). A review of MPA program retention strategies provided by NASPAA and the literature reviewed in this chapter show that the following activities may be effective for programs to implement.

First, MPA programs need to recruit and retain diverse faculty, so students of all backgrounds feel welcomed and supported. The survey by Sabharwal and Geva-May (2013) demonstrated that programs with diversity in their faculty are also more likely to have diversity in their student bodies, compared to programs with less diverse faculty.

Second, MPA programs need to practice effective advising. While little to no research has been done on the role of advising in MPA programs, the area has been studied in detail in the general literature on directing academic programs (see, for example, White, 2015). Students also recognize the importance of advising to their academic success. In a recent survey of students at Hispanic-serving institution, students preferred academic advising versus the simple sharing of information about academics and, furthermore, more interactions with students and advisors appear to be a student-perceived predictor of academic success (Vasquez, Jones, Mundy, & Isaacson, 2019).

Third, MPA programs need to support mentoring programs and cohort models to help students learn from others who have been through the program and also from their classmates. Mentoring of students and faculty in public affairs programs are areas that have been covered in the scholarly literature (Fountain & Newcomer, 2016; Holzer, 1999; Poel, Arroyos-Jurado, & Coppola, 2006; Portillo, 2007). From a comprehensive study of mentoring among women and minorities in public affairs programs, Portillo (2007) argued for more support for mentoring and more encouragement among leaders that students participate in mentoring programs. While these recommendations seem straightforward, as Portillo (2007) argued, "Simple recognition of the situations that young minority and female scholars face may go a long way toward ensuring their success within our field" (p. 111).

Last, MPA programs need to create processes that allow for faculty discussions on retention issues. These processes can be accomplished through productive faculty meetings, advisory board meetings, and advising meetings with students. Additionally, a strong introductory to public administration course in a program can be beneficial. Such a course will help on-board students to public administration and also their MPA program, helping retain the students. Having a "welcome to the program" module for new students may also increase retention. At Augusta University, we have a module for all new students that they complete before starting that helps get them up to speed on what they need to know as new students in the program.

Case Study of Recruitment and Retention: Augusta University's MPA Program

To illustrate the recruitment strategies that can be used by program directors, we discuss the recruitment, marketing, and retention strategies of Augusta

University's MPA program (AU MPA).[1] Recently, the AU MPA program has experienced significant growth. From spring 2016 to fall 2017, applications to the MPA program increased by 200 percent, and enrollment increased by over 125 percent. In the past two years, there has been an increase in the size of the total student body from approximately 30 students to over 60 students. At the same time, the program has made progress toward maintaining a diverse student body and improving its retention rates, including the time to completion for its students. The MPA director and faculty have been able to accomplish these goals with limited marketing funds and other resources. Accordingly, the AU MPA serves as an excellent case study to illustrate how incremental and cost-effective efforts can improve the recruitment and retention of public affairs programs. These strategies are detailed in the program's strategic marketing plan and diversity plan.

AU MPA's Strategic Marketing Plan

Table 12.3 presents the program's marketing goals and strategies that have been put in place to achieve these goals. Overall, the program has been driven by the goal to increase enrollment. The marketing goals and strategies, as mentioned, have helped the program increase its enrollment. With its marketing plan, the program seeks to implement the following goals.

- Increase partnerships with other academic programs at AU.
- Increase partnerships in the field of public administration.
- Increase partnerships with public agencies and nonprofits in the program's community.
- Improve the program's website and social media presence.
- Improve marketing through traditional media.
- Encourage students and alumni to help promote the program.

To accomplish these goals, the program has put in place the following strategies. The program leadership acquired new promotional materials, including an updated brochure. The program's director regularly meets with classes on campus, organizes information meetings in the community, and holds other forums to promote the program. The program greatly improved its website. There has been a significant increase in traffic to this site. The program works with the university's Division of Communication and Marketing and the Graduate School to publish profiles of current students and alumni.

The program works with alumni to promote the benefits of earning an MPA to their professional networks. To accomplish this, the director updated the program's alumni directory. The program's director and staff have built a strong presence on Twitter and Facebook for the program.

TABLE 12.3 Augusta University (AU) MPA Strategic Marketing Goals and Strategies

Goals	Strategies
Increase partnerships with other academic programs at AU and in the field of public administration	The program works closely with the leadership of other programs on campus
	The program offers a Certificate in Nonprofit Leadership with the university's MBA program
	The program partners with the university's Cyber Institute to conduct a workforce study for the Augusta-Richmond Metropolitan Area. The workforce study receives significant attention in local media, helping promote the work of the MPA program
	The program's director works closely with NASPAA, including serving as co-editor-in-chief of the association's scholarly journal, the *Journal of Public Affairs Education*
Increase partnerships with public agencies and nonprofits in the program's community	The program's director regularly meets with classes on campus, organizes information meetings in the community, and holds other forums to promote the program
	The program partners with the university's Cyber Institute to conduct a workforce study for the Augusta-Richmond Metropolitan Area. The workforce study receives significant attention in local media, helping promote the work of the MPA program
Improve program website and presence on social media	The program greatly improves its website
	The program maintains a dedicated staff position for social media promotions
	The program's director and staff have built a strong presence on Twitter and Facebook for the program
Improve marketing through traditional media	The program leadership acquires new promotional materials, including an updated brochure
	The program has been featured in local news stories
Encourage students and alumni to promote the program	The program works with the university's Division of Communication and Marketing and The Graduate School to publish profiles of current students and alumni
	The program works with alumni to promote the benefits of earning an MPA to their professional networks. To accomplish this, the director updates the program's alumni directory

The program's director works closely with NASPAA, including serving as co-editor-in-chief of the association's scholarly journal, *Journal of Public Affairs Education*. The program partnered with the university's Cyber Institute to conduct a workforce study for the Augusta-Richmond Metropolitan Area. The workforce study received significant attention in local media, helping promote the work of the MPA program.

Over the past five years, the AU MPA program has made changes to its admission standards and curriculum that have helped the program recruit and retain students. First, in 2016, the program implemented an accelerated degree option where undergraduate students with a certain GPA can complete both their BA and MPA degrees within five years. Similar BA-MPA degrees have been used as a tool to recruit adult learners by offering clear pathways toward degree completion (Kohler & Cropf, 2007). The AU BA-MPA program was created to recruit adult learners but also to be an attractive option for excellent undergraduate students who have a goal of public service. The program serves as a mechanism to recruit new MPA students, but also as a tool for the university to retain its excellent undergraduate students in one of its graduate programs. Additionally, the BA-MPA program helps decrease the time to completion for the program's students.

Second, the AU MPA program implemented a graduate-level certificate in nonprofit leadership. The certificate helps the program recruit students and serve their career goals. The Augusta-Richmond Metropolitan Area has one of the largest concentrations of nonprofits in the nation. Nonprofit organizations comprise 5 percent of gross domestic product (GDP), and importantly the nonprofit sector in recent years has been growing faster than the for-profit sector (Lambert, 2013). By design, students can complete the nonprofit certificate with their MPA and do not have to earn any additional credits. Given the certificate's flexibility and the career outlook for nonprofit management, the certificate in nonprofit leadership has helped the AU MPA recruit students since it was created in 2016.

Last, the MPA program has restructured its core curriculum to give students more flexibility to build elective focus areas. Currently, students complete 21 hours of core classes and 15 hours of electives. For the core classes, students take courses dedicated to key concepts and practices in public management and starting in 2017 students complete a course on leadership and ethics. The course is taught by a practitioner who can link the theory on the topics to practice. So far, students have thoroughly enjoyed the course, and it has helped with recruitment. Also, students have been attracted to the program by having the ability to craft several electives. Increasing elective offerings distinguishes the AU MPA from many other public affairs programs and also Master of Business Administration programs that are decreasing their electives. Having more electives allow students to get creative with their plans of study during their time in the AU MPA. The program offers two formal focus areas: Concentration in criminal justice and a certificate in nonprofit leadership. Students who do not use their electives to earn one of these foci build their concentration areas in local management, economic community development, cyber-security, and research-related coursework.

The AU MPA leadership and faculty are working on other curriculum changes for the future. The Augusta-Richmond Metropolitan Area has several ongoing development and planning projects. To capitalize on this opportunity, the program is creating a certificate in urban planning and development. Additionally, the program hopes to create an undergraduate degree program in nonprofit management to build pipelines for public service with many of the undergraduate students hopefully moving on to earn their MPA degrees from Augusta University.

AU MPA's Diversity and Inclusion Plan

The AU MPA program's diversity and inclusion plan seeks to accomplish the following goals.

- Recruit and retain a diverse study body.
- Recruit and retain a diverse faculty.
- Provide an educational experience that ensures graduates are culturally competent.

The program leadership and faculty implemented the following strategies to achieve these goals. First, to recruit and retain a diverse study body, the program is deliberately targeting efforts to recruit students from Paine College, a historically Black college in the Augusta community. The program is also highlighting its low tuition cost and planning long-term to create scholarships for minority students. Currently, the director helps students obtain graduate assistantship around campus that funds their tuition and works to ensure that this tool is used to help recruit and retain a diverse study body. AU MPA students complete a module of cultural competency in their first course in the program. The module asks students to reflect on issues of diversity in public workplaces and their daily lives. Through pre- and post-testing, we have found that students increase their self-reported perceptions of diversity and inclusion.

Second, to recruit and retain a diverse faculty, the program advertises position openings broadly, and the director works with associations in the field to help build diverse applicant pools. Currently, the program's faculty is diverse, including four women faculty members, an African American faculty member, and two white male faculty members. The program is open to using future faculty searches to increase the diversity of the program. Having a diverse faculty is important to show minority students that the faculty is reflective of them.

Last, to provide educational experience that ensures graduates are culturally competent, students participate in educational modules throughout the coursework and the program leadership provides speakers and other forums that help promote diversity.

Conclusions

MPA programs need to be sustainable in terms of enrollment and representative of their communities to serve the public. The leaders of public affairs programs are normally not experts in marketing, but MPA directors face a challenge to grow their programs, ensure diversity, and promote a climate of inclusion. They often have to accomplish these goals in an environment of scarce resources. The goal of this chapter was to provide MPA directors, faculty, and staff with strategies to recruit and retain diverse student bodies. We hope the strategies discussed and the profile of our experiences in the Augusta University MPA program will help public affairs faculty build diverse and inclusive public affairs programs.

Note

1. Please note that the information in this section is taken from the Augusta University MPA program's planning documents, internal records, and the program's director, who is a co-author of this chapter.

References

Andrews, R. & Ashworth, R. (2015). Representation and inclusion in public organizations: Evidence from the UK civil service. *Public Administration Review, 75*(2), 279–288.

Beaty, L. & Davis, T. J. (2012). Gender disparity in professional city management: Making the case for enhancing leadership curriculum. *Journal of Public Affairs Education, 18*(4), 617–632.

Brainard, L. A. (2017). Directing public affairs programs. *Journal of Public Affairs Education, 23*(3), 779–784.

Breihan, A. W. (2007). Attracting and retaining a diverse student body: Proven, practical strategies. *Journal of Public Affairs Education, 13*(1), 87–101.

Brooks, M., Jones, C., & Burt, I. (2013). Are African-American male undergraduate retention programs successful? An evaluation of an undergraduate African-American male retention program. *Journal of African American Studies, 17*(2), 206–221.

Brown, L. A. & Kellough, J. E. (forthcoming). Contracting and the bureaucratic representation of minorities and women: Examining evidence from federal agencies. *Review of Public Personnel Administration.* doi:10.1177/0734371X18822051.

Choi, S. & Rainey, H. G. (2010). Managing diversity in US federal agencies: Effects of diversity and diversity management on employee perceptions of organizational performance. *Public Administration Review, 70*(1), 109–121.

Clark, M. J. (1984). *Older and younger graduate students: A comparison of goals, grades, and GRE scores* (Research Report 84–5). Princeton, NJ: Educational Testing Service.

Eagly, A. H., Johannesen-Schmidt, M. C., & Van Engen, M. L. (2003). Transformational, transactional, and laissez-faire leadership styles: A meta-analysis comparing women and men. *Psychological Bulletin, 129*(4), 569–591.

Elliott, K. M. & Healy, M. A. (2001). Key factors influencing student satisfaction related to recruitment and retention. *Journal of Marketing for Higher Education, 10*(4), 1–11.

Elsharnouby, T. H. (2015). Student co-creation behavior in higher education: The role of satisfaction with the university experience. *Journal of Marketing for Higher Education, 25*(2), 238–262.

Farmbry, K. (2007). Expanding the pipeline: Explorations on diversifying the professoriate. *Journal of Public Affairs Education, 13*(1), 115–132.

Fountain, J. & Newcomer, K. E. (2016). Developing and sustaining effective faculty mentoring programs. *Journal of Public Affairs Education, 22*(4), 483–506.

Fox, R. L. & Schuhmann, R. A. (1999). Gender and local government: A comparison of women and men city managers. *Public Administration Review, 59*(3), 231–242.

Gibson, P. A., Leavitt, W. L., Lombard, J. R., & Morris, J. C. (2007). Acknowledging the "professional" in professional degree programs: Waiving the standardized exam for in-service applicants to an MPA program. *College Student Journal, 41*(4), 872–885.

Groeneveld, S. & Verbeek, S. (2012). Diversity policies in public and private sector organizations: An empirical comparison of incidence and effectiveness. *Review of Public Personnel Administration, 32*(4), 353–381.

Guy, M. E. (1993). Three steps forward, two steps backward: The status of women's integration into public management. *Public Administration Review, 53*(4), 285–292.

Harper, S. R. (2009). Race-conscious student engagement practices and the equitable distribution of enriching educational experiences. *Liberal Education, 95*(4), 38–45.

Hartlle, T. W., Joan, C. B., & Clark, M. J. (1983). *Older students and the GRE aptitude test* (Research Report 83–20). Princeton, NJ: Educational Testing Service.

Hatcher, W., Meares, W. L., & Gordon, V. (2017). The capacity and constraints of small MPA programs: A survey of program directors. *Journal of Public Affairs Education, 23*(3), 855–868.

Holzer, M. (1999). Mentoring as a commitment to teaching. *Journal of Public Affairs Education, 5*(1), 1–4.

Hsieh, C. W. & Winslow, E. (2006). Gender representation in the federal workforce: A comparison among groups. *Review of Public Personnel Administration, 26*(3), 276–294.

Kim, P. S. & Lewis, G. B. (1994). Asian Americans in the public service: Success, diversity, and discrimination. *Public Administration Review, 54*(3), 285–290.

Kohler, J. M. & Cropf, R. A., (2007). Creating an accelerated joint BA-MPA degree program for adult learners. *Journal of Public Affairs Education, 13*(2), 383–401.

Lambert, J. (2013). Infographic: What is driving non-profit sector's growth. *Nonprofit Quarterly*. Retrieved March 10, 2019 from https://nonprofitquarterly.org/2013/12/10/infographic-what-is-driving-nonprofit-industry-growth/.

Leavitt, W. L., Lombard, J. R., & Morris, J. C. (2011) Examining admissions factors in an MPA program. *Journal of Public Affairs Education, 17*(3), 447–460.

Lee, D. S. & Cayer, N. J. (1987). Recruitment of minority students for public administration education. *Public Administration Review, 47*(4), 329–335.

Lewison, D. M. & Hawes, J. M. (2007). Student target marketing strategies for universities. *Journal of College Admission, 196*, 14–19.

Light, P. C. (1999). *The new public service*. Washington, DC: Brookings Institution Press.

Loutzenhiser, K. K. & Orman, R. G. (2005, October). *What happens when you cross public administration with school serving adults?* Panel session at the annual meeting of the National Association of Schools of Public Affairs and Administration, Washington, DC.

Meier, K. J. & Stewart, J. (1992). Active Representation in educational bureaucracies: Policy impacts. *American Review of Public Administration, 22*(3), 157–171.

Menifield, C. E., Clay, J., Carruth, J. R., Cheever, K., Norris-Tirrell, T., & Norris, G. E. (2007). Waiving the MPA entrance exam: Impact on performance. *Journal of Public Affairs Education, 13*(2), 403–424.

Naff, K. C. (2001). *To look like America: Dismantling barriers for women and minorities in government*. Boulder, CO: Westview Press.

Network of Schools of Public Policy, Affairs, and Administration (2015a). *5 simple ways to market your program*. Retrieved March 10, 2019 from www.naspaa.org/principals/resources/5-tips.asp.

Network of Schools of Public Policy, Affairs, and Administration (2015b). *Peer examples*. Retrieved March 10, 2019 from https://accreditation.naspaa.org/resources/peer-examples/.

Oldfield, K. & Hutchinson, J. (1996). Using graduate record examination scores and partial graduate grade point averages to predict academic performance in selected classes at an urban Master of Public Administration program. *College Student Journal, 30*(4), 519–524.

Peltier, G. L., Laden, R., & Matranga, M. (2000). Student persistence in college: A review of research. *Journal of College Student Retention: Research, Theory & Practice, 1*(4), 357–375.

Pitts, D. (2009). Diversity management, job satisfaction, and performance: Evidence from US federal agencies. *Public Administration Review, 69*(2), 328–338.

Poel, E. W., Arroyos-Jurado, E., & Coppola, B. J. (2006). Women, mentoring, and a border university. *Journal of Public Affairs Education, 12*(4), 501–513.

Portillo, S. (2007). Mentoring minority and female students: Recommendations for improving mentor in public administration and public affairs programs. *Journal of Public Affairs Education, 13*(1), 103–113.

Primo N. (2013). NASPAA diversity report. *Network of Schools of Public Policy, Affairs, and Administration*. Retrieved June 4, 2019 from www.naspaa.org/sites/default/files/docs/2018-12/diversity-report-10-01-13.pdf.

Riccucci, N. M. (2009). The pursuit of social equity in the federal government: A road less traveled? *Public Administration Review, 69*(3), 373–382.

Rice, M. F. (2004). Organizational culture, social equity, and diversity: Teaching public administration in the postmodern era. *Journal of Public Affairs Education, 10*(2), 143–154.

Rivera, M. A. & Ward, J. D. (2008). Employment equity and institutional commitments to diversity: Disciplinary perspectives from public administration and public affairs education. *Journal of Public Affairs Education, 14*(1), 9–20.

Rogers, M. R. & Molina, L. E. (2006). Exemplary efforts in psychology to recruit and retain graduate students of color. *American Psychologist, 61*(2), 143–156.

Sabharwal M. & Geva-May, I. (2013) Advancing underrepresented populations in the public sector: Approaches and practices in the instructional pipeline. *Journal of Public Affairs Education, 19*(4), 657–679.

Selden, S. C. & Selden, F. (2001). Rethinking diversity in public organizations for the 21st century: Moving towards a multicultural model. *Administration and Society, 33*(3), 303–329.

Sinclaire, J. K. (2014). An empirical investigation of student satisfaction with college courses. *Research in Higher Education Journal, 22*, 1–22.

Soni, V. (2000). A Twenty-first century reception for diversity in the public sector: A case study. *Public Administration Review, 60*(5), 395–408.

Thompson, L. & Kroback, P. (1983). Predicting the success of students in an MPA Program. *Teaching Political Science, 10*(4), 182–188.

University of North Carolina Charlotte (2017). *Public service fellowship program*. Retrieved March 10, 2019 from https://mpa.uncc.edu/community-outreach.

Vasquez, S., Jones, D., Mundy, M. A., & Isaacson, C. (2019). Student perceptions of the value of academic advising at a Hispanic serving institution of higher education in South Texas. *Research in Higher Education Journal, 36*, 1–36.

Wechsler, B. & Baker, D. L. (2004). Going camping: A new strategy for preparing academically diverse students. *Journal of Public Affairs Education, 10*(1), 19–29.

Weikart, L. A., Chen, G., Williams, D. W., & Hromic, H. (2007). The democratic sex: Gender differences and the exercise of power. *Journal of Women, Politics & Policy, 28*(1), 119–140.

White, E. R. (2015). Academic advising in higher education: A place at the core. *The Journal of General Education, 64*(4), 263–277.

White, S. (2004). Multicultural MPA curriculum: Are we preparing culturally competent public administrators? *Journal of Public Affairs Education, 10*(2), 111–123.

13

CULTURAL COMPETENCY AND SOCIAL EQUITY IN PUBLIC AFFAIRS PROGRAMS

Susan T. Gooden and Brandi Blessett

In order for graduates of MPA programs to demonstrate cultural competency and appreciate the value of social equity, it is critical for both senior program administrators and program faculty to first lead the way. Deans, program chairs, and faculty need to assess the extent to which cultural competency and social equity permeate the organizational culture. As Pitts and Wise (2004) contend,

> A question for the public affairs community is whether the increased importance and relevance of diversity is reflected in the organizational culture of public affairs programs, or whether academic institutions, like many other organizations, ignore potential consequences related to diversity.
>
> *(p. 125)*

Put simply, graduates of MPA programs cannot be culturally competent or appreciate the value of social equity if such expertise is not held at the program level. This chapter discusses the general importance of cultural competency and social equity and applies this importance specifically to public affairs programs and the governing capacity of communities.

We present examples of how MPA programs can promote cultural competency throughout the student experience, and we discuss how public affairs' program leadership can routinely assess and evaluate their progress.

Cultural Competency and Social Equity in Public Affairs Education

In order for public administrators to carry out their mission of serving the public as a whole, they must have the skills to meet the diverse needs of all members of the population they serve. Such skills are commonly referred to as cultural competency (Norman-Major & Gooden, 2012). Cultural competency is fundamental to the implementation of good government and governmental organizations are "indispensable to a secure and civilized life" (Goodsell, 2004, p. 11).

As Cross (1988) discussed,

> [t]he word culture is used because it implies the integrated pattern of human behaviors that includes thought, communication, actions, customs, beliefs, values, and institutions of a racial, ethnic, religious or social group. The word competence is used because it implies having the capacity to function effectively.
>
> *(p. 1)*

Taken together, cultural competency is fundamentally about respect and understanding of diverse communities (Borrego & Johnson, 2012). Cultural competency also prioritizes cultural understanding. Such understanding ultimately leads to better service delivery because community strengths are valued and community differences are contextualized.

While cultural competency is important, it is also complicated. As Norman-Major and Gooden (2012) explain,

> [w]hile the goal is to increase cultural competence in public services to a wide range of people, we must also consider limits brought on by budget constraints and competing goals, values, demands and interests. Many questions are likely to arise: How many languages can be served? How much translation can we afford and what languages do we choose? How much accommodation is reasonable and affordable? Where does meeting the needs of one group potentially impinge on the rights of others? How do we balance varying ethics and cultural practices with the safety and well-being on community members?
>
> *(p. 10)*

A public affairs program that places a high priority on cultural competency prepares students to professionally address these important questions.

Addressing such questions requires prominent considerations of social equity. Relative to public administration, social equity is:

> [t]he fair, just, and equitable management of all institutions serving the public directly or by contract, and the fair, just, and equitable distribution of public services, and implementation of public policy and the community to promote fairness, justice, and equity in the formulation of public policy.
>
> *(Standing Panel on Social Equity, 2000)*

As Frederickson (2005) explained,

> [i]t is time for public administrators of all kinds to ask the so-called second question. The first question is whether an existing public program or proposed program is effective or good. The second question is more important. For whom is the program effective or good?
>
> *(p. 35)*

Cultural competency and social equity are important for public administrators – the daily operators of government. "The answer to Frederickson's second question requires consideration of how opportunity is structured in the United States. Social structures, including public bureaucracies, are important transmitters of opportunity" (Gooden, 2014, p. 16). It is a core responsibility of public affairs educators to equip students with the skills to research and learn important historical context, identify and examine structural gaps between democratic ideals and the realities of policy implementation and practice, develop skills to assess inequities by applying rigorous quantitative and qualitative skills, and evaluate and improve the capacity of governmental organizations to successfully navigate these uncomfortable or "nervous" areas of government.

Importance of Public Administration Programs and Governing Capacity of Communities

Public administration programs educate and prepare professionals to work across government jurisdictions, in nonprofit and philanthropic institutions, as well as in neighborhood associations as organizers and advocates. The breadth and depth for which public administrators affect the lives of people in and across the country cannot be understated. To be relevant and legitimate in a democracy, public institutions have a responsibility to meet the needs of all citizens (Frederickson, 2010). The reality is that social equity considerations have not always been given the same value and legitimacy as normative concepts of effectiveness, efficiency, and economy (Gooden, 2014). However, in the twenty-first-century globalized society, social equity has to be a foundational component of research, pedagogy, and service. The implications for people and communities are far too important to ignore.

Social injustice manifests itself in any number of ways daily for everyday citizens. For example, crime and criminality have been disproportionately attributed to the behaviors of people with marginalized racial, sexual, and gender identities (Gaynor, 2018). Public administrators made decisions regarding exclusionary zoning and highway and public housing construction that displaced Black residents and destroyed their neighborhoods in many central cities across the country (Alkadry & Blessett, 2010; Alkadry, Blessett,

& Patterson, 2017; Dantzler, 2016). Disparate health outcomes, for example, disproportionately affect people of color largely, but Black people specifically. At every economic level, Black people face greater health disadvantages than their white counterparts, which is related to higher morbidity and mortality, higher prevalence of chronic conditions, and poorer health outcomes (Institute of Medicine, 2003). Using the Social Determinants of Health Model (SDOH), Blessett and Littleton (2017) suggests integrative and collaborative approaches between public, nonprofit, and private actors are necessary to drive change. In other words, integrative in that policy actions take into consideration all of the factors related to the SDOH model: Neighborhood and the built environment; health and health care; social and community context; education; and economic stability. Collaborative strategies recognize the ability to leverage assets and interests across multiple sectors in order to create long-lasting change.

Public administration classrooms are opportunities to raise the level of consciousness around inequity and disparity. Many public administrators start their careers as street-level bureaucrats, which means they interact directly with citizens during the regular course of their jobs; their work within bureaucracies affords them wide latitude in job performance; and in this role they have an extensive impact on the lives of citizens (Lipsky, 1971). These intimate interactions inform the impressions and perceptions citizens have of government and the administrative state. When interactions are less than desirable, distrust and hostility can fester between administrators, institutions, and communities. The ability to prepare students to be mindful in their engagement with diverse constituents and cognizant of the ways institutional practices have and continue to sustain inequity are important acknowledgments. Moreover, Lopez-Littleton, Blessett, and Burr (2018) argue

> The next cadre of public service personnel will set agendas, allocate resources, and be responsible for the development and implementation of public policies. Program graduates will be lawmakers and responsible for creating a fair and just society for future generations ... In other words, government actors must consciously develop strategies for working toward racial equity and identifying structural racism (systems or practices that negatively affect racial and ethnic groups).
>
> *(p. 455)*

Prioritizing knowledge, skills, and behaviors that seek to advance equity are significant for effective service delivery. In this regard, public administration curricula should advocate for ethical practices, professional standards, and accountability measures to promote equity, justice, and fairness for all factions of US society.

Public Administration Curricular Examples

Given the Network of Schools of Public Policy, Analysis, and Administration's (NASPAA) accreditation standards, many public administration programs offer similar core curricula including courses such as an introduction to public administration, human resources management, financial management, research methods, organization theory and behavior, and a capstone course. Below, we consider how cultural competency can be integrated into four of these courses: the introduction to public administration, research methods, organization theory and behavior, and the capstone.

Introduction to Public Administration

Introduction to public administration (hereafter called Intro) classes are designed to orient students to the field of public administration. Most Intro classes introduce students to the founding thinkers and eras of the field. *Classics of Public Administration* by Shafritz and Hyde (2017), now in its eighth edition, is commonly used because of its chronological overview and topical content. While insightful for demonstrating the evolution of the field, the text is limited in offering time-specific social, political, and cultural context to further situate the discipline. Of the 54 chapter excerpts included in the book only eight women are included in what is considered a seminal public administration text (see Table 13.1). A quick overview reveals the dominant perspectives that contributed to the knowledge production of public administration theory and research were by white men. The contributions of women and people of color have increased over time, but those voices have to be included as a supplement to traditional public administration texts.

Since public administration does not happen in a bubble, students should be made aware of the environment for which the discipline evolved. As an interdisciplinary field, public administration classes can integrate diverse perspectives to better contextualize the short- and long-term effects of public administration on groups or communities. For example, Woodrow Wilson offers his analysis on "The Study of Public Administration," which is framed from an objective, apolitical, and technical orientation. Wilson (1887) argues for civil service to be treated like a business; it is sensitive to public opinion, and administration lies outside the sphere of politics. During the time of Wilson's publication, the political, economic, and social context of the United States was in flux. Chattel slavery ended in 1863 with the signing of the 13th Amendment to the Constitution. Despite an "end" to the practice of slavery, Black people where still treated as second-class citizens across all factions of society – in public and private institutions, by political rhetoric and public discourse, as well as in the media through its imagery. Despite attempts to isolate public administration of the environmental conditions of the time, not having discussions about race and

TABLE 13.1 Women Published in Classics of Public Administration

Author	Title	Year	Theme
Jane Addams	Problems of Municipal Public Administration	1904	Early Voices and the First Quarter-Century
Mary Parker Follett	The Giving Orders	1926	Early Voices and the First Quarter-Century
Alice M. Rivlin	Systematic Thinking for Social Action	1971	From JFK to Civil Service Reform
Naomi Caiden	Public Budgeting Amidst Uncertainty and Instability	1981	From Reagan to Reinvention
Martha Derthick	American Federalism: Madison's Middle Ground in the 1980s	1987	From Reagan to Reinvention
Camilla Stivers	Toward a Feminist Perspective in Public Administration	1990	From Reagan to Reinvention
Lois Recasino Wise	The Motivational Bases of Public Service	1990	From Reagan to Reinvention
Rosemary O'Leary	The Ethics of Dissent: Managing Guerilla Government	2006	Public Administration in the Twenty-First Century (through 2011)

racism, systemic oppression, and inequality does not help the field evolve in a way that is responsive to the needs of all citizens.

A counter-narrative to Wilson would be the inclusion of essays from *The Modern African American Political Thought Reader* edited by Jones (2013). This text is a compilation of essays from Black thought leaders across US history. Organized in a similar way to the "classics," the eras include: The Antebellum Era: The Rise of Abolitionism; Reconstruction and Beyond: Debates over the Negro Problem and the Creation of Civil Rights Discourse; Black Nationalism: Its Roots and Development; Radical Black Feminism; Modern Black Conservatives: Why Black "Neo-Cons" Matter; and The New Black Moderate: Obama and Beyond. The diversity of arguments presented are from men and women, conservatives and liberals, radicals and moderates. Students can use the readings to examine the Black political discourse when compared to normative policy discussion and political rhetoric.

To the extent that public administration is taught without context, Jones' book is a way to bring race and culture into the landscape of US public administration. Table 13.2 uses Black political thought to illuminate structural barriers and institutional practices that limited access and opportunity for Black people in the United States. Too often attention is paid to individual failures, rather

TABLE 13.2 Counter-Narratives in Public Administration

Eras of Public Administration (Shafritz and Hyde)	Modern African American Political Thought (Angela Jones)	Context
Period 1: 1887–1926 (Public Administration Dichotomy)	The Antebellum Era: The Rise of Abolitionism	The politics–administration dichotomy is advocated as best practice during the time Black people have been held captive and in bondage for 400 years. Public institutions are inherently involved in maintaining the subjugated status of Black people and are therefore not objective in the administration of government.
Period 2: 1927–1937 (Principles of Administration)	Reconstruction and Beyond: Debates over the Negro Problem and the Creation of Civil Rights Discourse	Efficiency and economy are lauded as values of public administration. Equity does not make its way into the public administration lexicon for another 40 years. What is the consequence of not addressing equity for the most vulnerable citizens in the United States?
Period 4: 1948–1970 (Public Administration as Management)	Black Nationalism: Its Roots and Development/ Black Radical Feminism	The fight for Civil Rights is emergent during this era. The inability of the US government to be responsive to the needs of Black citizens results in the rise of Black Nationalist movements designed to illuminate the disparity that exists across the US context: Access to public facilities, education, employment, health care, recreation.

than public policy decisions, administrative discretion, public opinion, and political discourse as far-reaching factors that have created, reinforced, and sustained racial hierarchy. The ability to contextualize public administration education within the context of real-world events and perspectives affords students the opportunity to have difficult conversations and challenge normative assumptions about people and place, but also situates their role as public service professionals in ways that do not repeat past mistakes.

The juxtaposition of the two narratives is important. First, Wilson is known as the "grandfather" of public administration. As someone so foundational to the intellectual development of the field, it is problematic to not appropriately anchor public administration without an honest discussion of race relations at such a crucial time in US history. Second, developing a field without relevant cultural context results in a workforce that is uneducated about how public policies and administrative decisions produce divergent realities for people by race, class, gender, etc. Context always matters. Third, discussions of race are difficult but necessary to have, particularly if as public administrators the ethic of our profession is the pursuit of ideals like democracy and justice for all. Helping students make connections between historical practices and contemporary realities can illuminate practices that were legal, but unethical; policies that produce and sustain inequity; or language that characterizes people and places as deserving or undeserving.

Students in the Intro class could be assigned critical reflection papers that seek to deconstruct public administration theory and practice as normatively presented in the *Classics* with the political discourse offered by Black thought leaders. The writing assignment could require students to consider social equity as the framework to anchor decision-making, along with the traditional values of effectiveness, efficiency, and economy. In this assignment, students will have to reconcile all the values of the discipline and recognize the trade-offs needed to ensure that policy development and implementation, resource allocation, and engagement do not consistently burden or benefit any specific community.

Research Methods Courses

Embedding cultural competency into research methods courses requires active reconsideration of many common research practices. As Table 13.3 details, this includes examining researcher orientation, analyzing the overall research design, considering data analysis, and providing a thoughtful discussion of research findings.

As researchers, we all bring important pre-conceptions and bias to our work. A research methods course should include a candid examination of areas of cultural competency and deficiencies. It should also acknowledge the importance of considering cultural competency in the development of all research designs (not solely those that involve questions focused on gender, race, ethnicity, sexual orientation, religion, or immigration). "We each have our own way of interpreting data based on the cultural lenses through which we view the world and we must guard against this bias when we as researchers, regardless of our ethnicity, study cross-cultural issues" (Atkinson, 1993, p. 220).

All research designs should include a cultural competency assessment. This includes examining whether question phrasing and language is congruent with the culture of respondents, soliciting input from individuals who are more culturally knowledgeable if such expertise is not contained within the research team, and using labels that are most appropriate for the population. For example, when asking a respondent about gender, only providing two response options (male, female) does not reflect cultural competency. Expanding response options to include "transgender female," "transgender male," "gender variant/non-conforming," "not listed," and "prefer not to indicate" provides more inclusive and culturally competent response options. Pilot testing of survey questions, semi-structured interview questions, and/or focus group questions can provide informative feedback prior to actual question administration.

Data analysis also involves important cultural competency concerns. For example, collapsing racial/ethnic categories into broad labels such as "non-white" can lead to important data assumptions and misinterpretations. Does this category primarily include data from African Americans, Latinos, Asians, or some combination? It is important for readers to know who is included in the sample and to prevent general misapplication of findings. Additionally, researchers should consider cultural implications of eliminating small sample sizes from the analysis. For instance, if researchers routinely exclude analysis of American Indians because the researcher deems the sample size is too small, what are the long-term implications to advancing knowledge of this population? And what message does it send relative to their importance?

Reporting data findings and developing recommendations also requires cultural knowledge, understanding, and skill. For example, are the recommendations appropriate and feasible? Has a cross-cultural lens been applied to developing recommendations?

Throughout each phase of the research process, public affairs education should include a cultural competency and social equity assessment. This begins by faculty and students alike understanding that the research process is inherently subjective, and that objectivity operates on a continuum. One of the best protections against research bias is to engage in team-based research that intentionally incorporates multiple cultural perspectives.

Organizational Theory and Behavior

Organizational theory and behavior is a course that examines the theoretical and practical underpinnings associated with managing public-sector organizations. Students gain an understanding of the role leadership, organizational culture,

TABLE 13.3 Cultural Competency Guide for "Everyday" Public Administration and Policy Research

Item	Description/Examples	Assessment Questions	Ways to Improve
Researcher orientation	Level of baseline cultural competency of researcher; cultural subjectivity	• Which of the six stages in the Cross model most accurately describes me? • Do I routinely prioritize cultural competency in my professional development activities?	• Acknowledge the importance of cultural competency in every research design. • Commit to rigorous cultural competency standards in research design. • Assess cultural competency of self and all research team members. • Frequently invest in cultural competency professional and social development.
Research design	Research questions; survey questionnaires; semi-structured interviews; focus groups; spatial mapping	• Do I routinely consider cultural competency in "everyday" research designs that do not have a primary cultural focus? • Are my questions congruent with the cultures of my respondents? • Are my questions reviewed by a variety of subgroups for language, meaning, context, and appropriateness? • What category labels do I include as options for respondents to identify racial or ethnic minorities and why? • Do I use self-reported demographic data, especially in focus groups or semi-structured interviews?	• Make cultural competency assessment a standard component of all research designs. • Solicit input from individuals who are more culturally knowledgeable about the subgroups included in the research design. • Use racial and ethnic labels that are most appropriate for the populations included in the research design. • Avoid collapsing multiple groups into a single "non" or "minority" category. • If only broad pan-ethnic categorical labels are available from the public agency, be sure to understand and report which groups are specifically included within each category. • Allow individuals to self-report demographic data (e.g., racial and ethnic data; disability status).

| Data analysis | Statistical analysis; content analysis; mapping | • Does my data analysis consider the dominant group's performance to be the gold standard? If so, based upon what justification?
• How do I handle small sample sizes of population subgroups?
• If data are longitudinal or comparative, does my analysis consider operational differences in categories? | • Consider and justify appropriate comparative performance standards.
• Recognize the value of small samples in public policy research, especially for underrepresented or hard-to-reach populations.
• Balance methodological rigor with practical population considerations. |
| Report of findings | Discussion of findings; recommendations; conclusions | • Does my report of findings reflect cultural knowledge and understanding?
• Are my recommendations relevant and appropriate for the population subgroups in my analysis? | • Solicit input on recommendations from individuals who are more culturally knowledgeable about subgroups in the study.
• Use a cross-cultural lens when contextualizing findings and developing recommendations. |

Source: Gooden (2012).

and relationships (internal and external) have as factors that can enhance or diminish organizational objectives. Leadership is a key component in creating institutions that are inclusive and culturally competent. Organizational culture is reflected in the policies, protocols, and attitudes of people inside the organization, which dictate the type and quality of engagement that occurs with people external to the organization. It should be noted that diversity in organizations is important, but it is not the only factor to consider when trying to create culturally competent, inclusive, and equitable environments. A holistic examination of policies and practices is also needed to fully understand an organization's strengths, weaknesses, threats, and opportunities.

To give students the basic foundation of public administration theory and practice, standard texts can be supplemented with reports to contextualize real-life dilemmas organizations may face. For example, the Department of Justice's (DOJ, 2019) "Special Litigation Section Cases and Matters" website has a list of reports related to: Corrections, juvenile justice, law enforcement agencies, among others. Special Litigations reflect investigations conducted by the DOJ into public organizations that have violated the constitutional and/or civil rights of their respective constituents. As public agencies responsible for enforcement of the law, examining organizational policies and administrative behaviors through these reports offers evidence-based findings regarding organizational policies and patterns of practice that produce disproportionate interactions and outcomes for people and communities of color. Real-world analysis juxtaposed against theoretical discussions of organizational behavior help students reconcile theory and practice.

Students can use DOJ reports to interrogate organizational behavior and offer recommendations related to: Leadership development; cultural competence trainings and equity workshops; effective community engagement; the use of equity assessments; updates or revisions to bylaws, employee manuals, or HR protocols; and the pros and cons of incentive and disincentive structures, among other things. Once a topic was identified, students would be responsible for contextualizing their recommendations using peer-reviewed research, reports, and any other supplemental information necessary to justify recommendations. Each paper needs to identify stakeholders (internal or external) to the organization who would be affected by the problem, and a list of recommendations to address the issue. DOJ reports typically offer a number of recommendations at the end of their respective reports; students are not expected to duplicate recommendations, but rather identify additional strategies to support an improved outcome.

These are just a few examples of ways to raise the level of consciousness with respect to issues of equity and justice in public administration classrooms. The intentionality for which students are exposed to diverse material, forced to challenge personal and professional bias, and given the tools to pursue and promote equity programs graduate public servants who are better equipped to address the complexity of life beyond theoretical discussions and status-quo norms.

Practitioner-Based Capstone Projects

Capstone projects afford public affairs students with an excellent, empirically based opportunity to apply and sharpen their cultural competency and social equity skills. For example, one capstone team in an MPA program examined social equity relative to emergency 911 systems. Students quickly became aware of additional considerations in responding to emergency requests from those who are deaf or hard of hearing. They also became aware of the complexity and delays involved when responding to callers who do not speak English, and the wide range of languages that are spoken within a 911 service area. Students were able to better understand weaknesses in emergency system technology and how these weaknesses result in important inequities with real-life consequences.

Another capstone example involved the analysis of university support services for students who are Veterans. A major finding from this analysis was that data on Veteran status was not routinely collected. It revealed an important need to first identify and track Veterans in order to facilitate analysis of their college experiences.

Relevantly, requiring social equity analysis as a component of capstone projects not only builds student knowledge, but often benefits the government (or nonprofit) agency as well. It deepens their understanding of the significance of cultural competency and provides them with important analysis relative to social equity that can lead to increased agency awareness and analysis in their future work. Capstone projects provide a real-life connection to why cultural competency and social equity are critical, and often reveal fundamental gaps in the delivery of public services.

The Role of Leadership

Department chairs, program directors, and administrators are key allies in the integration of social equity and cultural competence into public administration curricula. Change starts at the top, through modeled behavior and a genuine interest in the professional development of faculty, staff, and students, as well as dedicated resources to support such initiatives. While everyone may not "buy in" to the need to integrate social equity and cultural competency into the curriculum, there should always be opportunities for people to engage. Program retreats can be used to introduce and reinforce pedagogical strategies for the development of cultural competence. Typically at these types of events, attendance is mandatory, so faculty are not able to opt out. Student learning outcomes can be mandated as part of curricula assessment, whereby each class has to address an issue related to social equity or cultural competency and is thus evaluated as part of an annual performance evaluation. Integrating social equity or cultural competence into a classroom should not be seen as a punishment; however, accountability mechanisms need to be in place to ensure that students are being prepared to meet the needs of the diverse world they will serve. Faculty should not have the privilege to prioritize their personal preferences around social equity and cultural competency when programs of public administration and affairs seek to advance public service values. For too long, the field of public administration has talked about the importance of social equity without enough action to make this value a reality.

Conclusion

This chapter underscores the foundational value of cultural competency and social equity to public affairs education. While this manuscript provides brief curricular examples, many scholars have heeded the call for cultural competency and social equity resources for public affairs. The *Journal of Public Affairs Education* has published several articles on these issues, including multiple symposia such as Blessett's (2018) volume focused on embedding cultural competence and racial justice into public administration programs. Wyatt-Nichol and Antwi-Boasiako (2008) examined the "diversity across the curriculum" standard as well as program directors' perceptions of the standard. Gooden and Wooldridge (2007) and Johnson and Rivera (2007) provided strategies to promote social equity and diversity into human resource management courses. Rubaii-Barrett (2006) provided practical and normative justifications for the use of learning contracts in diversity courses. In Gooden and Myers' (2004) JPAE symposium, White (2004) examined the extent to which courses in MPA programs included cultural competency, while Rice (2004) examined the teaching of diversity/diversity management in public administration education and its relationship to social equity. The list goes on but the larger point is that, 20 years ago, there may have been a reasonable claim that curriculum resources relative to cultural competency and social equity were limited, but this is certainly not the case today. The challenge now is for MPA program directors and faculty to hold themselves accountable for building and transferring knowledge in these fundamental areas.

Every MPA program in unique from the values of the program and university, composition of faculty, its location, and types of students (in-service, pre-service, executive cohorts) it serves. So, there are no universal standards of social equity and cultural competence that would be feasible for all programs. However, programs that want to assess whether they have moved the needle could develop a plan to identify the relevant knowledge, skills, abilities, attitudes, and behaviors necessary to be considered culturally aware and equity minded. These ideas and concepts could be mapped across the curricula and measurable data could be collected to determine if students are indeed learning. MPA programs do lots of assessment; more than anything, the need would be to incorporate social equity and cultural competency in similar ways to other learning outcomes to determine program effectiveness. The assessment does not have to be a heavy lift, it just needs to be prioritized to demonstrate its value to the overall structure of the program.

MPA directors articulate the priorities for their respective programs. Therefore, the ability to embed cultural competence, racial justice, and social equity into and across curricula can only happen with initiative and support from program leadership. While directives may seem forceful, the reality is that without such a charge to all faculty, public administration programs will continue to place the responsibility for integrating cultural competence and social equity on those faculty who find value in such discussions. This traditionally has meant that faculty of color and women have taken ownership for incorporating such dialogues in the classroom. The current approach therefore reinforces the subordinate status of social equity as a value in the field because not everyone has to engage with the content, which limits students' access and exposure to diverse ideologies and critical conversations about inequity, discrimination, injustice, and oppression.

Faculty, on the other hand, must also begin to recognize how their presence at the front of the room, the content covered (or not covered) in their courses, and the discussions they facilitate (or do not facilitate) affect a student's preparedness to enter the workforce. Public administration students need to understand the social, political, economic, and cultural factors that influence the way stakeholders are affected by public institutions, public policy development and implementation, and engagement with each other and public officials. The ability to thoughtfully integrate diverse ideas and perspectives into the classroom represents an important opportunity for students to think about their roles as public servants engaging with real people and complex problems.

References

Alkadry, M. G. & Blessett, B. (2010). Aloofness or dirty hands: Administrative culpability in the making of the 2nd ghetto. *Administrative Theory and Praxis, 32*(4), 552–576.

Alkadry, M. G., Blessett, B., & Patterson, V. (2017). Public administration, diversity and the ethic of getting things done. *Administration and Society, 49*(8), 1191–1218.

Atkinson, D. R. (1993). Who speaks for cross-cultural counseling research? *Counseling Psychologist, 21*(2), 218–224.

Blessett, B. (2018). Embedding cultural competence and racial justice in public administration programs. *Journal of Public Affairs Education, 24*(4), 425–556.

Blessett, B. & Littleton, V. (2017). Examining the impact of institutional racism in black residentially segregated communities. *Ralph Bunche Journal of Public Affairs, 6*(1), 1–13.

Borrego, E. & Johnson, R. G. (2012). *Cultural competence for public managers: Managing diversity in today's world.* New York: Routledge.

Cross, T. L. (1988). Services to minority populations: Cultural competence continuum. *Focal Point, 3*(1), 1–4.

Dantzler, P. (2016). Exclusionary zoning: State and local reactions to the Mount Laurel doctrine. *The Urban Lawyer, 48*(3), 653–673.

Department of Justice (2019). *Special litigation section cases and matters.* Retrieved June 18, 2019 from www.justice.gov/crt/special-litigation-section-cases-and-matters0#police.

Frederickson, H. G. (2005). The state of social equity in American public administration. *National Civic Review, 94*(4), 31–38.

Frederickson, H. G. (2010). *Social equity and public administration: Origins, developments, and applications.* Armonk, NY: M.E. Sharpe.

Gaynor, T. S. (2018). Social construction and the criminalization of identity: State-sanctioned oppression and an unethical administration. *Public Integrity, 20*(4), 358–369.

Gooden, S. T. (2014). *Race and social equity: A nervous area of government.* Armonk, NY: M.E. Sharpe.

Gooden, S. T. & Wooldridge, B. (2007). Integrating social equity into the core human resource management course. *Journal of Public Affairs Education, 13*(1), 59–77.

Gooden, S. & Myers, S. L. (2004). Social equity in public affairs education. *Journal of Public Affairs Education, 10*(2), 91–97.

Goodsell, C. T. (2004). *The case for bureaucracy: A public administration polemic,* 4th edn. Washington, DC: CQ Press.

Institute of Medicine (2003). *Unequal treatment: Confronting racial and ethnic disparities in healthcare.* Washington, DC: The National Academies Press.

Johnson, R. G. & Rivera, M. A. (2007). Refocusing graduate public affairs education: A need for diversity competencies in human resource management. *Journal of Public Affairs Education, 13*(1), 15–27.

Jones, A. (2013). *The modern African American political thought reader.* New York: Routledge.

Lipsky, M. (1971). Street-level bureaucracy and the analysis of urban reform. *Urban Affairs Review, 6*(4), 391–409.

Lopez-Littleton, V., Blessett, B., & Burr, J. (2018). Advancing social and racial equity in the public sector. *Journal of Public Affairs Education, 24*(4), 449–468.

Norman-Major, K. A. & Gooden, S. T. (2012). Cultural competency and public administration. In Norman-Major, K. A. & Gooden, S. T. (eds), *Cultural competency of public administrators* (pp. 3–16). New York: M.E. Sharpe.

Pitts, D. W. & Wise, L. R. (2004). Diversity in professional schools: A case study of public affairs and law. *Journal of Public Affairs Education, 10*(2), 125–142.

Rice, M. F. (2004). Organizational culture, social equity and diversity: Teaching public administration education in the postmodern era. *Journal of Public Affairs Education, 10*(2), 143–154.

Rubaii-Barrett, N. (2006). Teaching courses on managing diversity: Using learning contracts to address challenges and model behavior. *Journal of Public Affairs Education, 12*(3), 361–383.

Shafritz, J. M. & Hyde, A. C. (2017). *Classics of public administration,* 8th edn. Boston, MA: Cengage Learning.

Standing Panel on Social Equity (2000). *Issue paper and work plan.* Washington, DC: National Academy of Public Administration.

White, S. (2004). Multicultural MPA curriculum: Are we preparing culturally competent public administrators? *Journal of Public Affairs Education, 10*(2), 111–123.

Wilson, W. (1887). The study of public administration. *Political Science Quarterly, 2*(2), 197–222.

Wyatt-Nichol, H. & Antwi-Boasiako, K. B. (2008). Diversity across the curriculum: Perspectives and practices. *Journal of Public Affairs Education, 14*(1), 79–90.

14

COMMUNITY OUTREACH AND APPLIED RESEARCH CENTERS

Hunter Bacot

A tenet of many students and faculty in the field of public administration is serving others, or helping people. In the discipline, many MPA programs are engaged in community outreach through coursework and service obligations; also, most universities feature public administration programs as centerpieces of their community outreach efforts, for which university public service (UPS) organizations are also featured. As the core of public administration programs is to prepare students to engage the community, what better way to exemplify this commitment than through direct action, or involvement?

Recognizing that community service is a salient aspect of many universities' engagement efforts, public administration, public policy, and public affairs programs often serve as vehicles of interaction with communities across the country, even internationally. With the Network of School of Public Policy, Affairs, and Administration's (NASPAA, 2014) universal competencies emphasizing student training through public efforts "to lead and manage ... to participate in and contribute to ... to analyze ... to articulate and apply ... to communicate and interact" (p. 7), many programs manifest such learning through applied projects, experiential methods, or service-learning methods. As a result, many UPS organizations house MPA programs, or are closely affiliated with the public administration program on campus. Most universities have an engagement aspect to their mission, yet universities affiliated with the Coalition of Urban and Metropolitan Universities (CUMU) and the Consortium of University Public Service Organizations (CUPSO) demonstrate overt commitment to engagement, or as Dabson (2015) refers, commitment to the "civic infrastructure" (p. 2). Between these two organizations, 40 states have some formal institutional orientation to serving their citizens and constituents through university-based service (CUMU, 2019a; CUPSO, 2019a). Still, even in those states not represented by these two national organizations, there are university-based research centers and institutes that emphasize community engagement as part of their missions.

Recognizing the centrality of MPA programs to university outreach and engagement efforts, this chapter provides an overview of those public service organizations engaging their communities through outreach work; in fact, many MPA programs are a part of these public service outreach units and serve as examples of these public service efforts. The chapter includes a discussion of a sampling of programs successful at building community partnerships and engaging their constituent citizens and civic officials. Finally, the chapter moves to a discussion of MPA advisory boards and closes with an epilogue on MPA programs and UPS organizations.

The University Public Service Organization

Public service in higher education is a time-honored tradition. The Morrill Acts of the late 1800s formalized the unity of university and community. With their emphasis on extension services, the Morrill Acts and later the Smith-Lever Act focused the university on its responsibility for service and outreach in each state (National Research Council, 1995; an excellent synopsis of the legislation for land grant institutions is provided in Tables 14.1 and 14.2). These Morrill Acts (of 1862 and 1890) first provided land then funding for states to establish universities that offered instruction in "agriculture and the mechanical arts"; these universities often feature "A&M" as part of their names, or are known as "tech" schools (National Research Council, 1995). The Smith-Lever Act extended these efforts by establishing "cooperative extension services" that, in conjunction with the USDA, extended the university into the community through dissemination of "useful and practical information ... to consist of instruction and practical demonstrations ... through field demonstrations" (National Research Council, 1995, p. 9). These land-grant universities typically include "colleges of agriculture, home economics, forestry, and veterinary medicine" (National Research Council, 1995, p. 17).

Though obviously focused on agricultural assistance, the notion of universities being partners with their constituent communities is a long-standing tradition. These original extension agencies firmly placed the university in a role of "linking academic and research program[s] to societal needs" (Rahm, 1997). The post-World War II era witnessed another period in which universities invested in policy institutes on their campuses to educate and develop policy specialists to address contemporary issues across the country and answer "practical questions of public importance" (Kuklick, 2011, p. 688). As these university–community relationships evolved, the university's place in the community via practical, applied research became institutionalized. In fact, today it is common, as Dabson (2015) observes, that there is "an active partnership between the university and the communities it serves by: disseminating evidenced-based practical knowledge and connecting research and education to achieve important societal goals" (p. 1). These cooperative arrangements between university and community are now common practice across US universities.

The UPS organization epitomizes the community outreach and engagement featured in many university mission statements. These university organizations have become mainstays of the university and the communities they serve. Through their work featuring students as researchers, these UPS organizations are creating, building, and sustaining the "civic infrastructure" of our communities (Dabson, 2015, p. 3). Through training programs, professional development opportunities, and academic programming these UPS organizations service all sorts of professionals, from elected officials and government and nonprofit staff and leaders to those aspiring to be involved and looking for a pathway to do so.

Serving the public good or providing public service to communities, while a central feature of most universities, is especially important to UPS organizations. With so many of these organizations dotting the university landscape, a universal understanding of what it is to engage the public establishes and institutionalizes a common mantra of public service across these organizations. The leading national organizations tendering public services via the university setting are CUMU and CUPSO. To understand public service is to understand the appeal of these organizations, which reflect the missions of their constituent members. CUMU "is dedicated ... to the creation and dissemination of knowledge on the issues that face our urban and metropolitan campuses and the communities we serve ... [and] as those issues grow, so does the complexity of *community and campus-wide engagement*," while CUPSO institutions provide "students with opportunities to *learn about and actively participate in addressing public policy challenges*" (emphasis added; CUMU, 2019b; CUPSO, 2019b). With such statements guiding these organizations, it is apparent that public service holds an important place across universities, or at least these nearly 200 member universities.

Every state has a UPS organization conducting general or specialized research, which is typically focused on state or regional issues, or in the case of CUMU public service organizations on local issues. UPS organizations "have become the primary sources of U.S. research, discovery, and innovation" (American Academy of Arts and Sciences, 2015, p. 3). These UPS organizations also serve as conduits of research for other groups across the states, e.g., with the state municipal league and associations of counties. As such, these UPS organizations catalyze opportunities for local, state, and national agencies in a variety of research areas, which typically include "economic development and technical assistance" (American Academy of Arts and Sciences, 2015, p. 2). These UPS organizations generally serve as a major source of discovery and innovation in the United States. Also, positioned within major research universities, UPS organizations typically manifest strategies that promote stability and growth in their states, regions, and localities (American Academy of Arts and Sciences,

2016). In so doing, these research centers, like the universities within which these enterprises are housed, contribute to "economic growth, innovation, upward mobility, civic engagement, ... and are unparalleled in the level of service provided" (American Academy of Arts and Sciences, 2016, p. 12).

As examples of these service efforts, several longstanding and more comprehensive UPS organizations are delineated as examples of the standing these units command in their respective states and localities (* denotes an in-house MPA program; see CUPSO, 2019c).

- Rockefeller Institute of Government, State University of New York (SUNY) at Albany:

  The mission of the Nelson A. Rockefeller Institute of Government of SUNY is to improve the capacities of communities, state and local governments, and the federal system to work toward genuine solutions to the nation's problems. Through rigorous, objective, and accessible analysis and outreach ... aimed at improving how public institutions operate ... through research, expert advice, training for public service, and public dissemination and engagement ... The Institute's grounding in universities also undergirds how it performs its mission – to educate based on open inquiry and scientific principles, not advocate particular interests or ideological views (Rockefeller Institute of Government, 2017).

- Carl Vinson Institute of Government, University of Georgia:

  Since 1927, the Carl Vinson Institute of Government has been an integral part of the University of Georgia. A public service and outreach unit of the university, [it] helps governments become more efficient, effective, and responsive. Through training and development, customized assistance, application of technology, and studies relevant to government operations and decision making, the Institute of Government helps state and local government leaders navigate change and forge strong directions for a better Georgia, and helps international officials better understand and respond to global trends (Carl Vinson Institute of Government, 2017).

- Institute for Governmental Research and Service, University of Maryland:

  Founded in 1947, the Institute for Governmental Service and Research (IGSR) is dedicated to improving the well-being of individuals and communities through its work in areas of public health and safety, justice administration, health information technologies, leadership and governance, and fiscal and land use management.

IGSR partners with local governments, state and federal agencies, university researchers, and community organizations on projects that strengthen government effectiveness and efficiency, promote evidence-based practices, and improve policy and outcomes ... [through] evaluation studies, opinion surveys, data analysis, strategic planning consultation, training, and technical assistance (Institute for Government Research and Service, 2019).

- School of Government, University of North Carolina*

    Established in 1931 as the Institute of Government, the School provides educational, advisory, and research services for state and local governments [and] ... is also home to specialized centers focused on information technology and environmental finance. The School of Government works to improve the lives of North Carolinians by engaging in practical scholarship that helps public officials and citizens understand and improve state and local government [and] ... and also provides educational, advisory, and research services for state and local governments. The School of Government is also home to a nationally ranked graduate program in public administration ... (School of Government, 2019).

- Hatfield School of Government, Portland State University*

    The mission of the school is to attract, prepare, and renew leaders and managers for public service and non-profit service ... [the school is] involved in ... public policy and administration, civic leadership, and criminal justice [projects] ... Students participate in highly acclaimed programs in public administration, non-profit management, public health, political science, and criminology/criminal justice. [One of the school's centers], the Center for Public Service (CPS) works to enhance the legitimacy of – and citizen trust in – public service institutions and the people who work for them through applied research, training, education, and other talent-building programs and services that are custom-tailored for the specific needs of the public and non-profit sectors ... (Hatfield School of Government, 2019).

- Institute of Public Service, University of Tennessee:

    The Institute for Public Service was created in 1971 "to provide continuing research and technical assistance to state and local government and industry and to meet more adequately the need for information and research in business and government." To help meet this legislatively mandated mission, the Institute is composed of several agencies including the Municipal Technical Advisory Service, the County

> Technical Assistance Service, the Center for Industrial Services, the Law Enforcement Innovation Center, the Naifeh Center for Effective Leadership and the Tennessee Language Center ... [and] staff provide on-site technical assistance and training, as well as regional conferences and programs on a variety of issues (Institute of Public Service, 2018).

The integration of MPA programs with UPS organizations is a long-held tradition; many MPA programs are featured assets of these organizations, while other UPS organizations are closely allied with the MPA program. For example, a selection of MPA programs involved with UPS organizations is displayed in Table 14.1. Though admittedly only a sampling of UPS organizations, the information in Table 14.1 provides an idea of how these UPS organizations and MPA programs are integrated in outreach, service, and community-engaged research. Many CUMU and CUPSO member institutions have either a UPS organization or an MPA program, with many universities having both, and these programs are typically affiliated in some manner (CUMU, 2019b; CUPSO, 2019d). These program examples offer a glimpse of how UPS organizations extend their tentacles into the community and insert these programs into the community to expand the presence of the university and its constituent units into the community and connect with other affiliated constituents.

The listing of institutional affiliations with these two leading national umbrella organizations, which consist of universities or centers and institutes engaged in outreach and research, offers a glimpse of their prevalence across the country. The sharpest distinction between CUMU and CUPSO is the constituent focus; CUMU is oriented toward urban-based universities, while CUPSO is institute/center-specific in membership (CUMU, 2019a; CUPSO, 2019c). The primary benefit of these organizations is information sharing and cooperation for research, especially grant-funded collaborative research. For CUMU and CUPSO, the overall penetration across the country lacks a few states, but those ten states without representation on these lists have research-focused institutions or institutes/centers that engage communities within their states (Alaska, Connecticut, Hawaii, New Hampshire, New Mexico, North Dakota, Vermont, West Virginia, and Wyoming). For collaborative problem-solving and diversity of perspectives in research, shared connections through these organizations (or others similar) can provide much-needed experience with pitfalls and successes such that mistakes can be avoided and successes duplicated.

There are 40 states with an institution or institutions engaged with CUMU and/or CUPSO. Some state universities have only CUMU memberships (Arkansas, DC, Illinois, Indiana, Kentucky, Louisiana, Maine, Minnesota, New York, Nevada), while other states' centers and institutes are only members of CUPSO (Alabama, Arizona, Delaware, Georgia, Idaho, Iowa, Kansas, Mississippi, Montana, and South Carolina) (CUMU, 2019a). For CUPSO, its membership includes those organizations that have long-standing records of research and engagement in their states and communities (CUPSO, 2019e). CUMU, in representing universities, engages more centers and institutes focused on metropolitan-area research; in fact, of its 104 university members, many are located across 50 US metropolitan statistical areas (CUMU, 2019a, 2019b).

Across all of these UPS organizations, there are many of these units that either incorporate MPA students in their research and engagement through the in-house MPA program, or are using MPA programs among others to identify students to work as project researchers, grant-sponsored researchers, or graduate assistants. As evident through the research and community work conducted by these UPS organizations, these units epitomize the outreach and engagement promoted by MPA programs across the country. Moreover, through this engagement, MPA students are provided opportunities for immersing into the community and gaining invaluable training in conducting research for communities, government, and nonprofit agencies. As these UPS organizations are vital to their communities, these organizations provide applied, practical experiential learning opportunities for students, particularly MPA students.

As UPS organizations provide excellent "real-world" experience for both students and faculty, universities with an MPA program may want to initiate a public service organization to make explicit their connection to the community. In doing so, several factors must be considered in establishing a university public service unit; these factors are outlined below.[1]

Formation considerations. Is the UPS unit feasible – politically, practically, and formally – for the university?

Organizational considerations. Is the UPS unit to be a stand-alone unit or a division within an existing unit? Are there other entities that can be combined or subsumed to create a new UPS unit?

Administrative considerations. How should the organization be placed in the organizational chart administratively – should the unit have a placement under a senior administrative official (a provost or vice-chancellor), or is placement within a college (reporting to a dean) a viable administrative placement? How should the unit be developed – as an autonomous quasi-university unit, or a newly created nonprofit under the university's umbrella?

Funding considerations. Will the unit be fully funded by the university as an annual appropriation, through an endowment, or will it be self-sufficient? Will the unit be partially funded by the university (e.g., personnel and operational funding) or should the unit be self-sufficient in that funding is derived by contract services? Can it be a combination of funding, i.e., partially funded by the university with additional funding derived from services rendered to clients?

Unit structure considerations. As the unit is affiliated with the university, will the unit consist of academically based faculty (tenure-stream), professional researchers, and graduate students, or will the unit be a professional-based applied unit comprised primarily of a non-faculty administrator and professional researchers (non-tenure-stream)?

TABLE 14.1 Examples of University Public Service Organizations and MPA Program Integration

Institute	University	Relation to MPA (Within/Allied)
School of Public Affairs	American University	MPA is within School of Public Affairs
Government and Economic Development Institute	Auburn University	Allied with MPA program (offers research and engagement opportunities to MPA and other graduate students)
Brown Institute of Public Affairs	California State – LA	Allied with MPA program (shared faculty, who are given appointments as "Faculty Fellows" at the institute)
Maxine Goodman Levin College of Urban Affairs	Cleveland State University	MPA program is housed in the College of Urban Affairs
Institute of Government	Florida Atlantic University	Allied with MPA program (have MPA faculty on "Steering Committee")
The Metropolitan Center	Florida International University	Allied with MPA program (have MPA faculty and students on their staff)
Andrew Young School of Policy Studies	Georgia State University	MPA is within School of Policy Studies
Local Government Center	Montana State University	Allied with MPA program (MPA faculty work with center)
John Glenn School of Public Affairs	Ohio State University	MPA is within School of Public Affairs
Hatfield School of Government	Portland State University	MPA is within School of Government
Walter Rand Institute for Public Affairs	Rutgers University	Allied with MPA program (MPA faculty work with institute)
Rockefeller Institute of Government	SUNY at Albany	Allied with MPA program (MPA faculty and graduate students work with institute)
Maxwell School of Citizenship and Public Affairs	Syracuse University	MPA program is within School of Citizenship and Public Affairs

Center/School	University	Notes
Center for Public Service	Texas Tech University	Allied with MPA program (MPA faculty and graduate students work with institute)
Carl Vinson Institute of Government	University of Georgia	Allied with MPA program (MPA faculty and graduate students work with institute)
School of Public Affairs	University of Colorado, Denver	MPA program is housed within School of Public Affairs
Hobby Center for Public Policy	University of Houston	The MPP is housed within the Hobby Center for Public Policy
School of Public Affairs and Administration	University of Kansas	MPA is housed within School of Public Affairs
Ford School of Public Policy	University of Michigan	MPA is housed within School of Public Policy
Humphrey School of Public Affairs	University of Minnesota	MPA is housed within School of Public Affairs
College of Public Affairs and Community Service	University of Nebraska, Omaha	MPA is housed within the College of Public Affairs and Community Service
School of Government	University of North Carolina, Chapel Hill	MPA is housed within the School of Government
Fels Institute of Government	University of Pennsylvania	MPA is housed within Fels Institute of Government
Muskie School of Public Service	University of Southern Maine	No MPA program – but their Master of Policy, Planning, and Management is within the School of Public Service
LBJ School of Public Affairs	University of Texas, Austin	MPA program is within LBJ School of Public Affairs
LaFollette School of Public Affairs	University of Wisconsin, Madison	MPA program is within the LaFollette School of Public Affairs
Hugo Wall School of Urban and Public Affairs	Wichita State	MPA is within School of Public Affairs

Staffing considerations. Given the unit structure, will staff consist of full-time appointments housed within the unit, depend on half-time appointments of faculty or staff affiliated with the unit and whose appointments are in another university department, or will the staff consist of some combination thereof, i.e., a full-time staff, e.g., director, associate director, professional researcher, and an administrative support person and have faculty or staff affiliates from other university units (whose remuneration is an annual stipend for research that supports the unit, or some sort of compensatory release time)?

Service market considerations. Will there be, or is there, a target service/market for products and services of such a unit, i.e., are there local, state, or federal governments, nonprofit agencies, foundations, the private sector, etc., that the unit can assist with professional services?

Overhead costs and indirect rate considerations. Assuming an established target market, what is the indirect rate charge for likely clients contracting for services with the UPS? The indirect rate assumptions and the division of these derived revenues must be determined beforehand, as these rates are crucial for accurately forecasting revenues; indirect rates differ by a potential client's level or willingness to pay and are typically negotiable (university research and sponsored programs typically have these rates established for such purposes, but these can vary across university research units depending on their grant and contract activity). Indirect rates typically provide support for such things as unit salaries and fringe benefits associated with a project, maintenance, facilities, equipment, as well as other tangible items incurred in producing the work product, but are difficult to itemize or expense directly.

Budget considerations. These include decisions about the responsibility for what annual appropriations should cover – what costs will be assumed by the university and/or the unit? For example, decisions about the control and responsibility for equipment that is paid for/controlled by the university versus that paid for/controlled by the unit. These also include decisions about what costs the unit incurs, if any, for routine university services to be provided for such requirements as space, furniture, utilities, office equipment, phones, hardware/software, IT support, building maintenance, etc. These budget considerations must also include fund controls and accounting protocols with regard to how funds are raised, recovered, expended, and held (e.g., carry-over funds, overhead fund division, reserve funds, restricted/unrestricted unit accounts, etc.).

Outcome considerations. The unit must decide whether to have an internal "public affairs unit" (a division, a person, or contracted out) that, in addition to preparing grant applications, collateral materials, and finalizing research reports, would prepare an annual report detailing program accomplishments, program performance, and measuring unit effects (for university, constituents, community impact, and, if a state school, state legislature/legislators). Though an important consideration for establishing the importance of the unit to its constituents, it is especially important if the unit is supported by public funds.

Establishing a UPS is a tremendous undertaking by a university, but the rewards to the university are immense. As a community neighbor, the university must acknowledge its importance to the community through engagement, at which point the university becomes "integral to the social, cultural, and economic wellbeing of the community" (Friedman, Perry, & Menendez, 2014, p. 1). As universities have come to understand "their fortunes are tied in part to those of their neighbors and physical surroundings, [thus] many have expanded their efforts to engage new partners and address pressing community issues" (Friedman et al., 2014, p. 16). One such way universities commit to their community is through applied research conducted by a UPS unit.

Integrating Public Service in the Classroom

The academic benefits of these UPS organizations are acquired through MPA programs housed within, or having a close alliance with, these UPS organizations. Such interaction through location or association provides excellent opportunities for students to practice their learned skills within these community settings. In fact, interactions between these UPS organizations and MPA programs include:

- improved student preparation
- enhanced curricula opportunities
- applied, practical experiential opportunities for students (Dabson, 2015).

These university partnerships typically involve students, through centers employing students, in courses with service-learning based components, or an experiential learning focus with applied experiences. Many MPA programs use practicum, service-learning courses in which students conduct research or prepare a project for specific government units or nonprofit organizations under the direction of a faculty member. Such service-learning, experiential activities are the building blocks of public service for citizens and students. Service learning and experiential education are not new to higher education, but have received newfound priority in MPA programs in recent years. Also referred to as collaborative learning, some characteristics of service learning include an instructor as the facilitator of learning and student responsibility for individual learning as well as for promoting the intellectual development of the group (Kolb, 1984).

DeLeon and Killian (2000) note two broad categories of experiential education: In one, students go into the community to provide a service and observe the "real world"; in the other, the community is brought into the classroom. Although both approaches incorporate active learning techniques, taking students into the community creates direct experience. Some benefits of experiential learning that DeLeon and Killian (2000) note are the opportunity to process concepts and principles, practical experience, and the opportunity to collaborate with other people on real problems. Though challenging, these are the principles that align UPS organizations with pedagogical goals of MPA programs, and thus the integration of UPS organizations with MPA programs (see Shea & Weiss, 2013; Powell, Saint-Germain, & Sundstrom, 2014).

Students benefit tremendously from these interactive, research-based experiences; not only do they benefit from interaction with faculty and researchers, these students also benefit from skill training, development, and enhancement (American Academy of Arts and Sciences, 2015). These applied research opportunities for applied, practical learning are important to students, who "can contrast their experiences at one of these sites with what they learned in a course about how interest groups try to influence the policy process in their favor" (Smith, 2014, p. 129). In fact, a survey of the experiences of college graduates points to the importance of "what students are doing in college and how they are experiencing it" (Ray & Marken, 2014, p. 5), thus, among others, "working on a project that took a semester or more to complete" is indicated by graduates as being a key factor in their being prepared for life after graduation (Ray & Marken, 2014, p. 11). As a result, students engaged in applied, practical experiential projects are more likely to succeed in their work environments.

In embracing student researchers from MPA programs, UPS organizations provide a setting in which applied, experiential learning becomes an immersive experience for students, who are able to foster a deeper understanding of complex issues while engaged in service with a community partner. This approach to instruction "has proven effective with students at all levels, from preschool through graduate school" (Stout, 2013, pp. 218–219). These applied, experiential learning opportunities permit faculty to engage students in research, thus further developing their classroom knowledge and ideas through practice in the community.

MPA Programs, Public Service, and Community Engagement

Integrating students in community outreach is an important facet of instructional orientation across graduate MPA courses. These course engagement efforts integrate an outreach-oriented, service-learning approach that links the university and community, while providing practical, applied learning experiences for students and much-needed service for communities. In approaching instruction in this manner, MPA programs reap the benefit of such engagement efforts, i.e., those who are "learning through doing," enjoy greater retention rates, advanced leadership development, and higher academic performance. Direct involvement provides exceptional learning and engagement experiences for students (as well as participating faculty and researchers), which include:

- direct contact between students and community, requiring student preparation for community experiences
- engagement in projects and activities that are devoted to the public good
- service activity that is reciprocally beneficial to the community and students (thus, the program and university)
- structured reflection that enhances student understanding of connections between course content and service, as well as the university and its community
- recognition of how disciplinary knowledge contributes to applied research and translates into our understanding of the world in which we live

As a result, these unique advantages extend classroom learning beyond the campus and contribute to student success personally, professionally, and socially as they step away from the campus to engage their communities and, hopefully, in the process become better citizens.

One of the more popular modes of delivering the engaged classroom is through MPA capstone projects; these culminating or capstone projects are used in nearly all MPA programs across the country to immerse students and the program into the community (at 91 percent; see Peat & Desai, 2012). Nearly one third of MPA programs immerse students in the community via a capstone course *involving a project* that inserts students and faculty in real-word situations addressing policy or management challenges (Allard & Straussman, 2003; Flynn, Sandfort, & Selden, 2001; Peat & Desai, 2012); these "[c]lient-based projects pair MPA/MPP students with nonprofit and government agencies to address a current public management or public policy issue or need" (NASPAA, 2018, p. 36). To wit, "[m]any MPA/MPP programs use capstone courses to integrate the curriculum into a cumulative project" in their community and these projects enable students to apply their acquired "knowledge, skills, and competencies" (NASPAA, 2018, p. 36). Immersive, applied MPA capstone projects align with the mission of most UPS organizations; in fact, CUPSO "supports university-based public service institutes in their efforts to assist state and local governments on a range of contemporary issues and challenges" (Charney-Hostetler, Engel, & Von Lehman, 2015, p. 19). Given the number of UPS organizations that house MPA programs (see examples provided in Table 14.1), there is a definite connection between MPA programs and research efforts of UPS organizations. Thus, universities, whose missions encourage community outreach and engagement, underscore their commitment by supporting collaborative efforts between MPA programs and UPS organizations.

The Importance of the MPA Community Advisory Board

To support efforts to integrate, engage, and assist state and local governments on a range of issues and challenges, MPA program coordinators must cultivate and sustain relationships with these communities; of import to establishing community connections is the MPA advisory board. As a vehicle for cultivating community connections, the MPA advisory board is an excellent means for community outreach and engagement. MPA programs, based on their community connections, likely can benefit from making those community connections more formal through an advisory board. As MPA programs are more dependent on their communities for projects, internships, and jobs, establishing some formal means of liaison with the community is a must; the advisory board is the most common type of method for establishing and sustaining relations within the community. MPA advisory board members can also provide vital insights and perspectives about the profession.

According to Cuninggim (1985), the advisory board is "a voluntary, extralegal group of advisors and/or supporters drawn together to give aid in one or usually many ways to an educational institution or one of its subunits, a professional school, a department, or a major academic division" (p. 1). El-Refae, Askari, and Alnaji (2016) add that the advisory board's role is more than service to a department and contend that the "main role is to serve the university and provide it with feedback on what is important for companies/organizations outside the university that will hire their graduates" (p. 33). Thus, it is important to any organization that a professional board be established that serves to provide guidance, direction, and accountability to that organization; MPA programs are no different. To begin, "the advisory board members should be professionals who are well placed" in the community "and typically will consist of "alumni, scholars, experts 'leaders of the profession'" (El-Refae et al., 2016, p. 33). In addition, advisory board selection criteria should also include, "occupational expertise, industry perspective, peer recognition, interest in students, commitment, and diversity" (Kerka, 2002, p. 2). Finally, MPA advisory board members must share similar values as expressed in the MPA program's mission (El-Refae et al., 2016; Taylor, Marino, Rasor-Greenhalgh, & Hudak, 2010).

The MPA advisory board should actively participate in program affairs as needed, requested, and deemed appropriate. The members of the advisory board must be willing to serve as ambassadors of the program through their own or others' networks, remain abreast and advise on contemporary practices and current issues affecting public affairs and nonprofit administration, and provide leadership for the program, program coordinators, students, and program constituents. Moreover, individuals selected to serve on an MPA advisory board should be able to interact with and promote the MPA program. In a perusal of various MPA program websites, board members selected to serve on the MPA advisory board should be willing to assist the program coordinator with support for the program:

- mission and strategy
- proposals and ideas

- strategic direction for the program
- community connection and engagement
- performance and accountability
- assessment practices
- development and fundraising
- recruitment of students and faculty
- internships and placement opportunities for students
- promotion and publicity
- alumni relations

They may also lend their experience and talents to:

- further program credibility
- foster inclusiveness
- instill diversity of thought

For an advisory board to be successful, the MPA program coordinators must advance their participation by incorporating their thoughts and suggestions into program activities (or educating members as to why it cannot be done). Likewise, MPA board members are a program's constant link to the community, thus board members must be active participants beyond annual meetings, e.g., board members must relate community events, needs, and activities to the program. In this capacity, board members can use MPA programs as information clearinghouses in which the program can promote or inform their students and constituents of activities, jobs openings, events, and grant or funding opportunities. A strong, active MPA advisory board is a tremendous asset for the MPA program both internally to the university and externally to the community.

MPA and Public Service Organizations: An Epilogue

Despite the positive aspects of UPS organizations and the profound, constructive effects of the research emanating from these institutions to improve public programs and policies, the future is fraught with challenge. Catalyzed by the recession of 2008, a confluence of events burdened higher education, thus affecting many UPS organizations. Among the challenges faced in higher education that impinge on the viability of UPS organizations are retrenchment funding and other changes in approaches to university governance and finance models (Rich, 2013).

According to Rich (2013), amid fiscal retrenchment the public university model treats academics as "cost centers," thereby shifting emphasis to self-sustaining models of engagement; in so doing, UPS organizations suffer similarly (p. 263). Pushed in one direction to hold tuition steady and moderate student debt while pulled in the other direction through funding cuts, or at the least no new public funds, universities are caught in the middle of a financial vise. Such destabilization profoundly affects UPS organizations through a combination of changing institutional values and priorities from their public role to that of market-oriented, cost-effective programming, for which many university offerings do not measure well (see Rich, 2013); the view of education being a state priority has waned and thus too has its funding (Rich, 2013). MPA programs are also challenged by the lack of competitive appeal that public-sector employment once enjoyed. While at one time known for excellent benefits, decent salaries, advancement opportunities, and civil service protection, public-sector employment is now marred by stagnant wages and benefits, public ridicule, and reductions in force across all levels of government. As these dynamics have negatively affected public-sector employment, student recruitment has suffered similarly.

Yet, the tie that binds those with an affinity for public service is serving others and helping their fellow man; human nature, despite the challenge, is noble: Public servants care – they care about others, they care about their community, and they care about their fellow man. Such values cannot be erased by societal change and oftentimes these are emboldened. As Harvard president Faust (2009) proclaimed, "universities are about a great deal more than measurable utility ... [they serve] as society's critic and conscience." While the threat to the engaged university is viable, the capacity of UPS organizations is insuperable; the engaged university is too vital to the community in which it is immersed (Rich, 2013). By slowly recognizing engagement through research and service, universities are incentivizing community outreach and presence through their faculty (e.g., by crediting such service through their annual evaluation criteria for teaching and research). The UPS organizations have also recalibrated their operations to sustain their engagement and outreach capacity; many of the larger UPS organizations have long served their communities via a self-sustaining model, so for these organizations the change in university operations is not nearly as disruptive. In fact, as demonstrated later, these UPS organizations provide the path to continued success in public affairs education.

Smaller UPS organizations, whether facing fiscal shortfalls or ideologically driven audits, are not able to sustain and must either exist in name only, or be absorbed in other campus units (or sometimes both) (see Holmes et al., 2015). Though affecting smaller UPS organizations more, the situation is further compounded for UPS organizations due to their reliance on only a few major sources of funding and/or the fiscal inability/declining funds of many states and local governments (especially local governments) to continue to financially support such research derived from these organizations (Charney-Hostetler et al., 2015; Rich, 2013).

Yet, based on Evans, Morrison, and Auer (2019), the solution lies with UPS organizations, as it is these organizations that have the necessary relationships across "institutions of higher education and communities of practitioners and stakeholders" (Evans et al., 2019, p. 292). Those UPS organizations that are leading their states in community outreach and engagement are the very institutions, especially those that house MPA programs, able to deliver "educational experiences that help our students develop expansive, value-driven, yet critical frames for facilitating sound public administration and policy" (Evans et al., 2019, p. 292). To adapt to these changes and achieve in educating future public servants, Evans et al. (2019) point to three essential goals for success.

- Restore the efficacy of the educational experience for the individual student.
- Enhance the relevancy of our graduate programs on the whole.
- Restore the policy school's role in driving renewed valuation of public service as a noble profession.

Programs should not be driven by cost, but recognized for the opportunity to aid, assist, and improve civics, government, and nonprofit capacity to lead. Of course, the irony in this call for change is that this change already exists; to wit, Dabson (2015) calls for a focus on:

- improving policy making by providing credible research and evaluation information
- honing government management practices through research, training and technical assistance
- developing leadership skills among city, county, state and regional government and nonprofit leaders

Consequently, UPS organizations are seemingly positioned to provide the ideal setting for cultivating future public servants. Perhaps more so than ever, the ideal setting for reinvigorating interest in public service lies in either a UPS organization that houses an MPA program, or an applied, experiential MPA program, as these units appear already engaged in "sustained relationships between practitioners and educators" (Evans et al., 2019, p. 289). As noted in the beginning of this chapter, the crux of public administration programs is to prepare students to engage the community, thus to commit to developing our nation's civic infrastructure. With the public service infrastructure of formal institutional orientation in place in each state through university-based service and recognizing the centrality of MPA programs to university outreach and engagement efforts, the solution may be a more concerted effort to insert these programs into the community to demonstrate the utility of UPS organizations and MPA programs to community constituents.

Note

1. This information draws from Rich (2013) and CUPSO resources, especially Hoke (2013a, 2013b), as well as the author's experience.

References

Allard, S. W. & Straussman, J. D. (2003). Managing intensive student consulting capstone projects: The Maxwell School experience. *Journal of Policy Analysis and Management*, *22*(4), 689–701.

American Academy of Arts and Sciences (2015). *Public research universities: Serving the public good*. Cambridge, MA: American Academy of Arts and Sciences.

American Academy of Arts and Sciences (2016). *Public research universities: Why they matter*. Cambridge, MA: American Academy of Arts and Sciences.

Carl Vinson Institute of Government (2017). About us. *University of Georgia*. Retrieved April 23, 2019 from https://cviog.uga.edu/about-us/.

Charney-Hostetler, A., Engel, J., & Von Lehman, K. (2015). *What's next? A benchmarking study on the operations of institutes of politics and centers for civic engagement in higher education*. Pittsburgh, PA: University of Pittsburgh Institute of Politics.

Coalition of Urban and Metropolitan Universities (2019a). *CUMU members*. Retrieved April 23, 2019 from www.cumuonline.org/cumu-members/.

Coalition of Urban and Metropolitan Universities (2019b). *About CUMU*. Retrieved April 23, 2019 from www.cumuonline.org/about-cumu/.

Consortium of University Public Service Organizations (2019a). *Main page*. Retrieved April 23, 2019 from www.cupso.org/.

Consortium of University Public Service Organizations (2019b). *About*. Retrieved April 23, 2019 from www.cupso.org/about/.

Consortium of University Public Service Organizations (2019c). *Member roster*. Retrieved April 23, 2019 from www.cupso.org/members/.

Consortium of University Public Service Organizations (2019d). *Resources*. Retrieved April 23, 2019 from www.cupso.org/resources/.

Consortium of University Public Service Organizations (2019e). *Resources: Public engagement activities*. Retrieved April 23, 2019 from www.cupso.org/resources/.

Cuninggim, M. (1985). *The pros and cons of advisory committees, association of governing boards of universities and colleges* (ERIC Report ED263 811). Washington, DC: Institute of Education Sciences.

Dabson, B. (2015, October). *The role of public service in higher education*. Paper presented at the annual meeting of the Consortium of University Public Service Organizations, Charlottesville, VA.

deLeon, L. & Killian, J. (2000). Comparing modes of delivery: Classroom and on-line (and other) learning. *Journal of Public Affairs Education*, *6*(1), 5–18.

El-Refae, G. A., Askari, M. Y., & Alnaji, L. (2016). Does the industry advisory board enhance education quality? *International Journal of Economics and Business Research*, *12*(1), 32–43.

Evans, A. M., Morrison, J. K., & Auer, M. R. (2019). The crisis of policy education in turbulent times: Are schools of public affairs in danger of becoming irrelevant? *Journal of Public Affairs Education*, *25*(3), 285–295.

Faust, D. (2009, September 1). The university's crisis of purpose. *New York Times*. Retrieved April 23, 2019 from www.nytimes.com/2009/09/06/books/review/Faust-t.html.

Flynn, T., Sandfort, J., & Selden, S. (2001). A three-dimensional approach to learning in public management. *Journal of Policy Analysis and Management*, *20*(3), 551–564.

Friedman, D., Perry, D., & Menendez, C. (2014). *The foundational role of universities as anchor institutions in urban development: A report of national data and survey findings*. Washington, DC: Coalition of Urban Serving Universities.

Hatfield School of Government (2019). Mark O. Hatfield School of Government. *Portland State University*. Retrieved April 23, 2019 from www.pdx.edu/cupa/mark-o-hatfield-school-of-government.

Holmes, J., Hans, P., Long, S., Maxwell, A., McMahan, E., Parrish, D., & Perry, J. (2015). *Report Board of Governors' working group on centers and institutes*. Chapel Hill, NC: UNC General Administration.

Hoke, L. (2013a, October). *SCUPSO survey results: Operations*. A paper presented at the fall directors' meeting of the Southern Consortium of University Public Service Organizations, Washington, DC.

Hoke, L. (2013b, October). *SCUPSO survey results: Return on investment*. A paper presented at the fall directors' meeting of the Southern Consortium of University Public Service Organizations, Washington, DC.

Institute for Government Research and Service (2019). Capabilities. *University of Maryland*. Retrieved April 23, 2019 from www.igsr.umd.edu/about_IGSR/capabilities.php.

Institute of Public Service (2018). About the UT Institute for Public Service. *University of Tennessee*. Retrieved April 23, 2019 from www.ips.tennessee.edu/home/about/.

Kerka, S. (2002). *Effective advisory committees: National dissemination center for career and technical education* (Report NDCCTE-17). Columbus, OH: National Dissemination Center for Career and Technical Education.

Kolb, D. A. (1984). *Experiential learning: Experience as the source of learning and development*, Vol. 1. Englewood Cliffs, NJ: Prentice-Hall.

Kuklick, B. (2011). The rise of policy institutes in the United States, 1943–1971. *Orbis*, *55*(4), 685–699.

National Research Council (1995). *Colleges of agriculture at the land grant universities: A profile*. Washington, DC: The National Academies Press.

Network of Schools of Public Policy, Affairs, and Administration (2014). *NASPAA standards: Accreditation standards for master's degree programs*. Washington, DC: Network of Schools of Public Policy, Affairs, and Administration.

Network of Schools of Public Policy, Affairs, and Administration (2018, October). *Client-based capstone projects: Facilitating critical public service skills through lived experiences*. Panel session at the annual meeting of the National Association of Schools of Public Affairs and Administration, Atlanta, GA.

Peat, B. & Desai, A. (2012, October). *Graduate capstone courses: Components, uses, and assessment – survey results*. A paper presented at the annual meeting of the National Association of Schools of Public Affairs and Administration, Austin, TX.

Powell, D. C., Saint-Germain, M., & Sundstrom, L. (2014). Using a capstone case study to assess student learning on NASPAA competencies. *Journal of Public Affairs Education*, *20*(2), 151–162.

Rahm, D. (1997). The history of the land grant mission. *Iowa State University*. Retrieved April 23, 2019 from www.biotech.iastate.edu/publications/bioethics_outreach/forum/rahm.html.

Ray, J. & Marken, S. (2014). *Great jobs great lives: The 2014 Gallup-Purdue index report*. Washington, DC: Gallup.

Rich, D. (2013). Public affairs programs and the changing political economy of higher education. *Journal of Public Affairs Education*, *19*(2), 263–283.

Rockefeller Institute of Government (2017). About us. *University of Albany*. Retrieved April 23, 2019 from https://rockinst.org/about-us/.

School of Government (2019). About. *University of North Carolina*. Retrieved April 23, 2019 from www.sog.unc.edu/about/mission-and-history.

Shea, J. & Weiss, A. F. (2013). From traditional to client-based nonprofit management course design: Reflections on a recent course conversion. *Journal of Public Affairs Education, 19*(4), 729–747.

Smith, P. H. (2014). American politics and the liberal arts college. *Polity, 46*(1), 122–130.

Stout, M. (2013). Delivering an MPA emphasis in local governance and community development through service learning and action research. *Journal of Public Affairs Education, 19*(2), 217–238.

Taylor, E., Marino, D., Rasor-Greenhalgh, S., & Hudak, S. (2010). Navigating practice and academic change in collaborative partnership with a community advisory board. *Journal of Allied Health, 39*(3), 105e–110e.

15

CONCLUSION

Bruce D. McDonald, III and William Hatcher

Moving into the role of MPA director may feel like a glamorous opportunity at first. Trust is being placed in you to ensure the success of the program, but often the opportunity to serve is given with little to no training or preparation. Ph.D. programs prepare students for careers as researchers and teachers, not university administrators. Often, the first encounter we have with administrative roles is when we are put into the position. When this happens, where do you start?

Serving as an MPA director can be a rewarding experience, but the learning process for MPA directors is often a trial by fire. That is, after all, how we both got our own starts as directors of MPA programs. It is also the impetus for why we pursued the publication of this book. Effective directors not only need to plan course schedules and address student questions; they must meet the challenges of higher education administration head-on. They recruit students and provide program and career advice to those students. They balance concerns regarding equity among students and across colleagues. They oversee accreditation and lobby deans for additional resources. All this is done while supporting the students and encouraging the faculty, without adequate resources, and without much formal authority over the faculty, staff, and administrators at the universities.

Rather than discourage faculty from taking on the task of MPA director, we have sought to make up the difference, to provide a foundation for you that helps take you from a faculty member focused on research and teaching to an effective MPA director of a striving program. We need more, not fewer, excellent faculty who are willing to face the challenge of being an MPA director and to help ensure that our field has effective programs. We proposed the book you have read with this goal in mind. We laid out chapters on subjects that we wish we had known about as we took on our own roles and then sought out authors for those chapters, typically turning to the mentors who helped and advised us when we were newbies. For new directors we hope that this book can remove some of the guesswork by providing guidance on what you should do. For more seasoned directors, our hope is that this book can help you move forward at improving and expanding your program.

Resources for the New Director

Despite the lack of training at the department or institutional level, there are resources available that can help familiarize you, and can guide you, in your new role as MPA director. In addition to the other chapters of this book, the Network of Schools of Public Policy, Affairs, and Administration (NASPAA) plays a key role in director training and programmatic assistance. Each fall NASPAA holds a conference that is directly geared toward continuing education for program directors. Not only do panels cover core topics, such as student recruitment, managing certificates and concentrations, addressing diversity, and responding to faculty concerns, but they frequently include workshops aimed at developing the skills necessary for new directors. Many of NASPAA's core resources are posted on its website, including instructional videos on accreditation and a series of e-mail listservs that directors can join.[1]

There are also several academic journals that publish articles related to public affairs courses and program management. An overview of these journals is provided in Table 15.1. The primary source of published information comes from the pages of the *Journal of Public Affairs Education* (*JPAE*). Established in 1995 and published quarterly, *JPAE* is the official journal of NASPAA and is dedicated to the advancement of the scholarship of teaching and learning in public affairs (McDonald & Hatcher, 2018; Perry, 2019). Its utility, however, is not just in the form of peer-reviewed research on public administration education; rather, it publishes a wide variety of research on issues of importance to the management of MPA programs. Recent examples of this breadth include the integration of public service values into NASPAA programs (see Svara & Baizhanov, 2019), establishing and measuring student competencies (Jennings, 2019), and how to address issues of diversity in programs and departments (Bishu, Guy, & Heckler, 2019; Edwards, Holmes, & Sowa, 2019; Stabile, Grant, and Salih, 2019; Thomas, 2019).

Three additional academic journals publish research on topics relevant to program management. The first of these, *Teaching Public Administration* (TPA), is the European equivalent to *JPAE*. Published three times a year by the Joint University Council of the Applied Social Sciences in the United Kingdom, TPA takes a broader perspective for its focus by publishing a range of scholarship of teaching and learning as it applies to public organizations. Although only the occasional piece is focused on issues related to program management, TPA publishes a

TABLE 15.1 Public Affairs Journals

Journal	Description
Journal of Public Affairs Education	The journal of the Network of Schools of Public Policy, Affairs, and Administration, the journal focuses on research that specifically applies to public affairs programs. Published research includes topics related to classroom teaching, but also program administration and accreditation.
Journal of Political Science Education	Published by the American Political Science Association, the journal focuses on issues that relate to teaching and learning within political science. Although most research is focused at the undergraduate level, the relationship between political science and public administration allow for a general application of the material to teaching some MPA courses.
Journal of Nonprofit Education and Leadership	Focuses on research that can improve the education and training of leadership within the nonprofit sector, though most research takes a more direct focus on the act of leadership rather education for leadership.
Teaching Public Administration	Published by the Joint University Council Public Administration Committee, the journal primarily focuses on the scholarship of teaching and learning as it applies to public organizations.

range of research that addresses the public administration classroom across a variety of cultural and governmental situations. The *Journal of Political Science Education*, published by the American Political Science Association, takes a similarly broad perspective, albeit from a heavily undergraduate, political science perspective. The final journal is the *Journal of Nonprofit Education and Leadership* (*JNEL*). *JNEL*'s mission is to publish research that can improve the education and training of leadership within the nonprofit sector, though most research takes a more direct focus on the act of leadership itself rather educating students on leadership. Other public affairs journals do, upon occasion, publish research on topics of teaching public affairs courses or the directing of MPA programs. These occasions, however, are more infrequent than they are common.

Other Resources within Higher Education

The issue of program management within a university setting is not limited to public affairs programs. As a result, a number of resources have emerged that focus on leadership within higher education more broadly. Tables 15.2 and 15.3 provide an overview of those resources that we have found most helpful in our own careers. The first set of resources are six books on serving as a chair or administrator within higher education. Rather than addressing leadership in the context of a public affairs program, they each focus on the general issues that emerge within the context of higher education more broadly. Examples include managing conflict within a department, mentoring faculty, and addressing diversity.

The second set of resources that are listed are the leading academic journals on higher education. Much like the more public affairs specific journals listed in Table 15.1, these journals publish peer-reviewed research on the issues and challenges facing higher education, while also giving attention to issues on departmental management and instructional design. Given the generalist perspective of higher education that the journals take, finding public affairs specific topics is difficult; however, the breadth of focus does allow for a more comparative approach. Through a comparative approach, it is often possible to find issues similar to what you are facing within the pages of the journals, even if the issues happened to take within a different discipline.

Of the journals listed in Table 15.3, *Higher Education* is the journal most directly applicable to those in the role of an MPA director. *Higher Education* publishes interdisciplinary research that relates to the common challenges, issues, and developments that instructors and administrators of higher education face. As a result of this focus, MPA directors and public affairs faculty can look at how other disciplines have sought to solve similar problems to those that they face. Examples of recent articles published by the journal that testify to this include an article on respecting voice and the co-creation of teaching (Cook-Sather, 2019), an article on gender segregation in higher education (Barone & Assirelli, 2019), and a study on research collaboration in higher education (Hammond, 2019).

TABLE 15.2 Books on Serving as a Chair or Administrator in Higher Education

Resource	Description
The Essential Chair Primer: A Comprehensive Desk Reference J. L. Buller (2012)	This book addresses issues of managing an academic department in the format of short vignettes of practical tips for the complicated scenarios that administrators will face in any academic program.
A Toolkit for Department Chairs J. L. Buller and R. E. Cipriano (2015)	The book uses case studies and problem-solving activates to provide department chairs with a foundation to manage effectively. This book makes a useful resource for a department chair that is looking to improve in their role of leadership.
The Department Chair Primer D. Chu (2012)	Focuses on exploring and understanding functions of a department or program leader. The understanding that is provided is matched with tips and recommendations on how to address the circumstances that arise from the context of the chairs function.
The Department Chair as a Transformative Diversity Leader: Building Inclusive Learning Environments in Higher Education E. Chun and A. Evans (2015)	Focuses on the role that the department chair can play in ensuring diversity in higher education. Particular attention is given toward the role as it relates to increasing the number of minority students in the academy.
Building Academic Leadership Capacity: A Guide to Best Practices W. H. Gmelch and J. L. Buller (2015)	Turns attention away from the role of the chair and gives it to the effective development of a program. This book intends to provide readers with what it takes to lead a program and how to structure that leadership in order to meet the needs of the stakeholders.
A Guide for Leaders in Higher Education: Core Concepts, Competencies, and Tools B. D. Ruben, R. De Lisi, and R. A. Gigliotti (2017)	This book is an excellent resource as it addresses the challenges to leadership that chairs and administrators face. Attention is geared less toward how to direct a program and more toward what it takes to be an effective leadership in higher education.

TABLE 15.3 Generalist Journals on Higher Education

Journal	Description
Higher Education	Focuses on publishing interdisciplinary research that relates to the common challenges, issues, and developments that instructors and administrators of higher education face.
Journal of Higher Education	Publishes empirical and theoretical work that addresses the functions of higher education and the role that higher education plays within society. Research that is published can take an interdisciplinary orientation, but generally focus on issues within higher education rather than its administrator.
Review of Higher Education	Takes a broad perspective to higher education by focusing on all issues that impact higher education. Although articles are research-based, they all incorporate practical applications for instructors and administrators.
Research in Higher Education	Publishes research on issues related to postsecondary education, with a particular preference for articles related to education policy issues. Frequent topics include student retention, equity, assessment, program governance, and curriculum design.

A Community of Directors

There is an old adage about university administration: Look for new friends amongst those in administrative roles or outside higher education, because your departmental colleagues are no longer your friends. In many ways, the adage is true. As the director of an MPA program, your responsibilities are much more extensive than those of the typical faculty and pursuing those responsibilities may place you at odds with their performance. For example, working on class scheduling may force you to assign faculty to undesirable classes or times and managing the program's budget may lead to limiting travel funds in order to implement a new recruitment plan.

One thing that is clear from the research is that being in an administrative role is challenging and isolating (Brainard & Infeld, 2017; Evans, Morrison, & Auer, 2019; Hatcher, Meares, & Gordon, 2017). The good news is that you do not walk into your new position alone. Rather, you are entering into a new community of faculty who understand what you are up against because they have experienced it themselves. And this new community is more than willing to be there to help and support you in any way that they can.

The best example of the awesomeness of this community comes from Doug Goodman at the University of Texas at Dallas. I (Bruce) became MPA director at Indiana University South Bend in 2013 after a particularly disastrous accreditation cycle. We were a small program inside of a political science department, and the political scientist I replaced was no more prepared to deal with accreditation than I was to teach his courses in political philosophy. When our report came back from the Commission on Peer Review and Accreditation, the list of things to fix was long and, as an incoming MPA director, I had a year to do it and no idea of where to start. I remembered, however, that Doug Goodman had said during our site visit that I could give him a call when the report came back. Doug will never understand how instrumental his time and guidance was in helping me address the accreditation issues. As a new MPA director, "WWDD?" (What Would Doug Do?) was written on the white board in my office.

Since those early years I have maintained the same willingness to help new directors as issues arise. Doug and I are not alone in this. Will, the co-editor of this book, frequently talks to directors when the need arises, and having had Doug Goodman as a professor, he can also attest to the value of "WWDD?." The desire to help new directors, as we were, after all, has been the impetus of this book and the supportiveness of those in administrative roles is so great that we had to turn authors away from this book project because we simply could not accommodate them all. All that said, you should take away from this book that there is a community who is there for you, even if only to lend you an ear when you need to vent.

But the question is, how do you find this community? Most of us attend NASPAA's conference each year and NASPAA's e-mail listservs are always a quick way of reaching a group of experienced directors at once. Interestingly, the "PA Twitter" community has emerged in recent years as a new, albeit unconventional, tool for contact. We are both active on twitter, as is the *Journal of Public Affairs Education.* You are more than welcome to reach out to use on Twitter or by e-mail and if we are not able to help or there is someone better qualified to help, we are happy to make the introduction.

Being a director is a hard, long, and stressful job, as well as a thankless task. Through everything, do not forget that there is a community behind you and we have been where you are. There is, after all, nothing new under the sun.

Note

1. Information on NASPAA's listservs can be found at: www.naspaa.org/membership/engage-naspaa/join-listserv.

References

Barone, C. & Assirelli, G. (2019). Gender segregation in higher education: An empirical test of seven explanations. *Higher Education.* doi:10.1007/s10734-019-00396-2.

Bish, S. G., Guy, M. E., & Heckler, N. (2019). Seeing gender and its consequences. *Journal of Public Affairs Education,* 25(2), 145–162.

Brainard, L. A. & Infeld, D. L. (2017). The challenges and rewards of service: Job satisfaction among public affairs program directors. *Journal of Public Affairs Education*, *23*(3), 811–824.

Buller, J. L. (2012). *The essential department chair: A comprehensive desk reference*. San Francisco, CA: Jossey-Bass.

Buller, J. L. & Cipriano, R. E. (2015). *A toolkit for department chairs*. Lanham, MD: Rowan and Littlefield.

Chu, D. (2012). *The department chair primer*. San Francisco, CA: Jossey-Bass.

Chun, E. & Evans, A. (2015). *The department chair as transformative diversity leader: Building inclusive learning environments in higher education*. Sterling, VA: Stylus Publishing.

Cook-Sather, A. (2019). Respecting voices: How the co-creation of teaching and learning can support academic staff, underrepresented students, and equitable practices. *Higher Education*. doi:10.1007/s10734-019-00445-w.

Edwards, L. H., Holmes, M. H., & Sowa, J. E. (2019). Including women in public affairs departments: Diversity is not enough. *Journal of Public Affairs Education*, *25*(2), 145–162.

Evans, A. M., Morrison, J. K., & Auer, M. R. (2019). The crisis of policy education in turbulent times: Are schools of public affairs in danger of becoming irrelevant? *Journal of Public Affairs Education*, *25*(3), 285–295.

Gmelch, W. H. & Buller, J. L. (2015). *Building academic leadership capacity: A guide to best practices*. San Francisco, CA: Jossey-Bass.

Hammond, C. D. (2019). Dynamics of higher education research collaboration and regional integration in Northeast Asia: A study of the A3 Foresight Program. *Higher Education*, *78*(4), 653–668.

Hatcher, W., Meares, W. L., & Gordon, V. (2017). The capacity and constraints of small MPA programs: A survey of program directors. *Journal of Public Affairs Education*, *23*(3), 855–868.

Jennings, E. T. (2019). Competencies and outcomes in public affairs education. *Journal of Public Affairs Education*, *25*(1), 73–92.

McDonald, B. D. & Hatcher, W. (2018). From the editors. *Journal of Public Affairs Education*, *24*(1), 1–2.

Perry, J. L. (2019). The *Journal of Public Affairs Education* at 25: An agenda for the future. *Journal of Public Affairs Education*, *25*(1), 3–11.

Ruben, B. D., De Lisi, R., & Gigliotti, R. A., (2017). *A guide for leaders in higher education: Core concepts, competencies, and tools*. Sterling, VA: Stylus Publishing.

Stabile, B., Grant, A., & Salih, S. (2019). Gendered differences in choice concentrations in Master of Public Administration programs. *Journal of Public Affairs Education*, *25*(2), 207–225.

Svara, J. H. & Baizhanov, S. (2019). Public service values in NASPAA programs: Identification, integration, and activation. *Journal of Public Affairs Education*, *25*(1), 73–92.

Thomas, N. (2019). In the service of social equity: Leveraging the experiences of African American women professors. *Journal of Public Affairs Education*, *25*(2), 185–206.

INDEX

Page numbers in **bold** denote tables, those in *italics* denote figures.

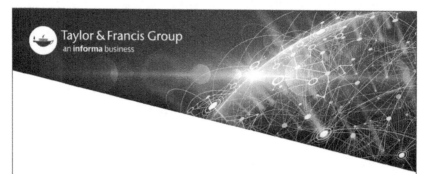

Made in the USA
Monee, IL
30 April 2021

67341852R00167